MANHUNTER

THE ART OF TRACKING

MANHUNTER

THE ART OF TRACKING

IAN MAXWELL

ROBERT HALE

First published in 2016 by Robert Hale,
an imprint of The Crowood Press Ltd,
Ramsbury, Marlborough Wiltshire SN8 2HR

www. crowood.com

www.halebooks.com

British Library Cataloguing-in-Publication Data
A catalogue record for this book is available from the British Library.

ISBN 978 0 7198 1076 3

Typeset by Jean Cussons Typesetting, Diss, Norfolk

Printed and bound in India by Replika Press Pvt Ltd.

Contents

Preface

Writing does not come easily to me. There is always something more urgent, exciting or compelling to do. Let's face it, I track because I like a bit of action, the outdoors, kit, nature and, yes, a challenge. It is ironic that the greatest challenge for me is to write a book. I hope that it will ignite your interest in an ancient art and, if you are already a tracker, the information here will help you to hone your skills.

I hope in this book to communicate the exhilaration I feel when I am tracking, though I fear that the English language is not sufficient to describe it.

When people asked me about ten years ago if I had written a book, tracking was becoming a forgotten art. I am grateful to many people around the world, and in particular David Scot Donelan, who kept the flame alive.

I have been teaching mantracking, wildlife tracking, counter IED, and survival skills through Shadowhawk Tracker School for over 10 years. We train people from all over the world. I have been lucky enough to work with some of the finest tactical and combat trackers on all but the coldest continents on earth. I have also travelled deep into the wilderness to track with indigenous tribespeople from Africa, Borneo, India and South America. I have spent a considerable amount of time with the US Border Patrol, and especially the Shadow Wolves, who are Native American trackers operating on the Tohono O Odam Reserve. They are also operational in Eastern Europe. A letter from them was part of the inspiration for this book. The letter read:

> Ean [sic] Maxwell
> It was a pleasure to meet and talk with you. I hope your time was well spent. Please take your knowledge and make good use of it. Your efforts are appreciated by all.

I am sometimes perplexed by the sheer number of individuals and organizations training trackers. It seems that there are several techniques taught by various people throughout the world. Some schools of tracking have broadly the same ethos, while other schools teach entirely different techniques. One thing is common to them all – they are all trying to find solutions for a complex discipline. Generally they seem to be divided between wildlife and mantracking; it is rare for schools to cross over these skills, and many schools teach either mantracking or wildlife tracking. This book demonstrates the importance of understanding both skills. The tracking of wildlife is an skill essential to mantrackers. It is important to distinguish between animal and human tracks. Knowledge of both greatly enhances the success of tracking operations. The techniques used

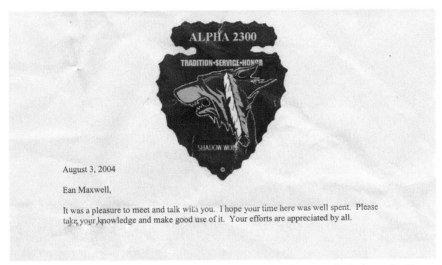

This is a letter from The Shadowolves. 'Ean' (Ian) has been spelled phonetically. The author of the letter has been removed to protect his identity.

These Argentinean trackers are without doubt the most sharp-eyed and cunning trackers I have had the privilege of working with.

by the various schools range from the Step By Step method, through to military-style tracking and the more spiritual approach which does attract a degree of debate from the non-believers, which is covered in Chapter 6.

Visual tracking techniques generally used by the military pay some attention to the senses, but these are not covered in detail here as some of these techniques present a danger to the tracker and some take too long to track the subject down. The X and Y formation, which are patterns the tracking team will form, is covered in Chapter 14. It is effective when manpower permits, and the spiritual approach does have its place when it is better understood.

It has been apparent that an alloy of techniques, which is flexible and incorporates the best ingredients from all tracking styles, will produce the most effective trackers. This book presents all these skills to make a highly effective tracking technique which you can apply under any circumstances and anywhere in the world.

The only aim of a tracker is to find the subject as soon as possible. The tracker will be driven by closing the time-distance gap, or by using cunning and guile to gather information from his surroundings to influence the outcome.

During this process, I have found from experience that tracking operations go through a number of phases, including mobilizing manpower,

A police dog handler is also a trained tracker.

skill levels, resources and ability to track effectively. Few organizations are able to provide a full complement of trackers – perhaps ten or more for one shift. Because of operational budgets, logistics and the susceptibility of trackers to get 'tracked-out', the operation will shift in size, techniques and effectiveness.

The Shadowhawk Phase Technique uses a number of skills, and is being employed operationally around the world. These techniques have their roots in Scotland, Africa, the USA and elsewhere.

In addition to native skills that go back millennia, this book also covers the latest cutting-edge techniques, including high-tech electronic devices.

Throughout, I have used terminology that seeks to standardize terms used in military, search and rescue, wildlife and law enforcement.

In recent years people have discussed the somewhat new term of 'mantracking'. There are other terms: 'human tracker', or just 'tracker'. Whether the term is new or old, the most effective way of describing someone who tracks humans is 'a mantracker'. The terms 'man' and 'mantracker' used throughout the book should be read as referring to both men and women.

Many techniques taught and written about can be overly complicated. Often, when the agency is called upon to track, they will deviate from a formalized technique because of operational reasons, and human behaviour. Therefore there is little to be gained by teaching techniques that will ultimately not be used. The Phase Technique is designed to be adaptable and seeks to simplify and provide operational solutions without loss of content or compromise.

The components of the Phase Technique, as described in this book, have been taught in Africa, Brazil, Argentina, Europe, USA, Canada and the Middle East. They are being used in the fight against armed poachers, in the global war against terrorism and in the gathering and interpretation of intelligence, tactical and combat tracking, wildlife tracking, search and rescue and counter-IED. They are also being used by forensic technicians to aid in the gathering of evidence. I have been called to court to testify as an expert witness, in cases where tracking was crucial to a successful outcome, and where the judge accepted the tracking evidence as the most important factor.

The reason that the technique is called 'the Phase Technique' is that individual trackers have varying skill levels. For example, a level one SAR Tracker may have less tracking ability than a tactical tracker, or vice versa, and although this could be addressed by 'dirt' time (i.e. time spent tracking in the field), the individuals will be going through a transitional phase of learning.

The term 'phase' also applies to operational tracking. It is very rare for a tracking team or individual to launch straight into action. There is the ramping–up process, while logistics are tackled, trackers sort out their kit and intelligence is gathered and then finally the follow-up commences. Often, a patrol or individual will be carrying out other duties and phase the tracking into their role as appropriate.

A good example is canine teams where the primary roles may be search and rescue, patrol-dog handlers, attack dogs, cadaver dogs or drug-detecting dogs. While using their dogs, they may happen across tracks, pick up on aerial spoor or be able to interpret bird dynamics. It may be that conditions are not suitable to deploy their dogs and the dogs are not able to interpret some types of spoor. In these circumstances the dog handler would switch to using his tracking skills.

I have seen this on several searches where the area was too busy with other people and pet dogs and in another situation where the surface was too hot for the dog's feet and our canine friend was returned to his air-conditioned compartment.

Equally, a search is a very dynamic situation, and resources including helicopters, quad bikes, horses and dogs will be phased in and out of the theatre of operation. The techniques have been used simultaneously in the same follow-up, by dog teams working alongside search officers and search and rescue personnel. None of them were specialist trackers, but all of them used tracking at one stage or another.

This book will describe how canine teams and mantrackers work together to provide the most powerful search tool available. I have also included some information about animals, where there is something to be gleaned from their behaviour which is of interest to trackers.

I have trained thousands of trackers, and worked with hundreds, and putting thirty-five years of following spoor into one book is a near-impossible task. There are so many things to be learnt in the field, and to this day I could spend another lifetime teaching all that I have learnt.

One thing I have discovered is the value of simplicity. That is not because I like shortcuts, but because if you complicate things they can start to go wrong when the pressure is on.

I hope that this book will be of interest to a wide range of people, from professionals in emergency services, those involved in sports such as hunting and stalking and those who want to learn about a skill that is deeply rooted in us all.

Ian Maxwell, ShadowHawk

CHAPTER 1

Background and History

Many thousands of years ago *Australopithecus* would have been able to smell his food and then, as time went on, he would have recognized tracks in the ground made by his prey. His eyes, mounted on the front of his head, were a highly effective hunting tool.

He was different from his predecessors who were browsers, grazers and scavengers because, armed with good eyesight and weapons, he would have tracked his prey efficiently using techniques that are probably very similar to those we use today. By this point in history our ancestors would have started to read tracks. They would have been able to work out whether the tracks were made by something that could be hunted for food or by something that was a threat to them or their family. Tracking had now become the tool of both the provider and the protector.

Over thousands of years tracking has remained essentially the same, although modern-day lifestyle has impacted on the level of, and the uses for, tracking. We no longer have to track our prey down but you could argue that modern shopping behaviour is an adaptation of our ancestral hunting and gathering skills. The hunt no longer occurs where we track down and kill our prey using our primeval skills: instead we hunt for the best bargains on the shop's shelves. I have observed classic hunting behaviour in supermarkets. Customers see a product that they want, yet they don't pick it up. They will often observe the product, possibly even study it in detail, and then go past it and around another aisle before returning to swoop in and pick it up. This is classic circling behaviour as used by predators when they circle their prey.

With civilization and agriculture came a fiscal society. Our ancestors were able to trade and purchase food. The need to hunt was eroded by shops and now supermarkets providing our food in exchange for money. The need to defend ourselves from other tribes and animals was largely taken over by governments and so that valuable skill started to slip into history. Yet the ability and desire to track still lies dormant in us.

Broadly speaking, we fall into two distinct types of tracker. One type of tracker is the hunter, characterized by the desire to hunt things down. Similar characteristics are displayed today in endurance running and persistence hunting.

The other is the cultivator, who has inherited behavioural patterns from when man started to cultivate land and created an agricultural society. The pastoralist is a different kind of tracker, being not so driven by the hunt. Despite the term, however, such people are crucial to a tracking team. The characteristics of both types of tracker are very strong, although it would take another book to describe the features. I am sure as you read this you are wondering which one you are.

On courses I will place an *assegai* in the sand without students seeing me do it. I make sure that there is a clear print, and then pick the *assegai* up. The way in which people describe what happened is a very good indication as to what kind of tracker they are. Some students will see only the basic fact of an imprint in the sand and cannot make any deductions about what they see. Some will go to great lengths to think it through and come up with an accurate description of what happened and their deductions. They don't express any interest in tracking down the person who placed the assegai.

A small percentage of these will make an accurate deduction; however, they go into extra detail. They will describe the fact that it has probably been placed by a hunter. They will therefore draw the conclusion that there is a potentially dangerous person in the vicinity armed with a spear. They express a strong desire to track down the assegai owner to establish if they are friend or enemy.

The first and second group tend to be the cultivators; however, the third group shows strong manhunting and tracking instinct. This group also make excellent pursuit trackers.

In many societies that I have visited there is a specialized warrior class of people, and without exception they are all trained in the art of tracking. I have found it interesting that there are specific codes of conduct to ensure that the warrior class is not corrupted, or use their powerful skills against society.

Some of the most outstanding groups of pastoralists I have met are the Samburu of Northern Kenya. They cherish their cows, which form an important part of their society. The Samburu have created a warrior class, whose job it is to protect the people, the village and the cows and to track down anyone who steals a cow from them. The warriors go through a rigorous training programme, not unlike a tactical tracker. They are taught to track, what to do in the event of meeting the enemy, stalking, weapons, survival and close-quarter combat. I once met a Samburu warrior. Through the dust I could see a pole with a flag attached, waving in the strong, dry wind. As he approached I was warned that he was a very tough and aggressive warrior and that if he didn't like the look of me he was likely to want a fight. I was told that a week ago, he had eaten a whole goat in one sitting, and that he was a giant! As he approached, I was somewhat aware of his inquisitive mind, and his display of weaponry in the ready-to-use position left no doubt that he wanted a fight.

When we met, I chose not to shake his hand and told him that I was a warrior from a country a long way off and was looking for him. He was somewhat taken aback by the fact that he had effectively become the quarry. We instantly struck up a bond and quickly got down to talking about knives, spears, guns and fighting. The day passed and we spoke through the night, at which time he told me he had been tracking me, and already knew who I was from my tracks in the dust.

When he learnt that I had a son, he invited him to join the Samburu and undergo warrior training, which would make him very proud. If ever I was in the area, I put a message out and a couple of days later he would wander into camp.

In Europe there are records of professional trackers from AD 500 onwards. The continental Germanic tribal leaders, and later their kings, made references to trackers in the laws they issued. Under Germanic law trackers were tasked with finding poached wildlife, stolen livestock and people. There is reference to the amount a tracker was paid: three *solidi* for a horse and two *solidi* for a cow (*solidi* was a form of coinage).

The word spoor, originally Dutch, translates to sign, tracks and trail, but this is only part of the complete term. In Dutch, tracking is translated as *spoorenkunde*, which is divided into three different levels: *spoorzoeken*, *spoorlezen* and *spoorvolgen*.

Spoorzoeken translates as finding and identifying tracks and sign. *Spoorlezen* translates to reading and interpreting sign and tracks. *Spoorvolgen* translates to the follow-up, where the tracker follows the track and sign.

Some of the earliest documented tracking comes from Rogers' Rangers, named for Maj. Robert Rogers, who used a blend of skills from Native American tactics and his own, somewhat innovative combat skills. The 28 'Rules of Ranging' are a series of rules and guidelines originally created by Rogers in 1757, during the French and Indian War (1754–63). They were intended to serve as a manual on guerrilla warfare for Rogers' Ranger company, a 600-strong contingent whose members were personally selected by Rogers. His rangers undertook a harsh training programme, which gave them the tools to live off the land and carry out reconnaissance duties but, interestingly, his rangers spent many hours learning tracking skills, which feature in the 28 rules of ranging. These rules came to be tested on many occasions.

US Ranger commander Lt.-Col. William Darby read the rules to the 1st Ranger Battalion prior to action during World War II, and a modified version of the rules is still followed by the 75th Ranger Regiment to this day. They are considered the model for all Ranger activities.

The Plan of Discipline, as extracted from Major Rogers' journal and intended for his Rogers' Rangers in 1759, includes the following advice:

... If you march over marshes or soft ground, change your position, and march abreast of each other to prevent the enemy from tracking you (as they would do if you marched in a single file) till you get over such ground, and then resume your former order, and march till it is quite dark before you encamp, which do, if possible, on a piece of ground which may afford your sentries the advantage of seeing or hearing the enemy some considerable distance, keeping one half of your whole party awake alternately through the night.

... Some time before you come to the place you would reconnoitre, look for footprints, make a stand, and send one or two men in whom you can confide, to look out the best ground for making your observations. ...

It is very interesting that Rogers formalized his rules of ranging, because this was probably the first and the last time that tracking was written about until the Boer Wars. Some cultures don't have a name for tracking, or a translation from English. Many of the societies that I have worked within simply don't have a term for the process. As a child growing up in the bush, the tribes that were around, the Bemba, Ngoni, Matabele and Mashona used tracking in everyday life, but it was the Europeans that gave it such a title.

History books tell us that tracking was used extensively in the Wild West, and the many Indian wars that raged as Native Americans resisted the settlement of Westerners. The iconic symbols of Geronimo and Cochise of the Apache tribes were glamorized by TV and movies. It is clear that Geronimo was an expert tracker and he used his tracking and stalking skills to slow down the US Cavalry. There are stories of Geronimo sneaking into US camps and removing gun parts, a clever trick indeed. Had he removed complete guns the Cavalry would have detected something was going on, and would have prepared for Geronimo's night-time forays. Instead they would not have suspected anything was missing. This is a tactic I use to this day, but it falls under another chapter.

During the Indian Wars a young American settler, Frederick Burnham, was growing up. He witnessed the killing of settlers by the Sioux and he became a scout and tracker by the age of fourteen. He was soon to be employed by the US Cavalry and picked up lots of skills from Native American trackers during his experience scouting and tracking in the Chiricahua Apache and Cheyenne Wars. In 1893 Frederick Burnham appeared in Africa, employed as a soldier of fortune to scout for the Shangani Patrol in Matabeleland. It was during his experience on this patrol that he claims to have tracked by touch at night to retrieve two of his colleagues from the bush. The accounts of his tracking, stalking and scouting make for interesting reading, but it is one of the earliest chronicles of tracking.

In 1876, Robert Baden-Powell had joined the British army, and was soon to be posted to Africa. He enhanced and honed his military scouting skills among the Zulu in the early 1880s in the Natal province of South Africa.

Baden-Powell's skills had impressed his superiors and he returned to Africa in 1896, and served in the Second Matabele War, in the expedition to relieve British South Africa Company personnel under siege in Bulawayo. This was a formative experience for him, not only because he had the time of his life commanding reconnaissance missions into enemy territory in the Matopos Hills, but because many of his later Boy Scout ideas took hold here. It was during this campaign that he first met and befriended Frederick Burnham, who introduced Baden-Powell to the American Old West and to tracking.

Both men were to spend their time fighting the Boers in South Africa. The Boers had a tactical advantage. They employed guerrilla warfare and used their skills as hunters. They were well camouflaged and concentrated on making the first shot count, based on the fact that, if you didn't hit the animal you were hunting with the first shot it would bolt. They also knew the land and environment.

To combat the Boer Commandos, Lord Lovat, from the North-east of Scotland, was given money to raise a private army. He recruited gamekeepers and ghillies who knew how to track and stalk animals and also had considerable expertise in apprehending poachers. They wore tweed, which to this day is still one of the best fabrics available for camouflage, and could stay out for days on end, living off the land. They were perfect scouts, and were a match for the Boers.

This was a turning point for tracking. The Lovats had adapted their uniforms and were wearing one in dark green, now known as Lovat green. Baden Powell had started to formalize his accounts of tracking and chronicled it in his books, including tracking games.

Although others were using tracking skills, the collaboration between Burnham and Baden-Powell, in their theatre of operation, meant that many features of tracking became formalized. Baden-Powell established the Scout movement and the little-known Legion of Frontiersman, which was a small paramilitary cadre of men, with tracking and survival skills, who could be deployed at short notice to areas of the Commonwealth.

It was evident that small élite tracking units were highly efficient and they were deployed in the many wars that followed.

As time went on, winds of change were sweeping across the colonies and South-east Asia. Countries were involved in freedom struggles. Some were involved with Soviet and Communist backers. These wars were fought in hostile landscapes, where the locals knew the terrain, and like the Boers were able to conduct guerrilla tactics. In 1948 in the jungles of Malaya, the deployment of large numbers of troops was not working, and so the SAS were deployed. The SAS comprised a small group of hand-picked men, capable of great stealth; these men worked closely and successfully with native Iban trackers. Soon the tide of the war began to turn against the insurgents.

Between 1952 and 1962 in Kenya, gangs of Mau Mau were attacking White settlers. The colonial Kenyans hit back, but the Mau Mau would simply fade into the jungle once they had struck. As in Malaya, local trackers were used, but for the first time, suspicions were being raised about the accuracy and loyalty of the native Kikuyu trackers.

Back in the jungles of South-east Asia, in 1963 war started in Indonesia. It was here that the British adopted tactics similar to those of the Boer Commandos and Lovat Scouts. Training that focused on hunting skills was introduced. Skills such as stalking, endurance, tracking and local knowledge were drummed into the troops.

However, the tracking carried out in the jungles of Malaya was still done mostly by natives. For some reason, the British did not fully embrace tracking. This may have been through lack of time to maintain the skill-set, or lack of confidence.

It was not until the Zimbabwean freedom struggle in 1970 that mantracking was to make a big comeback. Veteran Rhodesian SAS soldiers who had been in Malaya and Kenya were approached by Allan Savoury. Savoury was an excellent game ranger, who used tracking techniques to hunt elephants and run down poachers. His timing was good, because he had the ear of senior officers, who not only knew the benefit of tracking, but also knew the disadvantages of using local trackers. During the Zimbabwean freedom struggle, local trackers had in fact led troops into landmines.

In some areas of Botswana South Africa Bushmen were used to track but because of cultural variations it was difficult to work with them. There are stories of a follow-up using Bushmen, when midway along the spoor, the trackers would lie down, with no indication of when they would wake again. The reason for this is difficult to understand; it could be that they were tired, hungry or under the influence of hallucinogenic drugs.

Savoury, who was an expert tracker and able to survive in the bush, was given permission to raise and train his own unit known as the Tracker Combat Unit, composed of game rangers, hunters and ex-soldiers. Savoury caused concern when he said he loved the bush so much, if he had been born black, he would have joined the freedom fighters. Yet again a small, élite unit was formed consisting of yesteryear trackers. The Tracker Combat Unit underwent a metamorphosis, but they continued to get results from their tracking skills.

In Australia there is a wealth of experienced Aboriginal trackers. They have lots of stories of success, including the hunt for Ned Kelly. In the north of Australia there is a unit called Norforce. The regiment's lineage goes back to 2/1 North Australia Observer Unit (also known as the

'Nackaroos'), which was formed in 1942 as part of the defence of northern Australia from the Japanese during the Second World War, performing reconnaissance, scouting and coastal surveillance tasks across the Kimberley and the Northern Territory. They are reputed trackers of considerable reputation, of whom some 80 per cent are Aboriginal.

There are many other excellent tracking and reconnaissance units throughout the world, including the Ladakh Scouts of India. However, military tracking seemed to have reached an evolutionary stasis until quite recently.

During the 1970s the US Border Patrol were beginning to give greater priority to tracking. They were already using tracking to apprehend people crossing from Mexico into the USA. Two US Border Patrol agents, Jack Kearney and Ab Taylor, published books which gave blueprints for learning how to track. They had been called on several occasions to search for missing people and, as a result, started teaching search and rescue organizations. They were teaching the step-by-step method, which is dealt with in Chapter 6.

In the years that followed, the USA bolstered its Achilles' heel with Mexico by creating a structured force of trackers. Usually, there was the lineman, who was the first line of defence. He was backed up by Borstar (US Border Search and Rescue) and Bortac (US Border Tactical Unit). All of these units could call upon specialist trackers who used a range of assets from quad bikes, horses, elevated surveillance through to aerial surveillance. There was also an organization called the Shadow Wolves, founded in 1972 as an initiative undertaken by the US to track drug smugglers on Native American lands the American South-west. The Shadow Wolves comprise an Immigration and Customs Enforcement tactical patrol unit based on the Native American Tohono O'odham Nation in southern Arizona. Shadow Wolf officers are known for their ability to track aliens and drug smugglers as they attempt to smuggle their illegal commodities across the border. The name refers to the way the unit hunts like a wolf pack. The unit boasts an esteemed history of tracking passed down from generation to generation. Despite having access to high-tech equipment, the unit relies mainly on traditional methods of tracking. Officers may spend hours or days tracking in the field following spoor until arrests and seizures are made.

The Shadow Wolves consist of personnel from tribes such as the Apache, Sioux, Navajo, Lakota, Kickapoo and Chicasaw as well as the Pima and Tohono O'odham. They learnt from their elders that it is possible to 'hear' things that are silent and to 'see' things that are invisible on a trail. I was lucky enough to track with them and bring some of those skills into the Phase Technique, which is described later in this book.

In addition to the specialized tracking organizations, there were several organizations teaching search and rescue tracking and wildlife tracking alike, but it was not until 1998, when David Scott-Donelan wrote his fine book *Tactical Tracking Operations*, that we saw the emergence of tactical tracking spreading to law enforcement and the military alike.

There was little or no convergence between search and rescue (SAR), military and wildlife tracking until recently. I have always maintained that it is best to take someone who is a wildlife tracker, who is used to living in the outdoors, and teach them to mantrack. However, this is easier said than done. Many budding mantrackers want a quick fix to track humans, and are not really interested in tracking animals. However, perhaps because of the war in Afghanistan and a better appreciation of military methods, I have found a re-emergence of the desire to track animals, merged with mantracking. This has the advantage that the tracker can distinguish between animal tracks and human tracks. Skilled IED operators will go to great lengths to conceal their footprints and use livestock, including goat herds, in an attempt to obliterate human tracks. A good tracker will be able to recognize human tracks amongst animal tracks. While there will always be the use for a specialist tracking hunter force there is a present trend towards counter-IED tracking. This combines the very latest in technology, linked with the ancient art of tracking.

Who knows what will happen in the future. At the time of writing, the USA is developing robot soldiers and they may one day be the quarry, or able to recognize spoor, but they will never be able to out-compete the cunning and motivated human tracker.

CHAPTER 2

The Qualities and Skills of a Tracker

COUP D'OEIL: POWER OF THE GLANCE

I once asked a Bushman, 'What makes a good tracker?' He replied, 'Hunger.' I took him to mean two things. Hunger for food will sharpen the senses, and hunger for knowledge will improve your tracking database and chances of survival.

The tracker needs to have good level of fieldcraft and be able to survive and operate in environmentally hostile regions on his or her own. Fieldcraft comprises the skills and techniques involved in living and travelling in the field, especially while remaining undetected. These skills and techniques include acquisition of drinkable water and food, application of camouflage and navigation. Other skills include using features to conceal ground movement and obstacle crossing. Techniques for lie-up positions, observation, counter-surveillance, including survival, evasion and escape techniques, are also key skills.

Additionally, the tracker will require stamina and a skill-set that will aid in the search for dangerous people and missing persons.

The tracker needs to be a detective. He has to work from the facts alone, but if he is to be successful, he will also need to use his intuition to anticipate the movements of the quarry.

In the military terms a good general is said to have 'coup d'oeil'. In French this means 'power of the glance', and it is the ability to immediately make sense of the battlefield. While not every tracker will achieve this, it will enhance performance.

All my hunter force trackers have gone through a rigorous training regime. Not only are they expected to track, but to be self-sufficient, being able to think for themselves in stressful conditions in the field. They are expected to be good team members, but free-thinkers at the same time. I have found that if their free spirit is inhibited, their ability to apply themselves to a difficult quarry is hampered. Most of them are individualists to varying degrees, but at the same time they have the ability to fall in with others, and be members of a highly disciplined group.

They need to be able to know about all manner of equipment, and be able to draw upon skills like natural navigation, which is where they can use nature and natural features to guide them, for example tree growth being more abundant on the south side in the northern hemisphere and on the north side in the southern hemisphere, or buffeted growth showing the direction of the dominant wind. Natural navigation is a vast subject – however, being able to get an idea of direction by the sun is the most useful of all. To do that, they have to be able to observe well, and grasp every piece of information in detail, without taking notes. It may be minutes or years before they will need to recall that information.

I find if I take mini mental snapshots of information, including landscapes, for a maximum of three seconds I am able to remember most things in detail. I have tracked all over the world, and there are very few places where I cannot remember the tracks in minute detail. Not only that, but I can remember the noises and some of the associated smells.

I often get called to talk about tracking to the business community because they are curious to see if they could adapt parts of the philosophy of tracking to give them a competitive edge. Companies are keen to increase their performance by applying something which none of their competitors have tried, tracking 'tricks of the trade'. There are behavioural patterns, that as a tracker, I will always recognize in animals and humans.

The first one, I am personally guilty of. I pointed out to them that I had circled them at least twice, once when they were entering the venue and then after they were seated. There was a moment of uncomfortable silence, in which they realized their vulnerability. It is a behavioural pattern that the hunter will use and the prey will recognize. The circling behaviour is used to weigh up the prey, to get a feel for it, and the landscape. Where is the best place to launch an attack? Where is the best cover? What direction is the wind and where will they flee to? Are there any elements of the environment that can be used as a vantage point? Very few people will detect this behaviour consciously. However, I think most people will detect it subconsciously. The circle is best portrayed in the African bush, where the lion will circle buffalo or wildebeest before the rush to separate the young or injured from the herd.

So the question is, do you have to be a hunter to track? The answer is no, because we know that all complex animals use some form of detection for food, mating or feuding.

Like all tools, its efficiency is dependent on the method of use and the skill level of the user. The qualities and skills of a tracker can mean the difference between life and death – literally, your own life or, in search and rescue (SAR), the life of someone else.

The key is to remain the hunter and not become the hunted. They say that in nature the game is only predator and prey. The mantracker has to have the ability to remain the predator.

Seventy to eighty thousand years ago Palaeolithic man was a scavenger, relying on other animals to do the stalking and pursuit. Once the prey had been killed, man would move in to take his share of the food. Only after these scavengers discovered the spear were they able to develop skills to hunt bigger prey. Within our genetic makeup, this hunting gene still exists.

Later, during the Neolithic period, settlement and agriculture was coming into play and hunters declined in numbers and became localized to arid areas and jungles. This is still manifested today by the Bushmen of the Kalahari, who by no choice of their own ended up in the deserts of the Kalahari. Another good example of modern-day jungle settlement is the Iban tribe of Borneo. Both these groups are natural trackers and hunters, and throughout history have provided trackers for the military during times of conflict.

As time passed, more people became pastoral and agricultural, and our skills as trackers and hunters declined. The flame almost burnt out, but some of the skills still remain in certain people. Some are clearly still hunters and others have a pastoral style to their tracking. I have found that the division is very clear. The hunter type of tracker enjoys the chase, and once the chase has come to an end, will have a burning desire to go on the chase again. This type of person is generally the mantracker.

As it goes, the more successful cultures are those that took to growing crops on fertile land and establishing infrastructure, while those that continue hunter-gatherer lifestyles have a less developed infrastructure and occupy less desirable regions. Pastoral trackers are still good at what they do, and tend to be good at tracking and bringing in the livestock. A prime example of this is the Maasai tribe in Africa. Goats and cows are currency to them and they make excellent trackers. However the tribes have warriors within who, on the whole, are not overly interested in the welfare of the livestock and have developed their tracking skills specific to mantracking so that they can pursue people who steal their livestock. If someone steals their livestock the warriors will use mantracking to reclaim their cattle and it is likely that an armed skirmish will ensue.

Despite popular belief a manhunter doesn't have to be a Native American, Australian Aboriginal or Bushman of the Kalahari. There is a tracking instinct deep within every man, women and child. and we need to examine how those skills can be used in the modern age.

The common perception is that tracking is mainly a visual skill, and that good trackers have eagle eyes. Military trackers are referred to as VTs, or visual trackers. A VT will have a keen eye for visual signs, but without additional skills a VT is only slightly better than an untrained tracker in that he might be more clue aware. A good tracker has a multitude of skills and qualities. Not all trackers will be the best at all roles. Within my teams I have people who are excellent at bird dynamics but not so good at ground spoor. It is worth bearing in mind that, as a tracker gets older, his vision may weaken, but this is often compensated for by experience.

Key tracker skills include an inquisitive mind, being able to interpret spoor and the ability to anticipate the mind and movements of the target. Empathy is the greatest skill of all and ego the greatest enemy.

It would be an ideal world if only the 'good guys' could track, but in reality the 'bad guys' make good trackers too, and outwitting them is a cat and mouse game. In fact I have my suspicions that both the 'good guys' and the 'bad guys' sometimes enjoy this game of wits, albeit sometimes the outcomes are unpleasant. The cunning and guile of a tracker is always being matched, whether they are the pursued or the pursuer.

Tactical decision-making, knowing how to set a trap and when to strike is like a game of human chess.

I have often tracked on patrol, accompanied by local forces. On one occasion, while training military police in the jungles of South America, we were penetrating deep into the jungle to track and intercept armed poachers who had control of the area. The rangers had been unable to make arrests and the poachers were armed with guns and had the benefit of dense jungle to protect them. The poachers' senses were tuned into the slightest change and they were able to read the silent messages of the jungle. They were masters of moving silently and were well camouflaged and they would disappear into the jungle leaving little behind them other than a hot fire. They were aware that once they disappeared into the jungle they would have reversed the odds in their favour and that pursuit would not be safe. Booby traps, coded messages cut into a tree or a pile of stones and the advantage of silence meant that they had become the hunter and we the hunted, which was an unpleasant feeling.

On every patrol we were one step behind them, finding active poaching camps but no one in them. It then became clear that, in the village drinking dens, word had got round that a 'gringo' tracker was in town, and was patrolling into the jungle. This made the poachers hypersensitive.

I left for the jungle a day early, giving the impression that I had quit the area, and with two scouts set up in the jungle, moving closer to the camp hour by hour. After four days, we were based only a hundred metres from the poachers' camp and knew exactly where their trails, escape routes and booby traps were.

A briefing was given and a well-armed patrol entered the jungle to intercept the poachers. We could tell that they had entered the jungle from a river two kilometres away, because we could see holes in the dense growth on the riverbank. On investigating several holes, we saw that one had fresh tracks in the mud. The bird behaviour changed and we could see that the animals had become jumpy.

Two kilometres in dense jungle is a long way, but during the day it was as though the poachers were playing a boom box through the jungle. We could smell the clean smell of detergent and could hear the sharp 'ching' of machetes as they cut through the undergrowth.

As though prompted, the poachers calmly gathered their belongings and again disappeared into the jungle, shortly before the patrol arrived in camp.

The poachers were under the illusion that again, they had turned the tables on us, but within half an hour we had tracked down all six of them. As the patrol had closed in on the camp, and the poachers moved out, we tracked the poachers' exit from their escape route and followed them closely. They were stunned by what had happened, and despite their predicament there was mutual respect. Without the ability to second guess their movements and understand their motivation the operation would not have succeeded.

This jungle tracking operation included all the skills and qualities described in this book that a tracker needs. These are what we will go on to discuss next.

PHYSICALITY AND MENTALITY

Mentality

A common misconception that men make better trackers than women is fuelled by the desire of modern men to be the providers and protectors, the alpha males.

A vast amount of ethnographic and archaeological evidence demonstrates that the sexual division of labour where men hunt and women forage was uncommon among hunter-gatherers. Most of the gathering was done by women, but they also hunted small game, while the men hunted the large and more dangerous game. In other studies where women hunted, it was found that 85 per cent of women hunted the same quarry as men and had a 31 per cent success rate as opposed to 17 per cent for men.

I have found that women make excellent trackers. They have an eye for detail, and their senses are very receptive. However, I have found that they generally need to get results quickly. If the tracks are not easy to follow, and hours pass by, they have difficulty staying in the tracker's mindset. Men, on the other hand, also make excellent trackers, but seem to have a greater stamina for remaining in the mindset for longer, especially during times when tracking results are poor.

All trackers must prepare physically and mentally for the follow-up. They must expect the best of themselves, and think positively; in turn this will stimulate chemicals in the brain that induce positivity. Positive thinkers literally have a different chemistry from negative thinkers.

However, before a positive mental state can be achieved, negative thoughts need to be acknowledged and worked through. In other words, to expect the best, you will also have considered how to deal with the worst.

So the tracker must ask, 'What is the worst-case scenario?', consider the negative scenarios and prepare emotionally for every one of those eventualities, decide how they could be dealt with, then set them aside. Once this has been done there are no longer any negative thoughts left. The focus is then 100 per cent on a positive scenario, with an expectation of a successful outcome.

On numerous courses I have had students who were afraid of the dark, of insects and a whole range of other factors which would affect their ability to track. For example, on one course we had a forensic scientist who was afraid of ants.

Fears should be tackled early, otherwise it is too easy for coils of rope to become snakes, and fear takes over. In the darkness we lose our ability to see in colour and we see in shades of grey through the peripherals of the eyes. This is when most people allow fears to creep in to their mind.

It is not advisable to have a tracker who is afraid of the dark, or who has any fears that will impact on the follow-up.

It is important to rationalize any fear. Instead of 'Oh no, it's dark', try changing it to 'Oh yes, it's dark'. You'll find that by simply replacing the word 'no' with 'yes' will have a positive outcome.

While being positive is important, it is also important that the tracker does not have a strong ego, as this will ultimately reflect on ever-changing conditions. The ego is the tracker's worst enemy because with the ego come strong opinions and self-importance. Considering that empathy for our quarry and the ability to get into their mind is one of the most important skills, it is not surprising that this does not work well with ego. Often, during the learning phases of tracking, ego creeps in, and with that comes pride. When things don't work out for that person, and they are in the 'red zone' (see below), it is very difficult for them to accept their vulnerabilities and the fact that they may be on the wrong track. In these circumstances, they tend to get frustrated with themselves and sometimes they can get very angry.

The illusion of an easy-going, happy-go-lucky tracker is a good one, but don't be deceived; under that façade there could be a devastatingly effective tracker.

At the same time as being positive, the tracker must deal with fact only; it is very easy to see things that aren't really there. Usually this happens when trackers are tired, when it's very easy to see 'faces in the clouds'.

Often, when there is a sequence of events, all leading towards one conclusion, but with one crucial fact left out, it is human nature and a trick of the mind to fill in the gap. I come across this frequently when contacted by people who have seen large panther-like cats in the UK. Often they will have seen something, and then come across tracks, which to the untrained person look massive. Then, as far as they are concerned, they saw a panther with green eyes. When I attend, it is not possible to discern whether they have actually seen a panther or not, because they are so convinced. However, the track that they thought was from the panther, is indeed clearly that of a dog. On several occasions the media have been keen for me to confirm that the tracks are those of a big cat and they are always disappointed to find out that they are dog tracks.

That said, being of an analytical nature can be a double-edged sword in tracking. While it is good to analyse the tracks, it can have a negative effect when on the follow-up, because over-analysis tends to hamper the ability to use intuition, otherwise known as hunch tracking.

Mantracking requires immense mental concentration and can quickly drain the reserves and place stress on the tracker. It is crucial that a tracker recognizes the fact that they have entered the 'red zone' and are approaching the state of being tracked-out. This effect is where the brain has become tired, and the eyes have been overworking. Effectively, at this point, the tracker will have shut down and will not be able to see any tracks. I have had one tracker in this zone who was standing right next to an obvious track but couldn't see it, even when it was pointed out to him.

Being in the 'red zone' is an everyday event for trackers and being able to spot it in another tracker is a useful skill. However, with experience, trackers soon learn to recognize it themselves. Once a tracker knows that he is tracked-out, he should pass the trail onto someone else with fresh eyes so that they rotate the work. Often people ask, how long does it take to be tracked-out? Or, when working in formation, how often should the tracker be changed out? There is no definitive answer. The answer is that when the tracker enters the 'red zone', it's time to change about.

Attention to detail is essential, to the level that a small hair, a drop of blood, or a stone out of its socket can be spotted on a trail. This is especially important for the manhunting tracker. Anything that is out of context and a minute change in the baseline should be detected. Not only will the quarry leave behind clues as to their passing, but the possibility of booby traps exists, which could be a trip-wire at ankle height or, if specifically counter-tracker, at head height. On numerous occasions I have spotted booby traps, simply by noticing that some leaves were upside down, and when investigating I have found fully loaded traps.

In Africa, paying attention has paid me many dividends. By keeping an eye on the tracks of a black rhino or lion, I could see if they were in an aggressive mood, or in need of a kill.

Often on a course I ask students to select a leaf on a tree and, without marking it, to return to it later in the day. I am always astounded that every student has returned to the same leaf, and in one case, a year later, a student was still able to identify his leaf amongst many hundreds of thousands. I also do the same with small stones. The students will select a small stone; look at it for thirty seconds and then return it to me. I jumble the stones up and put them in the middle of the classroom. On every occasion the students have selected their stone correctly – in fact some students have kept their stones to remind them of the importance of paying attention to detail.

While this is a light-hearted exercise it has an important message: attentiveness can mean the difference between life and death.

Tuning-in to the Senses

I have found that when there is peril, my senses are super-tuned. I can hear a pin drop; I can smell the slightest scent carried on the wind; I can see in high definition; and I can feel the slightest change in temperature of the wind on my skin. Ideally the tracker should be in this state of mind continuously.

Being receptive to senses is possibly one of the tracker's most important skills. Not being tuned in could cost your life, or the lives of others. I have found that some people have lost this ability, possibly because our senses are overloaded by modern-day life.

The smell of soap being carried downstream on a river is a giveaway that someone is washing upstream. The sight of bubbles gives the same indication. On several occasions, usually during cooler times, I have felt the body heat of someone carried on the wind. If someone is smoking upwind they are virtually raising a flag above their head.

The tracker must have finely tuned senses to maintain his advantage.

Visual acuity

Most of the time a tracker is relying on his visual skill, as that is our most powerful sense. He must be able to spot the smallest detail, the smallest item out of context, and be able to do this both close up and from a distance. He must be able to use peripheral vision and immediately go back to splatter vision, where one item is being looked at to exclusion of other items (see Chapter 3). At this point he is using the power of predatory binocular vision. In this mode of stereopsis we are effectively seeing something from two different angles, and the brain processes the information so that we are able to judge distance. Herbivores tend to have eyes on the sides of the head, which gives peripheral vision and an effective measure against predators. However, peripheral vision is not natural to humans, so we have to train our eyes to work in both peripheral and binocular vision. Interestingly, information received through peripheral vision is not questioned by the conscious brain, and being able to track in peripheral vision, as described in Chapter 3, helps us to be more instinctive.

The hardest visual skill of all is to acquire the ability to look *through* something, rather than directly at it. An example of this is to look through the leaves of a tree to the other side. The reason why this is hard is that in the modern world we only look at what demands our attention. Good examples of this are flashing neon advertising, or the bright brake lights on a car, when they are activated in front of us. In a ferocious consumer market, products compete with each through colour, and we have got used to it. The brighter the better for consumer products. The more muted colours found in nature don't exist in the consumer market. We are continuously bombarded by these bright colours, through the media and right up to the point where we enter a natural environment. When I receive new trackers I have noticed that their eyes get tired very quickly. This is because their eyes have become lazy. When they arrive into camp their eyes don't know where to look because colours are muted. Having said that, it is exactly the opposite for search and rescue people. They are well adorned in high visibility clothing. The protective fluorescent apparel does its job well, which is to drag the attention of the eye from their surroundings to themselves, ensuring that they can be seen. When working with search and rescue, there is a whole new set of rules for training the eyes not to be distracted by their safety clothing. What I do is glance at their high visibility clothing several times, then immediately glance to the nearest muted feature behind them. I find that this helps to train my eyes so that their effectiveness in seeing difficult spoor is not hampered by their brightly coloured garments.

By the time we get into nature, often the more subtle spoor is there, but 'invisible'. Because our eyes are trained to look at what demands our attention, they will be drawn to look at straight outlines. Try looking at a door from a few metres away. At first you will think you are looking at the door, but in reality you are looking at the straight lines of the door, usually the vertical lines. You won't be looking at the centre of the door. In fact this is the case in nature as well; you will be drawn to the straight lines of tree trunks and other features. To exploit this we make camouflage shapes that disrupt the outline of humans, and they are generally curved in some form or other.

Being able to see minute detail and paying attention to it is very important. Once I was called by the police to track a missing person. In these cases, I always re-create the position of the person. For example, the majority of people are right-handed, which means they will stand to the left of a car-boot latch, unless they are holding something in their right hand.

In this area there were a number of tracks in the mud. To be sure that we were about to track the right person, a confirmed identifiable signature track was required. I was informed that the missing person had a dog and inside the boot of their car there were dog hairs. To the left of the boot latch I found a footprint with a matching dog hair squashed into the mud. This had to be the track we wanted to follow.

I often watch people on courses think that they cannot see a track. I can see it and I know they can see it, it's just that their conscious mind cannot believe it. I watch them move to every angle in an attempt to see the track. The way I know that they can see the track is that their head cocks towards the track, the eyes focus and then their head cocks back. They saw the track at the time the head cocked towards the track.

The key to this is to remove the over-analysis of the track and override the conscious mind. Intuitive shooting is done by 'ready, fire'. I usually hit my target this way. I have used this technique in the bush to be able to shoot a charging animal. To go through 'ready, aim, fire' causes the mind to stall, so I teach the technique of ready, and straight to fire, without aiming. Once this is mastered, the tracker improves significantly in spotting difficult tracks.

The next technique is to train the eyes to look ahead and then down. The skill here is to look at the horizon, and then draw the eyes back to the ground, about the height of yourself ahead. If done continuously it can be very tiring and you will soon feel the muscles around the eyes tire. I find that if you do a commentary it helps to learn the technique.

Patience, Determination and Perseverance

Never give up; never give in. Patience and silence are two of the most important qualities of a tracker. In fact, silence is not just golden, it is a weapon. On many of my follow-ups the quarry has been located just when most people would give up. Tracking painstakingly for hour after hour, and day after day, takes significant patience, especially when the trail goes cold. Often people training to be trackers become impatient and frustrated because they want to see more of the track. There is a fine line between positive determination and negative stubbornness, which has a negative effect on performance. Often it is when things are getting tough and the tracker is in the 'red zone', that the line is crossed. He becomes frustrated and wants to see the tracks, but cannot see any obvious spoor – so what does he chase? This is the point at which injuries occur, and the tracking team's performance will drop.

Perseverance is a key factor that can make the difference between a good tracker and an excellent one. I have never tracked anyone down without perseverance. I always think about how long it would take to track someone. A lead-time of twenty minutes can mean a full day's follow-up, if you are lucky! When you pick up spoor, it could go anywhere, uphill and down glen. It could involve torrential rain, freezing temperature, scorching sun, stinging plants, biting insects and dangerous animals. It could go on for hour after hour, when you see the sun rise one morning and are still tracking at sunrise the next day, without a break.

Tactical patience: the five-minute rule

The best results often come after patiently lying in wait, or waiting for further information. It is all too easy to lose patience, which in turn leads to negative frustration and then mistakes will happen and the harmony of the tracking team will fall apart. It is very tempting to throw in the towel when things are not going your way. I have a rigid rule under these circumstances. When your back is to the wall, things are looking bad and everyone has had enough, sometimes you want to break cover, head for camp or just give up. In these cases use the 'five-minute rule'. No matter what is happening, the trackers must remain on location for an additional five minutes. This rule has saved the day on more than one occasion.

Within a tracking team there will be varying levels of skill and personality. I have found that, rather than change the personality, it is better to maximize the individual skills. Let the hunters be the hunters and the bean-growers be bean-growers.

As described in Chapter 6, a tracking team should include micro-trackers and macro-trackers. The latter are more common, but to find someone who is interested in the minutiae of details is a more difficult prospect, because that person has a completely different mindset from the macro-tracker.

Generally, once the tracking team is operational in the field there is no formalized rank. Having said that, the teams will need to be controlled from within the group. This senior role is usually the result of having won respect. In some cultures trackers with white hair are revered, and in others someone who has taken the life of the enemy is respected. If neither of the above applies, there are other ways of winning respect.

I have found that being humble and showing interest in various cultures is a good start. Once in the field I will not feed or drink at the expense of another, and will never be the first to request a break. Once I have settled in, I will show the team that I am of equal or greater mettle than their own. This can involve traditional initiations or just stepping up to the mark when there is some kind of competition going on. I have fought in traditional stick fights and taken part in long-distance runs through snake-infested *kopjes* (low-lying hills with bushes) just to establish respect.

Courage

'The one with blood' is my name in parts of Africa and, strangely enough, with a Native American tribe. This description is reserved for the spirited person who will rise to any challenge, and is brave. It is a curious description, because I have been in many dangerous situations, some of which were long and enduring experiences, and some in which the danger lasted for seconds. I have faced many dangerous animal charges, but the most frightening was when a tiger charged. The roar of a tiger cannot be described: it is designed to stun its prey. When I was in India a tiger emerged from the jungle and within seconds it was charging. I was stunned by the roar and froze to the spot. The tiger sprung towards me and at the last moment, when only a metre or two away, it veered off. I was able to describe the feeling; I felt neither brave nor scared. One thing I do know, however, is that if the scared feeling had come through, the tiger would probably have sensed it and finished me off.

Being too brave can get you into trouble, but so can being too cautious. Both, however, are important parts of being a tracker. It is a fine balance between being too cautious and too brave.

Sometimes I like to see trackers work like lions. The nature documentaries show spectacular feats of stalking and an action-packed chase and kill by the lions. To get the cliché footage they film literally hundreds of hours and it has to be edited down. I have watched by day, and through the night, with night-vision equipment, which is almost suicidal! Lion are not brave or courageous; they attack only when they have judged that factors are stacked in their favour. At dusk, they usually start to move with a stretch of limbs. They then move off a fair distance, into their hunting ground. It is rare for a lion to attack outside of its hunting ground (however, if you stumble into the area it knows inside out, it is likely that you will get eaten!) Once in the hunting ground, the lions move a little and lie down, all their senses fully attuned. They are hoping that, by lying still, their prey will run into them. If nothing happens they move a short distance again.

Guile

All trackers should have a degree of guile. It is something that I can spot in a tracker a mile off.

The Special Boat Service (SBS) motto is 'By Strength and Guile'. It used to be 'Not By Strength, but Guile'. I prefer the latter, because it implies that you do not need strength to succeed.

Every tracker is an opportunist, because you only get what you are given. Sometimes there is nothing, and then something will appear, and it must be grasped and used. This applies to food and water. On courses, there is an exercise in scavenging. There is a bit of surprise when I give people their briefing. It can range from scavenging old tins to chicken eggs. If they operate close to human populations then they need to sneak in like a fox, and sneak out again without drawing attention to themselves. They are encouraged to do the unexpected!

An Open Mind

An open mind is an essential tool for a mantracker. The Australian aborigines believe in full circles, but when they paint them, they leave a small gap so the circle is not complete. They believe that if you leave a gap, then thoughts from outside the circle can get in. To let thoughts in is essential; after all, how will you be able to read the mind of your quarry if your own mind in closed?

I have tracked feignocides (faked suicides), and come across acts by humans that are unimaginable. The levels to which humans can go to are extraordinary. The feignocides are the most remarkable follow-ups. Often they have time to make elaborate plans, using information easily gained from the internet and books, so they can be hard to find.

On one occasion I was called to an incident where a mobile phone and a pile of bloodied clothes were found on a busy, fast road used by hundreds of trucks a day. At first sight it looked as though someone had wandered onto the road and been hit by a vehicle, which would probably have continued without the driver knowing that they had collided with someone. The phone had intentionally been damaged, although not so badly that information about the owner could not be identified.

The road was closed and I used techniques described in this book to corroborate the fact that it was believed that the person in question had been fatally injured and carried away from the scene. It was clear that someone had been to the site where the clothes and phone were found, but it was equally clear from the grass flagging that they had left the site. Several days later I found out that they had used a stolen relative's credit card and been located safe and sound. It transpired that they wanted to go off-grid to avoid debt and had staged the phone and clothes on the road so that it would look like a fatal accident without the body.

On another occasion the target spent several weeks planning his disappearance. He told everyone close to him that he was depressed and suicidal. He then cleared out his bank account, took a rope and ladder from his garage and parked up in a remote area. The fact that the rope was missing from the garage indicated that he had planned to hang himself in the woods.

I was called to the area after dark. Tracks led from his vehicle to a ladder up against a tree, but there was no rope. Tracks then led away from the ladder into a large wasteland of bogs and sinking sand. I continued to track him, expecting at any moment to see him swinging from a tree. The trail continued for a couple of kilometres to a road and then completely disappeared. I searched for several hours into the early hours for any spoor, but nothing was there. At sunrise I left the area and had a few hours' sleep. I returned to the last-known spoor only to find his fresh tracks on top of mine, so I could time them to within four hours. I followed the tracks and the target was found close by. It transpired that he had left the area the night before. His plan was to leave his past life behind, and his new girlfriend picked him up at a prearranged location (where I had lost his tracks the night before). During the night they had an argument and decided that he should return to his wife. To facilitate this, he was dropped back into the woods, walked some distance and sat down. This area had been searched using police dogs the night before and it is very unlikely that they would have missed him.

In recent years I have filmed a number of programmes for Discovery Channel. One such programme was to investigate the Yeti that is said to roam the Himalayas. Anyone who has been to the Himalayas will understand the vastness and rugged terrain. Despite the temptation to be cynical, I duly accepted the quest. I did not carry out any research before I left, because I did not want to have any preconceptions.

On arrival in Katmandhu I met the President of the Nepal Mountaineering Association, Ang-Tschering Sherpa. He is a well-respected man, not just in Nepal but around the world. He explained to me that the Yeti was indeed still alive. There were three kinds of yeti: the spiritual, the meat-eater and the vegetarian. Over the years the Sherpas had tried to kill them off because according to legend the Yeti had allegedly fathered a child to a Sherpa women who had died in childbirth. I was later to discover that Yetis probably do exist, with one contender being the Himalayan Black Bear. This animal has a ferocious temper, a white crescent on its chest, and leaves a footprint of the back foot placed indirectly on top of the front foot that is remarkably similar to that of a human footprint, but twice as big.

Inquisitiveness

Any tracking scenario will consist of many layers of information, from information about the quarry to the environment. The list is endless, but the tracker will need to have the desire to peel back the layers, sometimes looking at the same quarry from different angles. As each layer is explored, he must never accept the information at face value. He may be told something verbally, but will then need to investigate what the tracks are saying. No stone should be left unturned.

My teams always apply the Rule of Second Penetration. This means that once they have come to a conclusion, whether it is a fact or a trail end, they will not accept the first finding. They will push past the trail end, or information, and more often than not, on the second penetration they will uncover something that will affect the tracking. It is more than going one step further; it is the philosophy that there is always more than meets the eye.

Physicality

As with mentality, some of the physical requirements of trackers can be deceptive. That is to say, some things that might appear desirable at first sight may not necessarily be so. That said, fitness and endurance are, of course, essential. Often a tracker will cover small distances steadily and then the pace of the follow-up will change and pick up and speed is required. This sporadic level of exertion can go on for days and often, just when the going gets the hardest, that is when the quarry is found. This can play havoc with the body, especially when someone is used to a

rigid routine. I have found that changing routines before a patrol is bene-
ficial. The reason for this is that the biological clock can be altered to suit
the purposes of the follow-up. I find that, in the field, it is impossible to
stick to a routine. Often your routine will be dictated by the quarry. If
they are moving, you are moving. It would be foolish to stop for a break
in the midday sun in Africa: it would be much better to push on and stop
in a shady area.

The longer you can be on the tracks while moving, the more you should
be closing the time-distance gap.

Trackers don't have to be as fit as international athletes, however, having
walked thousands of kilometres, up mountains, through deserts, forests
and jungles around the world, I can safely say that no tracker should be
unfit. Fitness is required to stay on the trail and may be required to beat
a hasty retreat. If unfit, you risk getting stranded in a dangerous, exposed
environment because you are tired. Remember that your day is dictated
by the quarry.

A tracker must be able to draw upon his physical and mental reserves
at any time. During a training exercise in New Mexico, a tactical tracking arrest was about to be made of several individuals, whereupon I
stumbled on a small rock, about the size of a tennis ball. It was enough
to break my ankle and rupture tendons. The medic could see I had gone
into shock with the pain and the prospect of what lay ahead and offered
to strap the ankle, but I would still have to walk to get out of the desert. I
chose not to remove my boot. The high desert in New Mexico has large,
dense clumps of grass which grow above the ground, otherwise known
as 'baby's heads' because they are about the same size as the head of a
baby. It is impossible to walk without standing on them. I knew I had a
problem, because it was several kilometres to the nearest road.

I have a number of survival tricks up my sleeve, which I have used
when in peril.

The fundamental thought is that nothing is crushing, and you just need
time to come to terms with your predicament. Knowing the situation was
dire, it was a case of mind over matter. Because trackers are likely to be
operational in remote areas where self-rescue may become a reality and
be mentally and physically demanding, I draw upon three small mental
tricks.

First, I set myself small, achievable targets that last no longer than
five minutes. It can be something as simple as getting to a shrub I have
spotted. The second thought that goes through my mind is the longer
something goes on, the less time it has got to go on. In other words, the
tough times don't last. Winston Churchill said when you get to Hell, just
keep on going. The third trick or technique was taught to me by a Reiki
Master, who said that I should imagine the sky swirling into the injury in
the colour of red and leaving the injury in the colour of light blue. There

is no scientific reason why it should work, but I found that it focuses the mind and helps me to think calmly.

Somehow, using these and other techniques, I was able to get out of the desert without being a liability to the tracking team. I felt I was able to continue tracking for another few days before going to hospital and so I taped the ankle with duct tape. I had to be selective about the angle at which I walked. On getting to hospital five days later, they wanted to put the ankle into a cast, but, because I was about to leave for Kenya to train combat rangers in the bush, I declined medical treatment and used a complete roll of duct tape to strap my ankle into what turned out to be a reasonably good cast that stayed on for three months.

Trackers tend to live a healthy lifestyle and have an interest in martial arts and fitness levels as they can see how it directly relates to performance. Many trackers are not able to run at speed, but because their stamina levels are very high they are able to walk and jog for long periods. A minimum target is a four-kilometre jog, followed immediately by a four-kilometre walk. It is a good idea to control fluid intake and carry a light load of about four kilograms.

There are many sports which are excellent to complement tracking. I train at Muay Thai, kickboxing, Kapap and compete in fights, sabre fencing and running. I find that these are useful, not only for fitness levels, but also for defence or when controlled aggression is required.

I would not, however, recommend bodybuilding as the body will require large amounts of energy to fuel the muscles, which in turn means that more food and water have got to be carried. In the rugged and dry northern rangelands of Kenya, close to war-torn Somalia, the indigenous people are lean and very strong, with masses of walking and running endurance. While training in that region I came across Special Forces from a Western army. They had built up their muscles by weightlifting and a specialized high-protein diet. The local tribespeople watched in amazement as they ate and drank their way through large amounts of food and liquids. All these supplies require lots of space and energy to be carried. The tribespeople commented on how they admired the British special forces, because they are lean, and according to them only need a small amount of food and cups of tea!

There is a large variation in physicality and mentality, and it is for the tracker and teams to establish what level suits the purpose. It may be that a good micro-tracker, or remote base controller, is not as fit as the on-ground tracking team. Equally the flankers in challenging terrain need to be very fit. The last but not least quality that a tracker needs is a sense of humour!

CHAPTER 3

Human and Animal Senses

'The Commonwealth of senses: there is nothing that sharpens a man's senses so acutely as to know that a bitter and determined enemy are in pursuit night and day.'

Frederick Burnham

The major senses can be categorized as follows: the eyes and forms; tongue and flavours; body and tactile sensations; nose and aromas; and ears and sounds.

Most people look but don't see, listen, but don't hear and touch without feeling. If a tracker can fine-tune his senses, so that he can use every bit of information, then it will give him the advantage. Sometimes the advantage is big, and sometimes there is marginal gain, but it could mean the difference between life and death.

Many neurologists disagree about how many senses there are owing to a broad interpretation of the definition of a sense. Our senses are split into two different groups. Our exteroceptors detect stimulation from outside our body (for example, smell, taste, and variations in ground levels). The interoceptors receive stimulation from the inside of our bodies (for example, blood pressure dropping or changes in the glucose level). However, it is generally agreed that there are at least nine different senses in humans, and a minimum of two more observed in animals.

Sense can vary from one person to another, with personal, religious and cultural factors coming into play here. Whereas one person may like the taste of one food item, another person may find the same item unpleasant.

There are nine senses, but for the purposes of tracking we are going to concentrate on the five traditional senses. However, we must acknowledge that the other senses have a bearing on our performance. For example, when the interoceptors are detecting a drop in performance in breathing, in blood-sugar levels, or as a response to pain, we must acknowledge them and address the issue. To ignore our interoceptors could have a disastrous effect on the performance of a tracking team.

Some of our senses are more dominant than others, depending on the environment. In the jungle where there is little light, and the field of view is small, our sense of hearing becomes more dominant. In open landscapes sight is our dominant sense.

Trackers must train so that they can detect the sounds of humans on the move, be it machetes or axes chopping wood, the sound of metal chinking on metal or the sound of voices. They must also be able to detect the smell of insect repellent, tobacco, camp fire smoke and differentiate between body odours dependent on diet. I was working with soldiers in Africa and for several weeks I ate goat meat exclusively. Within two weeks my body odour changed. Usually people new into the area will already be carrying a baseline scent and their supplies of toothpaste, soap and insect repellent will be used until they run out. So we can use such hints as changes in odour to build a picture of the quarry.

SIGHT

This is the part of the central nervous system that gives us the ability to process visual detail. It detects and interprets information from visible light to build a 3D picture of the surrounding environment. The visual system carries out a number of complex tasks, including the reception of light and the processing of monocular view from each eye to build up binocular perception. This process forms the identification and categorization of visual objects, including assessing distances to and between objects and guiding the body's movements in relation to visual objects.

I have watched animals at length, both predators at the top of the food chain and their prey. I noticed that most animals don't see much of the *substance* of something; they were much more interested in where things were going. If it moves, it matters. Moving targets may be threats, meals or a mate. The earliest eyes evolved not to detect objects, but to detect motion. Most animals live a life of regularity, and their eyes have evolved to warn them of interruptions to their usual programme. Rabbits' eyes are remarkably tuned into motion, which makes the rabbit incredibly efficient at spotting predators.

Humans, as hunters and foragers, take a more than usual interest in what things *are*, however they are still first and foremost tuned to detect motion. This makes a great deal of sense where prey and predator disappear and reappear constantly as they move through grass, run behind trees and peer around rocks.

In the bush they say that only prey runs. Movement will be detected by the eyes of the predator and the chase instinct will be activated. The chase instinct also exists in humans, and some people cannot resist a chase. But what about herbivores? I spent a great deal of time in the bush, living for weeks cheek by jowl with elephants. On one occasion, in the Zambezi Valley, I tracked into a herd of elephants. At midday this is a very dangerous situation because the herd have usually come to a stop and are scattered around an area of fifty metres or so. Each elephant was taking up shade from a small tree and they were about to enter their sleep cycle. Many a hunter has been killed at this point because they have walked right through the usual warning zone into the critical zone, close to the elephant, where they could startle a semi-conscious animal that will then attack. Despite their size, their grey, wrinkled skin is excellent camouflage.

By the time I was aware that I was circled by a large herd of elephants, I had no option but to freeze. I then slowly (probably about a metre a minute) moved to a small tree that would partially disguise my body shape. As I peeked around the tree to see where they were, the movement was picked up by a young bull. There was no warning and he went straight into a full charge. At this point I had no option but to run, which triggered the motion detectors in other elephants, and in no time at all I was being chased by six or seven adult elephants. As I ran, and was forced to dodge trees, the elephants simply trampled them, and closed distance very quickly. It was interesting, as I had an out-of-body experience, looking down on myself as my bush hat came off and the elephants ran over it.

And then they stopped dead. I froze again, picked my route and stalked off. I think my hat, having my scent on it, had confused them into thinking that they had caught me. They were paying a lot of attention to it with their trunks because it had my body odour and they thought they had got part of me. That gave me the chance to sneak off.

Although this experience involved elephants, it applies even more to mantracking, because you may have to freeze so that an animal doesn't bolt and thus give your position away, but also so that the quarry doesn't see you either. There are occasions when you are tracking and a member of the public will come nearby. This mainly applies to covert operations. If you are on the move, the best thing is to freeze, so that you don't trigger the person's motion detectors.

The eye is a complex organ, but as trackers we need to know how we detect movement and use night vision.

The function of the cones is to detect colour, details, and faraway objects. This is the central pit of the retina which allows for maximum acuity. Over 50 per cent of all vision comes from this small area. The rods are further out and outnumber cones, but are more widely spaced. The rods detect movement but do not give detail or colour, only shades of grey. Both the cones and the rods are used for vision during daylight.

As predators, using binocular vision means that naturally our centre of gaze is quite small, which means we are not taking in sufficient information. There are reasons for improving our peripheral vision. I am sure that some readers will have experienced the feeling that someone is looking at you, without you looking at them.

One of the factors that you could have noticed through your peripheral vision is called skin indexing. What that means is that the amount of exposed and visible skin has an index. Someone in a bathing suit has a greater visual skin index than someone who is wearing a uniform on patrol. So if we apply this to the human face, when a person is not looking at you, the visual skin index is smaller; as they turn to look at you, you will see the complete face and the skin index will have increased. My tracking team are all trained to detect an increase in skin indexing. I can sense when someone in the tracking team wants to pass a silent signal by the fact that they have turned their head towards me. This is because the surface area of the skin that is visible is larger and more easily detected by peripheral vision.

The other reason why you could have detected someone looking at you is because the predatory stare is kicking out lots of energy. Although this is not scientifically proven, I had my instructors select three of the most predatory-looking people on a course. We then selected trackers to stand in front of them. Each tracker reported an uneasy feeling. I then stood in front of them and I could really sense evidence of powerful predatory energy coming from their eyes. So, as trackers, we have to neutralize this sense of predatory energy and increase our peripheral vision. Staring at someone and direct eye contact should be kept to a minimum.

The FBI train in a technique called splatter vision, which is designed to reduce the predatory energy. This requires that they operate in peripheral vision, ensuring that they don't focus on any specific object until something moves. This means that they will spot movement in their field of view, perhaps a threat, someone reaching for a gun, at which point they will focus on the movement. If the movement is significant, they will take action. During the process of splatter vision the eyes are focused to the front. For the duration, the sense of predatory energy from the eyes will be increased.

To develop peripheral vision I get students to place their arms in front of themselves at shoulder height, fists joined together, fingers pointing down. I then ask them to open the index finger on both hands and pick a spot on the horizon to keep their eyes on. They will notice the fine detail in the fingers. They will then slowly open their arms, noticing that the fine detail will become blurred the further the fists get away from the middle. Eventually the fist will disappear from view. At this point they will move the index finger, and will immediately pick up the movement. The field of vision is likely to be in the region of 160 degrees. This should be practised regularly.

As the lead tracker, it can sometimes be difficult to stay in peripheral vision, because of the need to focus on the tracks, and undertake close inspection of spoor. It is therefore essential that the tracker is given protection by the flankers and controller.

Night Vision

Human eyes cannot function as effectively at night as the eyes of animals with nocturnal habits, but if a human learns to use their eyes correctly, night vision can be greatly improved. There are several reasons for the training and practice necessary to use the eyes correctly.

One reason is that the mind and eyes act as a team in order for a person to see well; both team members must therefore be used effectively. Also, the construction of the eyes is such that to see at night they must be used differently than during the daytime. Therefore, it is important for a tracker to understand the eye's construction and how the eye is affected by darkness.

Although there is no clear-cut division of function, generally speaking, the rods make night vision possible. The rods and cones function in daylight and in moonlight, but in the absence of these the process of vision is placed almost entirely on the rods.

In nocturnal animals the retina is mostly composed of rods, and some animals have a *tapetum licidum* (meaning 'bright carpet'). This is a thick reflective membrane, which collects light and re-emits some of it back to the retina a second time, giving the rods a second chance to absorb the image information, thus maximizing the little light available. As this light is reflected off the *tapetum*, the eyes will appear to glow, especially if light is shone directly into the animal's eyes.

The eye's adaptation to darkness is another important aspect of night vision. When a dark room is entered, it is difficult to see anything until the eyes become adjusted to the darkness. We know this from entering a tunnel or darkened room from daylight. In this process, the pupils of the eyes first enlarge to receive as much of the available light as possible. After approximately five to ten minutes, the cones become adjusted to the dim light and the eyes become a hundred times more sensitive to the light than they were before the dark room was entered. A chemical called rhodopsin is produced, which gives us night vision in about thirty minutes, and the rods become adjusted to darkness. When they do adjust they are about 100,000 times more sensitive to light than they were in the lighted area. After the adaptation process is complete, much more can be seen.

This entire process is reversed if the eyes are dazzled by white light. In a few seconds they lose their adaptation to the dark.

The adaptation process of the eyes must be considered by the tracker before and during night tracking. First, the eyes must be allowed to adapt to the low level of light and then they must be kept adapted. After the eyes have become adapted to darkness, the tracker must avoid exposing them to any bright white light.

To avoid loss of night vision we use green or red torches. The lights are always held at low level, and head torches should be worn around the neck. There is nothing more frustrating than someone talking to you with their head torch shining directly into your eyes.

In review, and in addition to the principles previously discussed, the following will aid the tracker in increasing effectiveness of night vision:

1. Adapt the eyes to darkness prior to entering it, and keep them adapted. About thirty minutes is needed to adjust the eyes to maximum efficiency after exposure to a bright light.
2. Close one eye when exposed to bright light to help avoid the blinding effect.
3. Do not wear sunglasses after sunset.
4. Move the eyes more slowly than in daylight.
5. Blink the eyes if they become blurred.
6. Concentrate on seeing objects.
7. Force the eyes to view off centre.
8. Maintain good physical condition.
9. Avoid smoking, drinking, and using drugs which may be harmful.

TOUCH

Touch is communication. From the moment a baby is born touch constitutes a vital component of communication and, in a very strict sense, enhances its survival. Every mammal uses touch as one of the first senses. This is demonstrated by the newborn finding its mother and breast-feeding.

It is amazing that one hair can pick up so much information. It can detect the smallest of insects landing and a change in wind direction. The sensation of touch has been studied for many years, and the studies have had many and varied outcomes.

I prefer to use the term 'feeling', because it engages a far more analytical process. For example, the fingertips in humans have a high concentration of receptors. Get two pieces of sandpaper of different grains. Simply touch both pieces and you will find it difficult to distinguish which one is the coarser. Now gently rub your fingertips across the paper and you will find it easier to distinguish each one from the other. Touching a pineapple is very different from feeling the texture and shape.

Because we mostly use our primary senses of vision and hearing during the day, touch is of limited use to a tracker. At night we have diminished vision caused by darkness. Even so, never ignore touch; it can be useful. By use of touch, great feats of night tracking by Baden-Powell and Frederick Burnham were achieved. They were touching tracks to find their lost colleagues and to work out information about the Matabele oxen. Having read it, one night during a course, I put the students to the test. I took them to a level area, which was pitch black. I then made holes in the ground with my tracking stick every thirty centimetres. They were then asked to find the holes. I watched in astonishment with night-vision binoculars as they all found every single track. At first it was a little bit tricky, as their fingertips felt their way over the mown blades of grass.

The other use of touch is to interpret substrates and camp fires. We can get a lot more information about soil from touching and squeezing it than we can from seeing it. When trackers approach a campsite, if there has been a fire they should always check the temperature of the ashes to establish how long it has been since the fire was extinguished. I am always amazed that, when trackers are undergoing their assessments, 80 per cent forget to check the temperature of the ashes. This is done by placing the back of the hand towards the heat source. This same technique can be used to check a lie-up, whether animal or human, to see if the substrate is still warm.

My trackers learn how to use touch and sound to travel by night without light. While they are walking their brains tune in to the touch (albeit through a boot) of the ground underneath, and the sound of their steps. They start practising on gravel roads, with two tyre ruts either side. In the middle there is a ridge of stones and vegetation. Either side of the road there are ditches, brambles and gorse. If they veer off they will have a painful fall into the ditch.

At first the prospect is daunting, but very soon they can feel the different textures. At the advanced stage of this training, trackers can travel silently, without light, at night by using the feeling of the ground underneath the boot.

We can also interpret action indicators in the ground, which are the result of people touching or being in close proximity to each other (as described in Chapter 10).

Different cultures have varying attitudes towards touching one another and this is dependent on personal space and familiarity. We can look at a set of tracks which will tell us whether or not two people know each other. Consider the following. Two sets of tracks close to each other, one male and one female. They are walking in one direction, then they stop and face each other. The tracks are so close that this could only have been an embrace. They walk on a little further; the female tracks split off to the other side of the road, and they now walk for fifty metres. The male tracks then cross the road and join with the female tracks, as they walk ten metres side by side. The tracks stop and there has been a struggle. The female is found lying dead and the tracks of the male lead off. The interpretation of these tracks takes into consideration the effects of touch. It would appear that the male and female knew each other. They were walking side by side, possibly holding hands, inside each other's personal space. They stopped and embraced, then parted, possibly as the result of an argument. They then came back together again, once again walking holding hands. They stopped and he killed her.

The establishment of these facts indicated that the female was murdered by someone she knew, and had travelled to the scene with them as opposed to a forced abduction. The fact that they were touching each other as they walked, and embraced, showed that she had not been abducted and taken to the scene to be murdered.

TASTE

The sense of taste is a chemical reaction that is essential to survival. It protects us from unsafe foods. If a tracker eats a poisonous or rotten substance, his sense of taste is likely to detect it as a threat to the body and he will probably spit the threat out immediately. That way, the toxins are prevented from entering the stomach.

The sense of taste also helps to maintain a consistent chemical balance in the body. We can use this information to build up a profile of some-one being tracked, because taste preferences change in conjunction with the body's needs. For example, a tracker may come across discarded items such as chocolate or boiled sweets, which would indicate that the target was in need of energy, or consumed sweet food, consumed foods containing salt such as peanuts or salt-dried meat (known as *biltong*) in an attempt to boost their intake of minerals.

SMELL

If you smell curry in the African bush, it could signify that someone in the vicinity is cooking a curry, but a more likely reason is the presence of a black mamba snake nearby. Although the human sense of smell is feeble when compared with that of many animals, our sense of smell is still very acute. We can recognize thousands of different smells and are able to detect odours even in infinitesimal quantities.

Our smelling function is carried out by two small odour-detecting patches – made up of about 5–6 million yellowish cells – high up in the nasal passages. For comparison, a dog has 220 million odour-detection cells. Humans are nonetheless capable of detecting certain substances in dilutions of less than one part in several billion parts of air. We may not be able to match the olfactory feats of bloodhounds but we can, for example, 'track' a trail of invisible human footprints across clean blot-ting paper.

The human nose is, in fact, the main organ of taste as well as smell. The so-called taste-buds on our tongues can only distinguish four quali-ties – sweet, sour, bitter and salt – all other 'tastes' are detected by the olfactory receptors high up in our nasal passages.

A recent study at the University of Pennsylvania suggests that, contrary to popular belief, blind people do not necessarily have a keener sense of smell than sighted people. In their experiments on blind and sighted people, the top performers on most tests were (sighted) employees of the Philadelphia Water Department who had been trained to serve on the department's water quality evaluation panel. The researchers concluded that training is the factor most likely to enhance performance on smell tests.

You can train yourself to smell more effectively by not smoking and making sure that, when a distinctive smell is detected that a source is found, thereby linking the smell to the source. (Although smoking does not always affect scores on smell tests, it is widely believed to reduce sensitivity.)

The importance of 'training' in the development of smell-sensitivity is all too often overlooked by trackers (see Chapter 4). Smell is an extremely useful tool for trackers. It is one of the ways we can acquire lots of information about the quarry without seeing them, and so on every tracking course we teach how to physically change the way that we acquire scents.

To do this I looked at how dogs smell for scent. First, they seem to take a small, short intake of breath, and blow out through their nose forcibly. This does two things. Scent molecules are carried in vapour and trapped in the mucus within the nose. The sharp intake and blow can clear some of the mucus which has molecules from other odours. The second thing it does is to clear 'dead' air from the nose. The second stage, when the dog inhales for a slightly longer time, is when the fresh odour is trapped in renewed mucus.

I think we have lost the technique of active sniffing because it is socially unacceptable, but to improve our sense of smell, we can do exactly the same as a dog. Blow the nose hard to clear mucus and the 'dead' air and start sniffing. You will find that your sense of smell improves greatly.

Now we have to understand how odours are influenced by the elements, and how this affects tracking. There is a great deal of research on search and rescue dogs, and how they operate. The same principles apply to humans, albeit we are not going to be able to outperform dogs. Even so, when scenting is combined with other senses, it is a very powerful tool.

Weather is one of the most influential factors, especially wind.

The quarry will create a scent cone, which may be coming from him, a camp fire or crushed vegetation. It could be anything that will cause molecules from the source to vaporize and form a scent plume. The cone is three-dimensional. The strongest concentration of scent is closest to the quarry. Dogs will often run in what appears to be a zigzag fashion. Effectively what they are doing is running until they hit the edge of the cone, where the scent runs out, and turning inwards to run across the cone again, the zigzag pattern getting smaller as they approach the quarry. When trackers pick up a scent, they could do the same as dogs.

I have used scent cones on many occasions, for example in the search for a dead body. I caught the smell of death on the wind and, before I knew it, I had overshot the cone, and assumed it was a gust of wind that had brought the smell. I stopped and walked back a couple of metres and caught it again. Occasionally during the process, the scent would disappear, and I would walk until I got it again. Eventually, purely by using the scent cone, I found the body which was concealed in the undergrowth on a disused railway.

Moisture and humidity can, in general terms, be good for scenting, especially during the night and just before dew forms. Heavy rain will move odours downwards on a sloped landscape, but it won't affect the movement of scent on a flat field.

Hot air rises, so scent will drift uphill. In flat, sunny areas during the daytime hours, it may rise a few centimetres or more above the ground.

In contrast, cool air sinks, so scent drifts downhill during evening hours. Depressions, water and shaded areas in the terrain — swamps, ravines, ditches, evergreens, to name a few — will draw and collect scent. Logging trails, roadways and other features act as funnels, channelling scent in a linear fashion — great distances, at times.

Scent pools are where the scent collects, and could be several hundred metres away from the quarry.

I have conducted some experiments on how vegetation affects the scent of an object. In order that I could see the effects clearly I used synthetic smoke. This experimentation was not about the volatility of the scent, but what happens when it hits a thick bush. Where the bush is directly above and close to the source of the smoke, it was quickly absorbed. For a couple of seconds, during that time, the bush caused it to dissipate, and slowed it down. Some started to rise upwards until out of the bush and then dropped again. What was very clear was that, for the tactical tracker, vegetation can be very useful in dissipating odours. If there are any smokers on a team, they should only smoke very close to the ground, and upwind of a thick bush, or tucked into ferns so that the smoke will be dissipated by the vegetation.

A smell can bring on a flood of memories, influence people's moods and even affect their work performance. Smell is such a strong sense that the retail industry has been using it for many years. We know that even certain branded foods contain a trace element of their brand smell. Department stores perfume the shop floor with brand smells that control our moods and are conducive to buying. Because the olfactory bulb is part of the brain's limbic system, an area closely associated with memory and feelings, it is sometimes called the 'emotional brain', thus smell can call up memories and powerful responses almost instantaneously.

During training I blindfold students, and provide them with various stimulants. They then have to write down what it is that they are feeling, smelling or hearing. There are a number of objects, one of which has a hint of lavender oil. On one occasion, when the students had finished and they read out what their findings were, I was impressed when a girl said that, when she smelled one of the objects, which had the lavender oil, she could see her grandmother right in front of her. She couldn't describe what lavender oil smells like, but was able to describe her grandmother in great detail.

I also include a cartridge which has just been fired, and so still contains the smell of cordite. Although cordite is easily detectable, this is only of use to someone who knows what it is.

As trackers, when we smell something, we must be able to picture it in our mind's eye. Freshly dug earth means that something or someone has been digging. Cordite means bullets have been fired. The smell of death is interesting, because the smell of a dead animal (apart from a pig) is very different from the smell of a dead human.

Because it is such a powerful sense, I have trained my nose to detect a library of smells, but to do this I try to avoid receptor blockers like cigarette smoke or vehicle pollution.

HEARING

The ear is surrounded by ear flaps that channel sound waves into your outer ear canal. The waves travel along this passage until they hit the eardrum and cause it to vibrate. As a result, the ossicles start moving. They, in turn, pass on vibrations to a thin layer of tissue at the entrance of your inner ear called the oval window. The movement of the oval window then sets off wave-like motions in the fluid in your cochlea. The hearing organ consists of thousands of sensory hair cells attached to a membrane. The movement of sensory hairs is then translated into nerve impulses, which travel along your cochlear nerve to your brain.

We are able to locate the source of sound because we have two ears. If a sound comes from the right, for instance, it will reach the right ear slightly sooner than the left ear, or it will be slightly louder in the right ear.

Not all sounds are normally audible to all animals. Each species has a range of normal hearing for both loudness and frequency. Many animals use sound to communicate with each other and hearing in these species is particularly important for survival and reproduction. In species that use sound as a primary means of communication, hearing is typically most acute for the range of pitches produced in calls and speech.

Certain animals have more sensitive hearing than humans, which enables them to hear sounds too faint to be detected by humans. Frequencies capable of being heard by humans are called audio or sonic. Frequencies higher than audio are referred to as ultrasonic, while frequencies below audio are referred to as infrasonic. Some bats use ultrasound for echolocation while in flight. Dogs are able to hear ultrasound, which is the principle of 'silent' dog whistles. Snakes sense infrasound through their bellies, and whales, dolphins, giraffes and elephants use it for communication.

When I am in the bush, although I am unable to hear ultrasound, I keep my eyes on animals that can. For example, on one occasion when I was tracking I could see that a male giraffe had his eyes firmly fixed on me from sixty metres away. At that point I needed to break cover and cross an open area. It was a perfect killing ground for lions, and was scattered with the bones of dead animals. There was significant risk in crossing the salt-pan, not only from lions but also from being spotted by humans. The giraffe towered above the thorny acacia trees, so I used it as my visual sentry for lions and humans. Because it would be able to pick up infrasound, it would pick up an approaching vehicle well before I could hear it. I used the five-minute rule and crossed, all the while watching the behaviour of the giraffe. If the giraffe had changed anything about its behaviour, perhaps running off in a different direction, it would almost certainly mean that another human was approaching. If it moved its gaze from me to another object, it could be a lion on the move, or another stationary human in an ambush position.

With regard to human hearing in the bush, rifle butt slaps or taps are a deadly giveaway. These sounds are easy to hear, and easily distinguished as a tactical or armed team. Under no circumstances should a tracking team use rifle butt slaps to attract the attention of other trackers.

For those who cannot make bird sounds, a verbal cluck is ideal. It is done by placing the tongue to the top of the mouth and clicking the tongue downwards. To all but the expert tracker, this will sound like a bird, and others will think no more of it.

One technique I favour is for trackers to carry low frequency dog whistles to attract attention. Low frequency is detectable by humans, especially if they become familiar with the sound. Once you can recognize the quiet hissing sound of the whistle, you will be able to detect it, but it won't be so obvious to other humans.

Sounds (voices in particular) can travel a long way, especially at night. Sound discipline within a team must therefore be very strict. Cracking twigs, and metallic sounds, including a rifle being cocked, are instant attention-getters.

When working in an armed team, the weapons will be carried with the safety catch on. There may be occasions when it is suspected that the quarry is nearby. Since most weapons need to be cocked, it is at this point that the armed tracking team is at one of its most vulnerable stages. The usual 'positive cranking' is an unmistakeable sound. Even if the quarry doesn't have any experience of weapons, they will instantly recognize the sound from films and TV. The crank gives the position away, and the human brain struggles for a moment between the auditory crank, the feeling of the crank, the visual ability to look at the cocking mechanism, and taking in the quarry. The brief moment of hesitation is because the entire process of cocking a weapon is the pre-warning to the brain that a loud bang is about to happen, and often in the heat of the moment there is a fumble, or perhaps even a premature misfire which, if the other sounds didn't alert the quarry, will certainly give them the location of the weapon being fired. In some situations, one round is already in the breech, and the safety needs to be taken off to fire. For an armed tracking team, it is better to reduce the sound of the cocking mechanism by doing it a bit more slowly, before entering the hazard zone.

During a follow-up any discussions the tracking team may have must be done close to the ground, at very least in kneeling position, but best in the prone position, and whispering only. That way the dispersal of sound is minimal.

There are a number of electronic devices specially designed to listen to human conversation. Such devices will fit into the ear, and will shut off if a loud bang is detected. They are of minimal benefit, as they also pick up other sounds, which can interfere with that of the human voice.

A great deal of reconnaissance can be done where the light of a camp fire gives way to darkness. From the edge you have good vision of the quarry, and they cannot see you. However, make a sound and you will have the eyes of everyone on you at the same time.

There is, of course, the exception for search and rescue. Although SAR teams want to make some noise, they don't want to create so much noise that they can't hear the people they are looking for.

In New Zealand they have been experimenting with Sound and Light Line Search. It is used primarily at night, for conscious missing persons. They create lots of light, and make sounds. The searchers are interspaced so that they are not tempted to talk; once they have made a sound they wait for a response. One of the pieces of clothing that they have found useful in this technique is a broad-brimmed hat. They have found that by tilting the hat to the correct angle can help to channel sound back to the ears.

To enhance our hearing we can cup our hands, placing the thumbs and index fingers behind the ears, one facing slightly downwards. This will help to locate the source of sound, and improve hearing. It is important that you practise this in front of a mirror, because a small gap between the fingers can cause a large proportion of the sound to be lost. Make sure that the fingers are closed, and that the ear flaps are not closed accidently.

All too often I see searchers with hoods up, woolly hat over their ears, or wearing Balaclavas. For extreme cold weather, I have a range of hats, that I can drop over the ears when stationary, or where there is a risk of frostbite. However, it is very rare that I will drop a hat over my ears or wear a hood up, and I never wear a Balaclava. Pushing the ear flaps down, and then placing a muffler over them, is killing off one of the most important and useful senses, in situations where marginal gain in performance can make all the difference.

THE COMMONWEALTH OF SENSES

Part of the learning process of tracking is to develop and enhance the senses. During courses I will ask how many senses there are. People are very quick to get the five traditional senses, and then they start suggesting the sixth sense – women's intuition, hunches, coincidence and extra-sensory perception.

There are several possible explanations for why such 'intuitive hunches' sometimes play out. One is that on a subconscious level we are always thinking and coming to conclusions, but that these register only as hunches to our conscious mind. Another is that we pick up telling cues from body language, environmental subliminal sounds or peripheral vision without being consciously aware of doing so. A third is that for each coincidence we remember we forget all the times we had a hunch and it didn't come to anything. A fourth possibility is that we modify our memories for our own convenience, creating a connection where it may not have existed. These sorts of explanations probably account for many intuitive hunches.

As trackers, we should be aiming at merging all the senses together, into The One Sense. Simply by using wide-angle vision you will sharpen many senses, because information that enters the brain from the peripheral areas of the eye goes straight to the subconscious mind without being questioned by the conscious brain.

If all the senses are fine-tuned, you will find that you will get more hunches and the intuition that we need to tap into will pay dividends.

CHAPTER 4

Building the Skill of Environmental Awareness

Awareness is the anvil of tracking. It is the single most important factor in a tracker's training. As will be described in this chapter, there are different levels of awareness, and an understanding of the subject will help the tracker. Whether it is in combat tracking, search and rescue or wildlife, without using awareness we lose a significant edge.

Trackers must be able to detect the presence of the abnormal and the absence of the normal.

Awareness is the ability to perceive, to feel, or to be conscious of events, objects, or sensory patterns. Events can be confirmed by a tracker without necessarily understanding what is going on. Awareness is a relative concept. A tracker and the quarry could be partially aware, subconsciously aware, completely aware or even unaware of an event. Awareness provides trackers with the raw material from which they develop subjective ideas about what is going on.

This form of primary consciousness has the capacity to generate emotions and an awareness of one's surroundings, but not necessarily an ability to talk about the experience. In the same way, people can become conscious of a feeling that they can't label or describe. I have come across this regularly when I have been tracking with others. Over the years I have spent time with some great trackers from various tribes and on several occasions they have anticipated what would happen next. Their intuition paid off and I wanted to know how they did it. Many of them were not able to describe why their hunch was correct. At first I put it down to their inability to describe things in English.

Sometime later I was tracking a group of people who were trying to avoid detection. They were very aware of us and extremely mobile. It became clear that in order to catch them we would have think more smartly than them. We eventually came to a river bank and picked up their tracks, which had scattered when they crossed the river. I knew that this had been done to tie up the tracking team as they worked out which track to follow. I also knew that there was a second group of people who had been waiting at the crossing. So, in fact, we had two groups to track, not just one. One of the groups was a diversion, and they laid a more clearly dominant and readable trail. Most trackers would have gone for that. If they had been caught, they would have been completely innocent. I had an hunch about which track to follow. I could not describe why I wanted to back-track our tracks and could not describe how to justify it. The tracking team reluctantly followed me and within half an hour we had picked up the group who were back-tracking on *our* trail. It was a very clever move by them but my hunch was correct. I then realized that it can sometimes be an impossible task to describe the reasons for a hunch to others, but it is important to listen to it.

CHANGES IN AWARENESS

Our awareness is always changing and it's important to understand how your brain contributes to your state of mind. While most of us focus on looking at our emotions in an attempt to become happier, more spiritual beings, our brainwaves and our subconscious mind also play a key part in our quest for fulfilment.

We easily forget that we are the controllers of our reality and that our 'reality' is not made up of outside influences but actually consists of our thoughts, beliefs and mindset.

Therefore, by learning about the deeper states of consciousness, you can open your subconscious mind and create your reality at will, and with precision. To do this, the first step is understanding your different brain frequencies. We have five (Beta, Alpha, Theta, Delta and Gamma), and each frequency is measured in cycles per second (Hz) and has its own set of characteristics representing a specific level of brain activity and a unique state of consciousness.

1. **Beta (14–40Hz) – the waking consciousness and reasoning wave:** Beta brainwaves are associated with normal waking consciousness and a heightened state of alertness, logic and critical reasoning.

   While Beta brainwaves are important for effective functioning throughout the day, they can also translate into stress, anxiety and restlessness. The voice of Beta can be described as being that nagging little inner critic that gets louder the higher you go into range. Therefore, as a majority of adults operate at Beta, it's little surprise that stress is today's most common health problem.

2. **Alpha (7.5–14Hz) – the deep relaxation wave:** Alpha brainwaves are present in deep relaxation and usually when the eyes are closed, when you're slipping into a daydream or during light meditation. These times are optimal times to programme the mind for success and these waves also heighten your imagination, visualization, memory, learning and concentration.

   Alpha brain activity is the gateway to your subconscious mind and lies at the base of your conscious awareness. The voice of Alpha is your intuition, which becomes clearer and more profound the closer you get to 7.5Hz.

3. **Theta (4–7.5Hz) – the light meditation and sleeping wave:** Theta brainwaves are present during deep meditation and light sleep, including the all-important REM dream state. This is the realm of your subconsciousness and is only experienced momentarily as you drift off to sleep from Alpha and wake from deep sleep (from Delta).

    Your mind's most deep-seated programmes are at Theta and this is where you experience vivid visualizations, great inspiration, profound creativity and exceptional insight. Unlike your other brainwaves, the elusive voice of Theta is a silent voice.

    For the tracker it is at the Alpha-Theta border, from 7Hz to 8Hz, which is the optimal range for the zone-in, zone-out (ZIZO) process as described in Chapter 4. Visualization, mind-programming and using the intuitive power of your mind begins. It is the time when you are just drifting off to sleep when you have all those amazing ideas that you should have written down. It's the mental state in which you consciously create your reality. At this frequency, you are conscious of your surroundings; however, your body is relaxed.

4. **Delta (0.5–4Hz) – the deep sleep wave:** Delta has the slowest frequency and is experienced in deep, dreamless sleep and in very deep, transcendental meditation where awareness is fully detached.

    Delta is the realm of your unconscious mind and the gateway to the universal mind and the collective unconscious, where information received is otherwise unavailable at the conscious level.

    Among many things, deep sleep is important for the healing process as it's linked with deep healing and regeneration. Hence, not having enough deep sleep is detrimental to your health in more ways than one.

5. **Gamma (above 40Hz) – the insight wave:** This range is the most recently discovered and is the fastest frequency at above 40Hz. While little is known about this state of mind, initial research shows Gamma waves are associated with bursts of insight and high-level information processing.

We can get into trouble if we cannot turn on the type of brainwave needed for the task at hand. For example, if we cannot turn on Theta brainwaves and Delta brainwaves, we will suffer from insomnia, among other things. It would be ideal to turn on the ideal brainwaves to deal with each and every situation.

Think of the brainwaves as the four gears on a car. Delta brainwaves (the slowest waves) are first gear; Theta brainwaves are second gear; Alpha brainwaves are third gear; Beta brainwaves are fourth gear. No one gear is best for every driving situation, and no one brainwave is best for all situations. We get into trouble if one of the gears on our car fails, or if we forget to use some of the gears, for example, if we start our car in first gear, then shift directly into fourth. The same is true of our brains. Sadly, many people often skip their second and third brain gears (Theta and Alpha brainwaves).

Creativity and peak performance are activities for which Alpha brainwaves are helpful. Recently, sports scientists have shown that increases of Alpha brainwaves (often in the left side of the brain) precede peak performance. One key difference between novice and élite athletes is in their brainwaves. Just before their best shots, élite marksmen and archers will produce a burst of Alpha waves in their left brains. Novice and intermediate athletes do not show this Alpha brainwave pattern.

Jeff Cooper, a former US Marine Corps officer, adapted a military colour code system in an attempt to create a training method for threat situations and alertness levels, relative to one's state of mind. As taught by Cooper, it relates to the degree of peril you are willing to do something about, whether the threat is real or imagined. This code system allows you to move from one level of mindset to another to enable you to handle a given situation properly. Cooper did not claim to have invented anything in particular with the colour code but he was apparently the first to use it as an indication of mental state. The code is as follows:

White: Unaware and unprepared. If attacked in Condition White, the only thing that may save you is the inadequacy or ineptitude of your attacker. When confronted by something nasty, your reaction will probably be 'Oh, my God! This can't be happening to me.'

Yellow: Relaxed alert. No specific threat situation. Your mindset is that 'Today could be the day I may have to defend myself.' You are simply aware that the world is a potentially unfriendly place and that you are prepared to defend yourself, if necessary. You use your eyes and ears, and realize that 'I may have to shoot today.' You don't have to be armed in this state, but if you are armed you should be in Condition Yellow. You should always be in Yellow whenever you are in unfamiliar surroundings or among people you don't know.

Orange: Specific alert. Your radar has picked up something that is not quite right and it has your attention. You shift your primary focus to determine if there is a threat. Your mindset shifts to 'I may have to shoot that person today', focusing on the specific target which has caused the escalation in alert status. In Condition Orange, you set a mental trigger: 'If that person does "X", I will need to stop them'. Your weapon usually remains holstered in this state. Staying in Condition Orange can be a bit of a mental strain, but you can stay in it for as long as you need to. If the threat proves to be nothing, you shift back to Condition Yellow.

Red: Condition Red is 'fight'. Your mental trigger (established back in Condition Orange) has been tripped: 'If "X" happens I will shoot that person'.

Black: Catastrophic breakdown of mental and physical performance. Usually over 175 heartbeats per minute; increased heart-rate becomes counterproductive. You may have stopped thinking correctly. This can happen when going from Condition White or Yellow immediately to Condition Red.

The colour code helps to explain a mental progression in a dangerous situation. As the level of danger increases, your willingness to take certain actions increases. If you ever do go to Condition Red, the decision to use lethal force has already been made (your "mental trigger" has been tripped).

MORE MINDSET THAN SKILL

It is important to note that situational awareness, sometimes referred to as 'atmospherics', is being aware of one's surroundings and identifying potential threats and dangerous situations. It is more of a mindset than a hard skill. Awareness is not exclusive to specialist government agents, corporate security teams or special forces. It can be exercised by anyone with the will and the discipline to do so. Situational awareness is not only important for recognizing threats to the tracking team, but is also used for the detection of the subject.

The main element in establishing this mindset is to recognize that threats exist. Ignorance or denial of a threat can make your chances of recognizing an emerging threat quickly – and thus avoiding it – highly unlikely. Apathy, denial and complacency can be deadly.

A second important element of the proper mindset is understanding the need to take responsibility for one's own security: you are your own health and safety manager.

Another important facet of this mindset is learning to trust your 'gut', or intuition. Many times a person's subconscious can notice subtle signs of danger that the conscious mind has difficulty in recognizing. Trusting your gut instinct and avoiding a potentially dangerous situation may cause you a bit of inconvenience, but ignoring such feelings can lead to serious trouble.

Finding the Right Level

It is crucial to stress here that situational awareness does not mean being paranoid or obsessively concerned about security. In fact, people simply cannot operate in a state of focused awareness for extended periods and high alert can be maintained only for very brief periods before exhaustion sets in. The 'fight-or-flight' response can be very helpful if it can be controlled. When it gets out of control, however, a constant stream of adrenalin and stress is simply not healthy for the body and mind and this also hampers security. Therefore, operating constantly in a state of high alert is not the answer, nor is operating for prolonged periods in a state of focused alert, which can also be demanding and completely enervating. The human body was simply not designed to operate under constant stress. All people, even highly skilled operators, require time to rest and recover.

Because of this, the basic level of situational awareness that should be practised most of the time is relaxed awareness, a state of mind that can be maintained indefinitely without all the stress and fatigue associated with focused awareness or high alert. Relaxed awareness is not tiring and it allows you to continue life while rewarding you with an effective level of personal security. When trackers are in an area where there is potential danger (which, in reality, is almost anywhere), they should go through most of the day in a state of relaxed awareness. Then, if they spot something out of the ordinary that could be a threat, they can 'dial up' to a state of focused awareness and take a careful look at that potential threat (and also look for others in the area). If the possible threat is simply a false alarm, they can dial back down into relaxed awareness and continue on their way. If, on the other hand, the potential threat becomes a probable threat, seeing it in advance allows a tracker to take actions to avoid it. In such a case he may never need to elevate to high alert, since he will have avoided the problem at an early stage.

However, once in a state of focused awareness, a person is far better prepared to handle the jump to high alert if the threat does change from potential to actual.

I experienced this in Kenya. While we were covertly observing an armed group from a high point, a black rhino on the plains below picked up our scent. (I had previously seen the rhino on the plains, but deemed that our high position was sufficiently far away that it wouldn't pick up our scent.) However, despite the fact that it was at least a kilometre away, it did so. Black rhinos can be very bad-tempered, and males will defend their territory to the death. The rhino turned and started to canter towards us. What had previously been a probable threat had now become a high alert. In no time at all the rhino was within two hundred metres and was in the mood for a tussle. By the time he had got to this point we were already bugging out to the back end of the hill and running to get downwind of him. It was an unnerving experience, because losing sight of a rhino doesn't mean that he isn't still looking for you. He could have popped up at any moment and charged. If the rhino had found us and charged, we would have had to fire a shot to warn off or kill the creature. But the sound of the shot would have had the adverse effect of alerting any poachers in the area to our presence and to our position.

Of course, when a person knowingly ventures into an area that is very dangerous it is only prudent to practise focused awareness while in that area. When the time of potential danger has passed, it is then easy to shift back to a state of relaxed awareness.

People can hone their situational awareness ability by practising some simple drills. For example, you can consciously move your awareness level up to a focused state for short periods during the day.

One skill that is useful is to look at the people around you and attempt to figure out their stories, in other words, what they do for a living, their mood, what they are focused on and what it appears they are preparing to do that day, based merely on observation. Employing such simple focused awareness drills will train the mind to be aware of these things almost subconsciously while in a relaxed state of awareness.

This situational awareness process also demonstrates the importance of people being familiar with their environment and the dangers that are present therein. Such awareness permits some threats to be avoided and others to be guarded against when it is necessary to venture into a dangerous area.

ZIZO – The Primer for Tracking

In many practices, changes in states of consciousness are induced by activities that create trance states, such as drumming, dancing, fasting, sensory deprivation, exposure to extremes of temperature or the use of psychoactive drugs. Native Americans used sweat lodges and vision quests prior to battle or hunting. Bushmen use a mixture of psychoactive drugs, drumming and dancing. Zulus use drumming and dancing.

As mantrackers, we cannot take part in most of these activities, so we need to find another method of getting to a heightened state of awareness.

This is where the process known as ZIZO comes in. This process synchronizes the tracker with his surroundings. It slows down and reduces Beta waves, caused by stress prior to the follow-up – for example, a kit malfunction, or something that was on the tracker's mind, which is not relevant to the follow-up.

1. Zone-in

The best way to zone-in is to move away from the noise and the sometimes confusing and highly charged environment prior to a follow-up.

I generally find that people are talking, smoking and fiddling with kit at this stage. For some reason, the stress level causes people who are normally familiar with their equipment to find suddenly that they cannot locate this or that, cannot undo a buckle or reach into a pocket, and find any number of reasons to fumble and cuss.

I move a short distance away, but not so far that I cannot still hear what is going on. I will look away from the mêlée of people and spend a moment clearing my mind of surging thoughts. Did I forget to close the house door; did I lock it? and other thoughts which are not relevant to the follow-up.

Once I have cleared these thoughts I let my mind go. I clear any previous conceptions from my mind and then start to visualize and work my mind into the subject.

I have developed the zone-in so that I can do it anywhere, including areas where there is a lot going on, like airports.

To practise the zone-in, find an area where you can sit. Spend thirty seconds scratching itches, adjusting your clothing and position, and then do not move for at least twenty minutes. Purge the mind of surging thoughts. It can be difficult for those people who are always on the move.

Once you have spent a short while zoning-in, you will begin to see your surroundings in high definition and your ability to maximize your senses will have improved. Be careful at this point, because I have found that during the learning phase there is a danger that trackers will fall asleep.

2. Zone-out

During the process of zoning-in, start the zone-out process and plot yourself into the landscape. Think about what is behind, in front and around you as well as things that you cannot see, such as a river or canyon. At this point you will be getting into the heartbeat of your surroundings.

Putting the ZIZO together will give you a massive advantage over the subject.

Every time I move from one environment to the other I ZIZO. It could be merging from a forest into a clearing, or vice versa. I will stop for a moment, before moving on. The more you practise the ZIZO the better you will get.

VISUALIZATION

A mental image is an experience that significantly resembles an object, event or scene, but occurs when the relevant object, event or scene is not actually present to the senses.

As contemporary researchers use the expression, mental images can occur in the form of any sense, so that we may experience auditory images, olfactory images and so forth. However, because sight is our primary sense we tend to focus mainly upon visual mental imagery.

Common examples of mental images include daydreaming and the mental visualization that occurs while reading a book. When hearing a song, a musician can sometimes also 'see' the song notes in their head.

Visualization can sometimes feel abstract, and some trackers have difficulty with it. This can be remedied by the tracker forming the size or shape of the object with his hands. Literally, while he visualizes it, he draws the outline or in some way mimics the object. In many tribes around the world they will shape-shift during a dance. For example, the Bushmen will sometimes mimic an eland or a kudu.

Visualization is a term that is popular with sportsmen and personal development gurus, as trackers we need to take it to another level. Not only do we need to visualize ourselves, but we need to visualize the landscape and the subject we are tracking.

Using the same method as sportsmen, we will visualize both internally and externally. We will imagine what we will feel like during the follow-up and how we will deal with factors as they are presented to us, such as coming out of cover to cross a river. We wouldn't just dive in, we would visualize the sensation of crossing the river; the cold water on the skin and the slippery rocks under the feet.

We also need to visualize externally – what we would look like crossing the river to an enemy, or sky-lining on a ridge, with the sun or moon behind us.

At this point trackers have a difficult task, because they have to visualize internally and externally, not just themselves, but the subject they are tracking.

The initial process for visualization starts towards the end of the zone-in. I would never, under any circumstances, consider tracking without the ZIZO. If you are going to be putting yourself in harm's way you need to know what is going on around you. You will be asking yourself questions like 'Are the people we're tracking aggressive, dangerous and cunning?'. If you decide that they are going to be cunning, then you will have to consider your own cunning. If they are going to be in-your-face aggressive, then you have to visualize how you will deal with that.

I find that if I visualize small details about the subject: hairstyle, gait and a multitude of other factors, I will also be asking myself if they are fit, well fed, well hydrated, and so on. The saying is: 'Think as smart as the animal you are tracking!' No words could be more accurate.

I think of the visualization process akin to looking in a mirror. The face looking back is not you; it is the subject you are tracking!

During the follow-up, tracks may be clearly visible and then they may seem to disappear. Experienced trackers are able to visualize what the track would look like and where it would be.

Tracker's Hard Drive

Once a tracker has seen a track, he should be able to place it on the brain's hard drive for recollection at a later date. For example, once he has seen a GSG9 boot pattern it will stay in his memory, along with thousands of other tracks.

A few years ago I was tracking someone in the bush. His track was very distinctive, because the front of his shoe was broken and his toe had worn the sole of his trainers so that his big toe could be seen in the tracks. I clocked it. About a year later the same tracks reappeared, and I was able find the person who was wearing them. This time he had climbed a tree in an attempt to throw off the bloodhounds.

When we are trying to visualize what the subject might be doing, you will be probably be imagining a bird's-eye view. However, for trackers, another method is to imagine that there is a mirror which is reflecting the subject's horizontal image back to you. So not only are you seeing him from above, but you can also see him from ground level. This is an advanced method of visualization, but is especially important for those involved in counter-IED activities, where a bird's eye view is not sufficient.

There are different kinds of visualization: for example, if I am tracking someone who has placed a booby trap, and I want to find them, I visualize a fishing hook at the end of a line, submerged in water. The hook leads up to the rod, back to the reel. That's the easy bit. Now I try to visualize the person when they were holding the rod in the water: what was their position, why did they chose this patch to fish from and what were they trying to catch, with what bait? Then I think what if I was the fish they were after, what booby traps might be out there, or IED? What have they placed as a decoy to the eye, or other bait that would draw me in to the hook?

When we track it is usually after the subject has left the area, so now we have got to think past the line and reel to the person who has left the scene. Where are they now, where did they come from and where did they rest up? Where did they get the bait? This is ideal visualization for counter-IED functions.

I have been called to give evidence as an expert witness in criminal cases. In every case, either for the prosecution or defence, the court has used visualization of the subject, as defined by the tracks. We can tell whether a person was acting in a suspicious or furtive manner from their tracks, but it is another thing to imagine the person in those tracks when they were made. Forensic tracking has grown in popularity in recent years and I have noticed an increase in the demand for my services of forensic track interpretation.

CHAPTER 5

'Mindology'

The human mind has undergone field trials for millions of years. It is perhaps one of the most studied and yet least understood subjects in the world.

Trackers need to be familiar with the psychology of the hunter and hunted; after all, the follow-up is always going to be a hunt. The tracker should be able to maintain his position as the hunter, and never become the hunted.

Not all trackers have a strong hunting instinct, although in some it is obvious because of their behaviour. The hunting instinct is associated with those who like the pursuit or chase, and when they achieve their target, they instantly want to move on to the next chase. Other people are content to track without the need for a chase.

Somehow we have to harmonize their abilities. If the tracker with a powerful hunting instinct is let loose he will probably look to dominate the surroundings, while the tracker with a lesser hunting instinct could well become the hunted!

Using the analogy of the 'evolutionary arms race', as predators develop efficient predatory adaptations, the prey will counter with defensive adaptations. This results in a selection pressure that is unequal because if a predator loses the race, he simply loses a meal. If the prey loses the race, he loses his life. The pressure is, then, greater on the prey to evolve new adaptations.

We can equate some of this to tracking. As we get better at tracking, our prey can get better at anti- and counter-tracking. In desperation the hunted can become dangerous and devious and tip the balance in his favour. The equation works like this. Suppose that both the tracker and the quarry start with 50 points each. If the tracker loses one point to the quarry, the score will be 49 to the tracker and 51 to the subject, which means the tracker has to somehow reclaim two points.

It can be likened to a see-saw with people of unequal weight. Naturally, the person with the greater weight has control. If he so chooses, he can keep his end down, leaving the lighter person with his feet off the ground, which is domination. The best option would be to keep the see-saw so that it can be controlled without domination, which can, to a certain extent, be inefficient. If the lighter person were to re-address the situation it would give them back some control.

NOOM

The Bushmen of the Kalahari have a term that applies to domination. The word 'Noom' or 'N'um' refers to the practice of survival. It is hard to give a direct translation, but what it means is that you should match the energy of your surroundings, and then add a small amount, so that you are not dominating, but are just ahead.

This concept applies to your personal well-being. In other words, if you are not prepared both physically and mentally you may get hungry, dehydrated or tired. Those very elements will diminish your *noom* and the quarry, or environment, will have the advantage over you.

I apply *noom* to everyday life and especially in the jungles and deserts of the world, where it is easy for the bugs, snakes and elements to take their toll and wear you down. To put it simply, if I don't wash my hands, I will get a stomach upset, which in turn will affect my ability to track efficiently. If I don't dress appropriately for the environment, I could get too cold or too hot. Wearing the wrong kind of camouflage or boots all affect *noom* and could have disastrous results.

Eat when you can, drink when you can and make sure your equipment and clothing are up to the job; that way you reduce the likelihood of losing your advantage during a follow-up.

What if the quarry also has a good level of advantage over the tracker? We then have to become *noom* thieves and start to pick away at this advantage by using psychological tricks of the mind, dummy trip-wires, keeping up the pursuit so that the quarry doesn't have a chance to sleep, rest or eat. By shaping the follow-up to the tracker's advantage, the quarry is forced into taking actions which they may not understand, or which may not be under their control. The key is not to give any indication to the quarry that they have the advantage. (This only applies to combat and tactical tracking, obviously not search and rescue).

Even though the quarry might be the enemy, it is important for trackers to have empathy for the subject and get to know their personal motivations. It helps to get inside their mind and this could help in anticipating their next move.

PSYCHOLOGICAL RESILIENCE

Tracking is always a roller-coaster of emotions. One minute it can be a massive high, because you have found fresh tracks, and within hours you are cold, wet, hungry, with no prospect of getting out of the elements and getting some sleep, on top of which the tracks have dried up. Our quarry has been playing tricks on our mind.

The factors mentioned above can break a tracker, with serious consequences. This is called buzz-kill. I can plan to defeat all but the most resilient trackers, if not within a long day, at least by the next morning.

This tracker has been defeated by 24 hours of physical and mental disruption. The temperature is extreme and he is no longer in control of his well-being and is in grave danger. He has removed his boots, which is a common behavioural pattern of people who are suffering from hyperthermia.

The tracker will have crashed and burnt: small problems seem insurmountable. The tracker desperately needs to re-*noom*, but to do this he must be mentally resilient.

The ability to adapt to adversity and overcome barriers is crucial to a tracker's strength. This skill — resilience — can characterize both physical and psychological strength. But while every tracker should be trained how to develop physical resilience, it is also essential to learn how to develop psychological resilience.

Resilience is an essential part of a tracker's positive growth and development. In addition to peak physical performance, every tracker must be well-balanced psychologically, spiritually and socially. Resilience is:

- The ability to maintain mission readiness before, during and after stressful situations.
- An important way to enhance effectiveness and decrease the adverse effects of stress in all aspects of tracking.

More than simply stress resistance, resilience is a proactive and adaptive process that emphasizes turning challenges into opportunities. For example, consider the differences between steel and rubber:

- A steel bar is capable of maintaining its rigid form while bearing large loads, but is susceptible to breaking.
- A rubber brick, on the other hand, bends easily under even small loads, and is extremely difficult to break.
- Moreover, once the load is removed from the rubber, its flexibility returns it to its original form.

The tracking team depend on you to have a flexible type of strength so that you can recover peak performance after a stressful event.

Like a physical skill, psychological resilience is a skill you can learn. All of my trackers go through rigorous mental resilience training. At Shadowhawk we offer a whole module which lasts days, during which trackers are given the tools to be psychologically resilient before being repeatedly tested to breaking point. The tools are:

- The ability to cope with changes.
- Being positive about abilities.
- Having a goal that needs to be achieved.
- Developing problem-solving abilities and providing solutions.
- The ability to adapt and learn.
- The ability to keep practising skills.
- In short, the ability to *noom* and re-*noom*.

Short-Term, Highly Achievable Tasks

Surviving either in the wilderness or even in urban areas can be difficult. Now add to the mix the fact that you are tracking a dangerous person, or even worse this person has turned the tables and you are now the one being tracked. The terms 'surviving' and 'tracking' are just words but, when translated to reality, there are literally hundreds of tasks that need to be taken care of, including finding food and water, and dealing with clothing, kit, the environment and emotions. People will be asking themselves lots of questions about when they are going to eat, drink and sleep. Remember that the quarry dictates our day, so we don't know where we might be sleeping, the distance we will travel, or many other important details. This all creates a stressful environment.

When there are so many factors influencing our day, things can get very tough, affecting our physicality and mentality in a negative manner. At this point some people go into a very dangerous overdrive and push on. Their brain is not working to its full capacity; their senses are dulled and their reasoning is questionable. Alternatively, some people will flop and the words 'I can't go on' will be muttered.

Then it is advisable to stop and take time out for safety (TOS). This can last ten minutes or thirty seconds. Once this is done, the trackers should concentrate on short- term, highly-achievable tasks.

If the task is too big – for example, if the team have to cross a mountain range before dark – then many will either flop, or go into overdrive. If the main task remains the same but is broken down into smaller tasks – for example to get to that rock in ten minutes – it is easily achievable and then another small task is undertaken. When it comes to micro achievements, it is a personal challenge/task that is best done internally. I find this ability to break down a larger task into smaller ones quite daunting and, when done under pressure, to be my most effective survival tool.

This kind of training pays off tenfold, as there is little that the trackers are fazed by. They can take the knocks and get straight back up for the fight-back.

CHAPTER 6

Types of Tracking

While the underlying skills have remained the same, tracking has evolved into distinct areas of specialization. This metamorphosis has its roots firmly based in our genome, but evolution has produced trackers who possess specialist genetic novelties.

To a certain extent this is the result of cause and effect. Among other factors, wars, media and money have all had an influence on modern-day tracking.

On the surface, people often think that there is a clear division between military-style tracking, search and rescue, nature tracking and the spiritual or 'energy' aspect of tracking. There are excellent schools based in the USA: the Scott-Donelan Tracking School, Tom Brown School of Tracking and Universal Tracking Services (UTS), to name but a few. There are also excellent tracking schools and individuals all over the world and, last but not least, the trackers themselves.

I have found that a large influence on the style of tracking is the individual person's perception of themselves. Some military-style trackers steer clear of nature tracking or spiritual tracking and vice versa. During operational tracking, the best trackers can tap into and cross the barriers that often keep them separated. This method of integration solves the problem of polarization of styles. There is no word that can replace the term 'spiritual' in tracking and it is a word that can have some trackers running for the woods.

However, there is an unlikely alliance between spiritual tracking and military-style tracking. In military tracking, the limits of human endurance and peril can be experienced. During this time, the senses are raised and somehow a connection is made to the environment and the subject being tracked.

MILITARY-STYLE TRACKING

Military-style tracking varies from other styles in that the trackers are looking to the spoor furthest away, so that they can move quickly. Other styles of tracking are looking to individual, or sets, of tracks for interpretation. Good military-style trackers can do both.

Historically this has left little room for the spiritual type of tracking, since it is mostly visually based, at least in the literature and training. However, we have for centuries used indigenous people to do our military tracking. Many of these trackers are deeply spiritual, and some take mind-altering drugs and participate in trance-inducing dances to enhance their tracking ability.

When I was in the jungles of Borneo, we had excellent trackers, some from the Iban tribe who were infamous headhunters. They have adapted successfully to the jungle and are both feared and revered by other jungle tribes, because of their known ability to track down the enemy.

They were deeply spiritual, especially about the jungle, and they would go to great lengths to appease the jungle gods. In that area the jungle is considered by them as feminine, and she could easily be upset or become jealous, yet they made excellent military-style trackers.

Military tracking is now becoming more mainstream, and is suited to someone who has already acquired good infantry skills. Certainly, there are exceptionally good trackers coming out of the various military schools of tracking; however, one of the pitfalls of generalized military tracking is its own 'self-limitation'. Depending on the country and tracker training ethos, it leaves room for additional skills. The limitations are the result of the cost of training, the level of the instructors and the ability of those involved to maintain a high level of skill in this specialized area while maintaining their main operational role.

Military-style tracking is divided into two sections: combat tracking and tactical tracking.

Combat Tracking

Combat tracking is where the target is hunted down and then neutralized, without being given the opportunity to respond to verbal instructions. In Africa, the tracking team would locate the target, extricate themselves and then an infantry or artillery platoon would take over and finish the job. There was never a question of issuing instructions, because the targets knew that they would be killed in a gun battle and were prepared to fight to the death. In this situation, trackers are aware of the war of attrition, the bottom line being 'don't take any risks; don't go in for the kill'. The vicious circle is very difficult to break.

Combat tracking is fading into the past, with the occasional flurry of activity. On many occasions the enemy have known what trackers can do and have been able to lure tracking teams into IEDs and ambushes. With modern-day surveillance and intervention from the air, the decision to deploy combat trackers is rarely done. People have realized the value of winning hearts and minds, and the value of taking someone alive. On several occasions when gun battles have taken place, the injured have been known to escape and die away from the initial contact area. It is then down to the authorities to prove that the person was shot legitimately and to identify the location in which they were shot.

Military tracking also includes the deployment of snipers, whose job it is to conduct reconnaissance. Snipers make excellent trackers and should be expert at anti-tracking and camouflage techniques.

Tactical Tracking

Tactical tracking is becoming more widespread. It is different from combat tracking in that, once the targets have been identified, they are given verbal instructions as to what they should do. If they comply with the instructions then they should not fear any further harm.

While I was with the US Border Patrol in California and Tucson I learnt the value of tactical tracking. On my first day I reported to El Centro Headquarters. The Chief was very welcoming and explained that they treat every prisoner with respect, authority and humanity. This was later to become apparent to me.

The same night I joined agents patrolling, on the lookout for illegal activities, including illegal migrants and drug smugglers. Within hours we were tracking down and apprehending people. Although the Mexicans vastly outnumbered the police, they gave themselves up and complied with instructions.

Both the US Border Patrol and Mexicans knew how to play the game. The Border Patrol did not want to use weapons or shoot at people because that would then give the Mexicans a reason to fight back with guns.

Every time that a group of Mexican were tracked down, they were given clear instructions in Spanish:

Detente, no te muevas.
Bajen las armas y las manos en el aire.
Ponte de rodillas.
Acuéstese en el estómago.
No mueva.

Which translates to mean:

Stop, do not move.
Put your weapons down and your hands in the air. [*They comply*]
Get down on your knees. [*They comply*]
Get down on your stomach. [*They comply*]
Do not move.

When these instructions are given, you have less than eight seconds to get those apprehended to comply with the first instruction. If they comply then they are likely to follow further instructions. However, if they do not comply with the initial instructions within eight seconds they are already weighing you up and considering how they could attack or escape.

The initial instructions must be forceful, fast and delivered with appropriate aggression. Sometimes this might mean overwhelming aggression and aggressive posturing. At the early stage, aggressive posturing is best practice. It must be emphasized that the aggressive posturing is likened to being a professional actor. At no point does the tracker actually lose his temper and become genuinely aggressive.

Once the instructions are obeyed the tactical tracker has good control, and is able to change his demeanour to suit the environment and target.

If this is done well, no one will get injured.

Counter-IED Tracking

In conflicts all over the world people have been making improvised explosive devices. They are cheap and easy to make. An IED could cost just a few dollars, but the cost of finding and diffusing one can be many thousands of dollars. Detecting IEDs is not just about technology; it requires a high degree of training and the ability to recognize changes in the local contextual environment. This book delivers many of the skills used to detect IEDs. Due to the ever-changing skills of the bomb-makers, this book should be used only to supplement formal training.

A great deal of research has gone into detecting IEDs, including sweep patterns. However, looking for disturbance on the ground may not indicate the location. It is entirely possible that the IED is concealed in a wall, tree or other object off the ground.

A good understanding of the principles of tracking will give the operative a valuable tool. By recognizing spoor and interpreting it, the operative may be able identify not only where the IED is placed, but who placed it there.

There is no 'one treatment' cure-all to IEDs, but tracking is a vital part of a complex scenario.

SEARCH AND RESCUE TRACKING

For many years the USA has known the value of tracking and has applied it to searching for missing persons. This is usually a two-way detection process. The trackers are trying to find the subject and the missing person is trying to find a way back to safety (with the exception of certain categories).

Great trackers and authors like Abe Taylor and Jack Kearney were both US Border Patrol agents who were using their skills day-in, day-out to track Mexicans, and it wasn't long before they were being called to search for missing persons.

During the 1970s and 1980s the step-by-step method of tracking evolved. There are some misconceptions that evolved with this technique.

Search and rescue (SAR) trackers tend to wear high visibility clothing. This search controller is a well-trained and experienced tracker.

The step-by-step method implies that you do not leave the last track until you have found the next track. The effect of this is that the tracker can become bogged down in the 'red zone' and not find the next track. Every search is an emergency and, for every moment that the tracker lingers on an elusive track that he cannot see, the time-distance gap will be increasing.

Step-by-step tracking makes use of a tracking stick on which there are markers that are used to measure stride and footwear size.

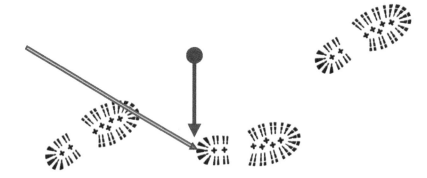

Place the point of tracking stick at the primary impact point of the second track.

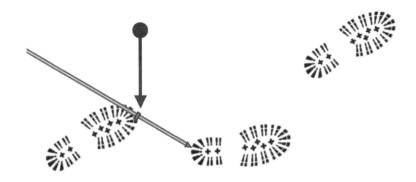

Move the first 'O' ring down to the terminal impact point of the first track.

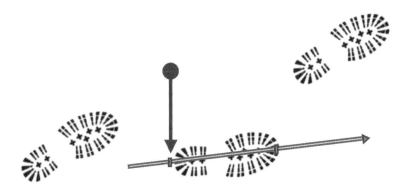

Move the second 'O' ring down to the primary impact point of the same track to provide a quick reference guide to the length of a track.

Since the step-by-step method was taught by Abe Taylor, Jack Kierney and Joel Hardin (the last-named also an ex-US Border Patrol agent), I was keen to investigate whether the technique is still used, so I visited the US Border Patrol.

I discovered that the technique is no longer used by the US Border Patrol. However, through training thousands of trackers, I have found that the step-by-step technique is a highly effective training tool.

By using the stick the tracker is able to concentrate on the arc of the stick, which is adjusted to roughly the equivalent length of a human stride. Within that arc, the next track should be found.

Not only does this help to concentrate the eye on where the next track is, it also helps to build up the tracker's confidence and ability to anticipate where a compression shape should be. However, the misconception that the tracker does not move until he can find the next track is wrong.

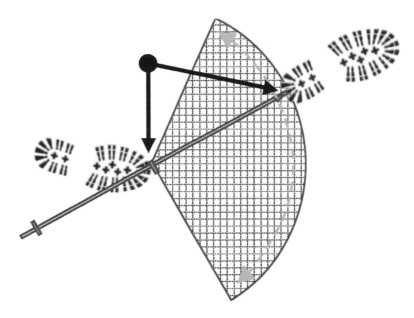

Keeping the first 'O' ring above the terminal impact point, sweep the point of the stick approximately 120 degrees in the direction of travel – the next track is likely to be within the arc.

The tracker should move as quickly as possible and can always bracket and mark the track and return to it later if necessary.

Search and rescue trackers come from all walks of life; they are highly dedicated and selfless in their endeavours. Throughout the world, search and rescue teams give many hours of their life to searching and will turn out free of charge. They are usually well disciplined and keen to add skills that will assist in their search for a missing person. However, mantracking has always had a rocky ride with search teams. Some search teams think tracking is an entirely separate resource, like search and rescue dogs.

It is very hard to find, train and retain a dedicated SAR tracking team. They cannot be mass-produced. Trackers and tracking techniques are frequently misunderstood because most people have a distorted view that tracking is a mystical art-form, without substance. That said, it is better to recruit SAR trackers from within a SAR team. For over ten years I have been doing just that. I have been training SAR organizations for a long time and found that on every course the delegates recognize the potential of tracking. However, only a small number of those same delegates have what it takes to be good trackers. That said, every SAR tracker who has attended my school will at least know where to look for tracks, and some of those talented people will be able to follow a complex trail.

ANIMAL TRACKING

In an ideal world, all mantrackers would be accomplished wildlife track-ers. The ability to track wildlife, and interpret wildlife behaviour, is one of the most powerful tools available. On countless occasions, interpreta-tion of animal behaviour has saved my life. If your enemies know how to interpret wildlife better than you, it may be impossible to track them down, because they will always be one step ahead. If they are in pursuit of you, every move you make will cause a ripple effect that will give your position away.

I have used game trails to find water. To do this, you have got to under-stand the matrix of tracks. If you simply follow a game trail, you could be walking in the opposite direction, away from the water. By looking at the junction of two trails, you will see that one will have a slight slant to one side: they will form an offset Y junction. You should follow the trail that becomes one: as the water source gets closer there will be numerous manifolds all leading to a dominant track. When you are very close to water, the dominant trail will scatter into capillary trails. The reason for this is that animals approaching water are very cautious of predators lying in wait, and they will use the cover of vegetation and their senses to make sure it's safe before approaching.

In some locations you could be tracking humans in the same area as deadly animals. The ability to read animal tracks will give you an indica-tion of what lies ahead. On one occasion I was tracking one person who had cut through an electrified fence. His intention was probably to cut through the fence at dusk, and then wait to see if it was detected. If not, a gang of poachers would have quickly infiltrated an area rich with rhino. They would have killed as many rhino as possible in one night and left by dawn with their rhino horn.

I was called when he cut the fence, which had caused a short circuit. I picked up his tracks at the fence, where he had been waiting to see if the cut in the fence had been detected. He had detected my approach and made off. By this time it was dark, and no matter how much you want to follow a track, it must be avoided at all costs after dark. You could easily walk into an ambush or booby traps. All that the people being tracked have to do is remain still and you could walk straight past them. So I decided to commence the follow-up first thing in the morning.

The trail led for a few kilometres along a dusty road. There were tracks from a cobra and a leopard on the road. He then went up the hill, with a *kopje* on top. The leopard tracks followed the same route and on one of his prints there was a leopard track on top of it. It was clear that the leopard had travelled that path after him, sometime during the night. My suspicions were that he knew the terrain well and knew that a leopard had its lair in the *kopje*. He was obviously planning on using the *kopje* for a high-point lookout, in the hope that if someone found his prints they would have to go past the lair to get to him. Big cats behave differently when they wake and so you can tell when you are getting close to a lair. The usual business-like trail in a straight line is replaced with random, more dispersed tracks. Approaching a leopard's lair is a nerve-racking experience. There are a number of possibilities: the leopard could be asleep and unaware of your presence or it could be awake and be in the lair, unaware of your presence, which is the most dangerous situation. Usually wild animals will give about 10 per cent of an opportunity for you to back off or for them to back off. Startling an animal doesn't give them time to think and they will go straight into an attack. Another option is that it has detected you and is waiting to defend the area. Last, but not least, it could be waiting in a nearby shadow, waiting to pounce.

This was a tricky situation to be in. The only option was to stop short of the lair, make some noise, and zone-in. After twenty minutes, I moved closer, and edged my way over the top of the lair and down the other side. The leopard was out and it had cleared the way for me to follow this man's tracks to the road where he had been picked up by security forces.

OTHER FORMS OF TRACKING

Track-biased Teams
This denotes a team which has a primary role that is not tracking. This could be canine units, military police, covert operators or search and rescue. They are deployed with another objective outside of tracking but are trained to use tracking as one of their tools.

Macro-tracking
The FAST (Fast, Adaptable, Sure Tracking) phase technique is designed to be used in tracking the target aggressively. For this purpose, I have divided tracking into two sections. Most trackers want a quick result and as such will look for the most obvious spoor. They will cast ahead systematically, often covering large distances, taking into consideration the landscape, often several kilometres ahead.

Because it is the quarry that dictates where a tracker goes, there are factors that the tracker may not be aware of. On one occasion we were tracking a group of armed poachers who had a couple of hours start on us. Air support was called in and unbeknown to the poachers they had started to move directly towards a heavily defended military base in the bush – and so were we. They would have been stopped by the fence and spotted by lookouts. The outcome of us shunting armed poachers close to the camp would have resulted in a gun battle and possibly the use of artillery. The military would not have known about our follow-up, and would probably have mistakenly opened fire on our tracking team, with disastrous consequences.

The big picture is crucial to tracking, but when things slow down because the spoor is lost, or the team is trying to find an initial commencement point, or corroborate spoor, it is essential that they look closer.

Micro-tracking

This is where trackers are seeing extremely small spoor. It could be anything from a grain of sand lodged in a leaf, to human hair or a single strand of burlap from a ghillie suit caught on a bush. This can be happening during a follow-up, or a specialist micro-tracker will be deployed to seek micro spoor.

This is a specialized skill, which is suited to a specific type of tracker, who has a sharp eye, patience and experience. One in ten trackers have the sharp eye required for micro spoor, and then they need to have the correct mindset. It can be a slow and laborious task, but when the tracking team is struggling to find spoor the micro-tracker could be the only chance of finding an ICP. Micro-tracking is also an essential skill for counter-IED detection.

Micro-tracking can cause the follow-up to slow down and therefore, while the micro-trackers are at work, the rest of the tracking team continues cutting for spoor. Obviously this is dependent on maintaining the safety of all trackers.

CHAPTER 7

When and Where to Use Tracking

I am never *not* tracking. I am constantly aware of my surroundings. All trackers should be continuously tracking from the minute they wake up to when they fall asleep.

When functioning this way, trackers' brains are operating in the Alpha–Theta border, the Gamma range for intuition and visualization and Beta when a high level of alertness is required. They are applying the principles of *noom*, ZIZO and awareness. This could be in the jungle, the desert, Las Vegas, London or Rio de Janeiro

There are no occasions when tracking cannot be used. However, there are conditions when tracking has to be managed, for example during the deployment of canine teams, a crime scene or dangerous environment.

There is a small amount of misunderstanding about when to use trackers. In areas where tracking has been used in the past, the benefits are better understood. To a certain extent, managers and commanders have the perception that trackers can only work when the area is uncontaminated by other tracks. Usually, by the time a tracking team is called in those who've called them are getting desperate because other resources have been unable to locate the subject. During the 'grey' timetable of a search, many people will have come and gone and almost certainly damaged spoor that trackers are looking for. One of the misconceptions is that, at that stage, there is no point in calling in trackers, and the other is that we are only looking for tracks in the ground. Nothing could be further from the truth. Experienced trackers are using all their senses continuously – they will be aware of scent alleys and will also be looking for aerial spoor, which is rarely damaged by other searchers. Even if all the tracks appear to be obliterated, the tracker only has to be lucky once, to find part of or a confirmed identifiable signature track. From that single track, a great deal of information can be gained. Information about where to deploy other resources, corroboration of direction of travel, physicality and mentality of the subject could be assessed.

I was involved in a search for a group of people who had been left behind by their coyote guide from Mexico. Quad bikes had been deployed to follow tracks, which were being corroborated by aerial support, who confirmed the tracks.

Once deployed, US Border Patrol quad bikes and aerial support can follow tracks over many miles.

Towards the end of the day we were called in and, within a few minutes, using basic tracking skills, we were able to see that they had been following the right tracks but in the wrong direction. The helicopter and the quad teams had followed tracks where they had *come from*, not to where they were going. Twenty minutes later we were finding the bodies of the mother, daughter and son. Although they were found quickly, they were unfortunately dead. In these circumstances, if a tracking team had been deployed immediately, there is a likelihood that the people would have been found alive.

Trackers do not find spoor all the time and there will be occasions when nothing can be found despite maximum effort. This said, trackers should be deployed urgently to any incident as they will be able to make an assessment as to whether tracking will be useful. They are the trackers, their skill level will have been maintained, so they alone should make the decision. As trackers we should always be prepared. Our kit should be in a state of instant readiness and we should be prepared to stay on the trail for at least twenty-four hours without back-up.

On one occasion I was called to a tactical follow-up. A vehicle had crashed at high speed while being pursued by police. The occupants of the vehicle fled the scene and one of them was believed to be carrying a semi-automatic rifle. The police did not have the skill to track through a hostile environment.

Immediately on arrival, a tracking viability assessment was made, and we commenced the follow-up, which lasted six hours. Because a weapon was suspected, and several people had fled the scene, helicopters and specialist firearms teams were deployed. Often helicopters and lots of activity can give the quarry a good idea of what is going on. When the helicopter has gone and police units are despatched to other calls, the quarry might begin to think that the coast is clear.

In the desert the escapees had made good distance and were concealed in a gully and able to watch the coming and goings at the scene from several miles away. What they hadn't seen was a deployment of trackers being dropped further down the road. We worked our way back to the scene, using camouflage and concealment techniques, and picked up the trail. We followed it and then waited for the quarry to break cover and move. When they were in the open we were able to use optics to see if they were carrying guns. As they emerged, it was apparent that they were not carrying weapons and so we were able to be more overt and increase the tracking cadence. They noticed us, which was our intention, and they were shunted straight into a cut-off team.

Tracking does not have to be in pursuit of people. It can be used by snipers employing anti-tracking skills, for gaining intelligence and training. We have had military instructors on our course. When recruits are undergoing training they are taught how to construct a hide for an observation point. The golden rule with a hide is that you never go in front of it because the outline, glint or movement could give its position away. When the recruits are left alone to man their hides, one of the common temptations is, in fact, to go in front of the hide to get a better look. When the instructors return, often the recruits will deny going against instructions. The instructors are then quick to point to the tracks at the front of the hide to prove their case.

The basic tracking skill of ground spoor awareness is the ideal tool for counter-IED training and application and would be an ideal skill-set for any infantry personnel.

Given that trackers should be included in any follow-up and that they are the only people qualified to make a tracking viability assessment, there are certain times of the day, month and year that are best to track in.

When it comes to a follow-up there are certain factors that improve our chances of finding tracks.

DAYLIGHT TRACKING

Light

We are not always lucky enough to be able to track on a bright, sunny day. In the northern hemisphere, winter light can be very grey and it can be hard to find any definition. Under these conditions, there is little you can do, apart from looking for other spoor.

It is in these conditions that we rely upon experience and speculative tracking. On the flip-side, a clear, sunny mid-winter morning is the best light condition any tracker could hope for. The sun angle is very low first

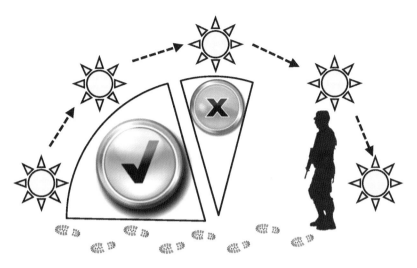

Low angles of light provide the best conditions to track as, when the sun is at its highest, its light washes the tracks thus making them difficult to see.

thing in the morning and last thing at night. At this time the shadows are long.

The tracker should keep the tracks between himself and the sun, which is easy enough if the tracks are heading into the sun. However, they may be leading away from the sun, in which case he must place his body so that he can occasionally look backwards.

It is the shadows that show up tracks, so it is vital that trackers exploit light in the morning and afternoon. It will pay dividends to be ready to track at first light, which is before sunrise. As the sun rises, colours will become visible.

When the sun reaches the highest point above, tracks in the ground are much more difficult to see, and give the effect of being bleached out.

In hot climates this may be a good time to rest; the temptation is to take a break, and this is where the mental and physical endurance of a tracker is tested because, in mantracking, this is the time when extra effort is required. At midday, the quarry is likely to be resting up and this provides the opportunity to close the time-distance gap. With the sun at its highest point, despite the tracks being harder to find, it is easier to find other spoor. Examples of this are blood spoor, broken or crushed vegetation, or discarded material. If spoor is there and the tracker can see it then the follow-up must continue.

Dew and Frost
Potentially useful features that may be present in the morning are dew and frost.

Dew

Dew is liquid moisture on the ground that is seen in the morning. It can be confused with rain, but the moisture does not result from rain. At night the ground will cool. If there is enough moisture in the air and the cooling is great enough then condensation will occur on the ground. The formation of the condensation is the same process that occurs when you leave a glass of ice water out when there is moisture in the air. You will see condensation forming on the outside of the glass. This is because the glass is cold and there is enough moisture in the air that the dew point is reached.

Because dew coats grass evenly with a layer of droplets that form a newly made baseline, it is ideal to track on and we can use it to age a track. However, it is essential that tracking commences before the dew evaporates, which will begin to happen as soon as the sun comes up. On courses I demonstrate this by the students laying a track after the dew point. Within minutes of sunrise the dew will evaporate.

If a tracking team can be on the tracks left in dew at dawn they could cover several kilometres, certainly across fields. By looking at tracks in the dew, you can count accurately the number of people involved and their direction of travel. You can also make an assumption that they travelled after the dew point, if the droplets are formed on vertical blades of grass. However, if they travelled before the dew point, droplets will have formed on the horizontal crushed blades of grass.

This track was made before the dew and frost came. Note that the grass is flat in the region of the track and vertical outside the track. Overnight dew settled on the flattened grass and turned to frost. Ice crystals then formed on the flattened, horizontal areas.

Frost

Ground frost forms in the same way as dew, except it occurs when the dew point is below freezing. In fact, true frost forms when the temperature is below freezing: the moisture goes straight from a gas to a solid. If the moisture goes from a gas to a liquid and then to a solid, the result will be frozen dew. You can tell the difference between frost and frozen dew by looking at them. Frost looks more feathery, brighter and you can see the crystal formations: frozen dew is solid and does not have quite the white appearance of frost.

Frost is not as time-critical as dew and it can linger for many weeks. It is a very useful tool for trackers.

If true frost has been stood on, the white feathery crystals are crushed and tracks are easy to find. Very often the blades of grass cannot bend because they are brittle and the cells are damaged when they are stepped on. When this happens the grass tends to go yellow. From this we can deduce that the tracks were made when there was grass frost. However, it may be that during the day rain has fallen, which then freezes to the already flattened blades of grass. This is frozen rain and does not have fine crystal formations growing upward. I have used this to age tracks in Poland.

NIGHT TRACKING

Tracking at night can be very dangerous, and should only be considered for search and rescue or in extreme circumstances for tactical and combat tracking.

Tracking at night has benefits for SAR, but for tactical and combat tracking all the quarry has to do is lie still, listen and watch for the trackers. They then have a number of options open to them. Attack you, wait until you have passed and back-track or stay still and build up a dossier of intelligence on the team. Depth of view is poor at night, and there is a very real possibility of falls, counter-tracker booby traps, or traps intended for wildlife in the area. Hazards also include predatory animals and venomous snakes and insects.

Light Discipline and Use

The human eye is not very well adapted for seeing in darkness and so we rely upon artificial light sources to illuminate our surroundings. It is good practice to improve our night vision naturally (see Chapter 3).

There are some light sources that do not bleach the rhodopsin. Green LEDs have proven to be very successful; red takes away contours, and tires the eye; blue is better, but not as good as green.

Ideally, all torches used after dark must be green, or at least have a red or green filter.

Red is a good light source. It does not show detail as clearly as green light.

Green is the best source of light. It does not affect the trackers' night vision and it shows crisp detailed information.

All members of my tracking team use green torches. White torches should be carried but are only permitted for an emergency. (Mobile phones and electronic devices are surprisingly bright when you are out in the open and so they are masked with tape or covered if it is essential to have them switched on.)

Torches must not be held higher than the waist, and at no time must the beam float around and illuminate the vegetation, tree canopy or any other object higher than the shoulders. The beam must stay on the ground unless there is a task that requires otherwise. Economy of beam is essential to reducing the amount of stray light. There are occasions when I will cover the light with tape and place a pin-prick hole in the middle, which is more than adequate for map-reading and small tasks.

Head torches must be worn around the neck and not mounted on the head unless there is a task that requires both hands to be free. There is nothing worse than someone else speaking to you when they have their head torch mounted and switched on. The beam only a matter of centimetres from your face can be blinding.

There should not be any camp lights that are derived from pressurized gas, paraffin or battery. The white light will prevent the production of rhodopsin.

If white light is used in a tactical or combat role, then it is essential that you reduce the sweep of the light, and make it random. Bear in mind that, as you sweep your torch, you are illuminating the area ahead for the quarry: once your beam is past him, he will move and take cover before your beam gets to him and once again illuminates his way ahead. Allied prisoners of war escaping from German prison camps perfected the technique of using the searchlights to their advantage.

In SAR there is a very good chance that the subject is lying up after dark. If he does not have a light source, he won't move far and the team can close the time-distance gap very quickly. In addition, because this is usually a two-way detection process, he is likely to make himself known.

In New Zealand they have conducted some research on using sound and light line search techniques. An experiment was conducted with different search subjects placed in different locations. Search teams used a sound and light line tactic in two-person teams. The detection index for a search team hearing a shout was 306 metres. The detection index for a subject hearing a whistle was 395 metres and seeing a light was 277 metres. There are conditions that can cause a variation on these factors including wind speed, direction, terrain and vegetation.

I have used some of the components from this technique. Usually, I am very strict on light discipline, however on one particular occasion I wanted to illuminate the tree canopy with my torch. This changes the distance from which a torch can be seen from a few hundred metres to several kilometres.

Attach a green LED torch to the end of the stick. By doing this, you will gain greater control over the angle of light cast around the track.

During darkness we have control of light angles, a luxury we don't always have during the day. To maximize this we can attach a green torch to the bottom of a stick at an angle. This is then held just above the ground and away from the body. This is a very effective way of following tracks at night.

I also use technology for tracking at night. I use night-vision binoculars and a heat detector. If someone is well camouflaged and they are not looking in the direction of the night-vision binoculars, they can be very hard to spot. However, with the heat detector attached to the binoculars, I can get a visual display from the detector or I can override the visual screen (so no visible light) and plug in an ear phone to pick up an audible sound when heat is detected.

Moon Phases

The moon can be surprisingly bright and it is an elementary mistake not to understand how to maximize its benefits and how dangerous it can be to you. Criminal gangs of poachers, insurgents and drug smugglers plan their activities around the phases of the moon.

As the moon reaches its highest point, even the smallest of items can be seen. On many occasion I have lain in wait and watched silhouettes of people being back-lit by the moon as they move through the night. They thought they were being smart by using the moon to light their way and didn't need torches. Big mistake!

Nocturnal predators know that their chances of a successful hunt are greatly reduced, because the prey will see them first. Experienced smugglers, poachers and insurgents know that there is an increased chance of being spotted so they lie low until the full moon starts to wax or wane.

Activities are increased at the new moon, through to the first quarter, then resume again at the last quarter through to the end. They are still active at full moon but only travel when the moonlight fades. However, movement of economic migrants through frontiers is often done at full moon. The reason for this is that the migrants are generally inexperienced at travelling through wilderness environments and cannot use torches, for fear of giving their positions away. They need light and their best option is to travel under a full moon.

OTHER CONDITIONS AND SITUATIONS

Weather

There are no weather conditions that a tracker cannot work in. If it rains, it can help to soften the substrate and assist with ageing. Long-leafed plants like ferns can bend and wilt with the amount of water on them. If someone passes by, the leaves that they brush against will literally spring back to their normal height, leaving the other leaves still wilting.

Urban Environment

Tracking in built-up urban areas can be easier than tracking in the wilderness. The abundance of urban gardens allows for excellent track-traps. Building sites in the hearts of the biggest cities provide sand, dust and dirt piles that are excellent for using the principles of transfer. There are literally thousands of clues in the city. In the summer, molten tar on the walkway or discarded materials offer clues, and of course people are forced to follow routes dictated by buildings and structures around them.

Through Water

During the summer months in the area where I live thousands of walkers take to the coastal path. There is a lot of china clay in the area and they can step into a puddle and make an excellent track. If the sun comes out, the track literally gets baked and becomes very hard. In this state I have observed one track last for more than a year.

When a person passes through water they can leave a perfect track in the mud or, indeed, cause silt to go into suspension, giving a characteristic milky appearance at the site, and some will carry downstream. Where the target walks on submerged stones, algae will rub off the rock. Where they exit, there may be tracks made visible by water on nearby stones or vegetation.

CHAPTER 8

Where to Look and What to Look For

Look for the shadows and you will find the leopard. People are often surprised that trackers can seemingly turn up a footprint or spoor and know what it is, the direction of travel and what the subject was doing at the time. The fact is that if you know where to look and what to look for the rest will fall into place.

There are some basic strategies for a tracker:

1. Gather as much information as you can about the subject. Time spent gathering information is not time wasted. If you come across someone on the trail, don't be afraid to ask them if they have seen the target (although this has to be moderated in combat and tactical tracking). However, never accept what they say as gospel truth. Sometimes people will deliberately give the wrong information and sometimes they will give what they believe was the correct information but which is actually wrong. In some parts of the world, locals will give you the answer they think you want to hear, not necessarily the truth.
2. Know the landscape. It may be that there isn't enough time to get to know the environment well. In these circumstances an experienced tracker will use other factors to help him understand. If there are no maps available, and using a local guide is not suitable, then it will be necessary to use natural navigation. This subject is so vast that it deserves a book in its own right.
3. Have an understanding of the flora and fauna, especially birds in the area of operation.

HUMAN PREDICTABILITY

Human behaviour is 93 per cent predictable, a group of leading Northeastern University network scientists recently found. Humans have a more complicated process of deciding on which behaviours to express rather than just following instinct.

Spontaneous individuals are largely absent from the population. Despite the significant differences in travel patterns, they found that people are equally predictable. The predictability represents the probability that we can foresee an individual's future whereabouts in the next hour based on their previous trajectory.

The travel patterns for someone we are tracking will be influenced by a number of external factors, which the tracker will take into consideration before and during the follow-up. By knowing and understanding the external factors that will affect the target's movements we can close the time-distance gap significantly. Humans are predictable, but one of the first skills of anti-tracking is to do the unpredictable! There are some assumptions that the tracker will have to make. Much of this information will come from knowing something about the target and the terrain. If they are competent in the wilderness, are they trained in survival, or even more dangerous, are they trackers?

Route Influencers
Route influencers will either attract or repel a human. There are no hard and fast rules, despite various publications about what people will or won't do.

Path of Least Resistance
This is the most important route influencer and is the bread and butter for tracking teams. A path of least resistance is what a human or animal will use to travel from one area to another. In the wilderness humans and animals have worn game trails that have become established. Often, these will cut through vegetation on either side. It makes sense to use these as travel will be quicker and there are fewer hazards involved.

One of the most common paths of least resistance is a dried up river bed, sometimes referred to as a gully or wadi. These have a number of advantages for travelling on. They are usually sunken and have vegetation growing along the banks, therefore they are good for tactical movement of trackers, but also the quarry is likely to use the same gully for evasion.

The advantages of using a path of least resistance are that it is easier and faster. Anyone being tracked doesn't need to hack their way through the jungle, the damage of which would be spotted by a tracker. The disadvantage is that trackers will be looking on the trail for tracks. If the target has followed a well-established trail, road or path, then it is possible that a cut-off team will be deployed further down the trail.

Tracking teams must, themselves, be extra vigilant on paths of least resistance. A path of least resistance is exactly where anti-personnel mines and other IEDS are placed, knowing that there is a strong likelihood that a human will use the path. The method of activation can sometimes be spotted. A trip-wire at ankle height is not always easily seen, but for counter-tracking, trip-wires are also placed at head height.

In some areas, more primitive traps are used. These can range from a small snare to spiked fall pits and to loaded devices of primitive arrows and spears, often laced with human faeces or poisons.

While I was tracking with the Brazilian and Argentinian forces in the jungle, the drug smugglers and poachers had well established trails through the jungles. They knew it, and so they established a complex system of paths and booby traps. Each junction had a code either cut into the vegetation or made by bending sticks. A small tree cut with one swipe of a machete, and then bent over a trail, would indicate that the trail was safe to travel on. If there was no stick over the trail, the unsuspecting tracker could walk straight into a primitive path-guarder stabber or arrow trap.

Funnelling or Pinch Points

Sometimes, manmade or natural barriers will funnel the target through a specific area. Among the most useful funnels for tracks are bridges over rivers, especially when the rivers are in flood. In Africa, the only way to cross a river is by bridge or boat. Because of crocodiles lurking silently in the water, very few people will attempt to swim.

When on patrol I would look out for landing points for canoes, perhaps only visible because of a small keyhole in the vegetation which, when investigated, could reveal an entire camp, or bridges which targets were forced to walk across.

At this pinch point the officer checks for tracks on a bridge over the Galana River.

Trackers examining a track trap for anything other than tyre marks.

Funnelling can be the result of many other features, including vegetation. There are parts of the world where vegetation is so thick or poisonous that the target will have no option but to follow an existing trail.

While on patrol in Africa, I would know that the locals were well aware of the preferred habitat of young male groups of Cape buffalo. They like to be in dense vegetation, usually close to water, where they can remain concealed. Passing too close or through these small patches is close to suicide. The Cape buffalo is likely to charge without warning and frequently kills the intruder. Locals, knowing the area, will not attempt to go through such vegetation, and will pass where there is open ground and equidistant from the clumps.

Track-traps

Interpretation of track-traps is something which is within the skill level of most officers and SAR teams. As the term suggests, it is where tracks of the target will be registered in an area where their directions were influenced, and where they have stood or left an action indicator in the ground.

The best track-traps consist of damp mud, which is high in plasticity. In this substrate extremely fine detail can be seen and will remain intact for considerably longer than sand or dust.

Tracks traps can be found anywhere, but river banks, and gravel roads and game trails make good places to look.

Barriers

General Considerations

Barriers are an extremely powerful influence on the course taken by the quarry. They will divert or delay movement or cause the quarry to turn back. Often, in fact, where physical barriers give way this creates a pinch point or funnel (see above) where the target is forced to take a particular route in order to cross or traverse a barrier. The impact of these areas may be dependent to some extent on the motive of the target. Examples are mountain passes, where it is a lot easier to wind one's way through the valleys than to go over the mountains. Similarly, where there is a body of water, especially fast flowing, and there is a bridge, the target is likely to use the bridge. In the latter case, by deduction, we may be able to discount perhaps several kilometres of river bank and go straight to the bridge, where we will look for tracks and track-traps. However, remembering that 7 per cent of people are unpredictable, we cannot completely discount the possibility that the target may have crossed the river by other means.

There are areas around the world where bogs, marshes and swamps exist. Over many years roads have been constructed above them to make transport easier. In northern Poland there is an area that I have tracked where the Tsar's Road, built on the orders of the last Russian Tsar Nicholas II, is raised above the marsh. In the depths of winter it is sometimes possible to leave the road to cross the marsh over a layer of ice, but in the summer it would be very difficult to leave the road. To go into the marshes with biting insects and dense vegetation would be a very unpleasant experience. However, even during the winter, dense vegetation still rises from the marsh and makes going hard, so it is likely that any given target will stick to the roads and pathways.

Manmade barriers

Manmade barriers create a significant influence on the target. Some manmade barriers will stop progress completely, and the target will either have to find some way to negotiate the feature or turn back. Manmade barriers include:

- Perimeter fences
- Roads, especially motorways
- Canals and irrigation channels
- Dams

In addition the state of the quarry's mind should be taken into consideration. A person who is on the run will come across other manmade barriers which could include:

- Well-lit areas
- Heavily populated areas
- Vehicular traffic
- Areas of intensive surveillance, which includes drones and geophones
- Religious, sacred and sites of superstition (although these can also sometimes be attractants)
- Tribal and gang territories

Natural barriers
In addition to very obvious barriers such as mountain ranges, cliffs, rivers, lakes and deserts, there are other potentially severe natural barriers. These include dangerous animals, and certain vegetation and biting insects, as touched on earlier. In Canada there is an area where a prison is located. Escapees from that prison have survived a couple of hours before giving themselves up – the ferocious black flies have forced them to surrender.

Along many river banks there are outcrops of razor-sharp grass that are impenetrable. In the Sonora Desert there is a plant called 'the jumping cactus', or choya. It is by far the most extreme plant I have ever come across. The reason why it is called the jumping cactus is because the spines are so fine and sharp, that even though you may have just brushed against it gently you will be covered in vicious barbed spines. My thick leather military-style boot brushed against one. I only realized when, at the end of the day, I took my boots off. As I removed the affected boot, the spine remained in my foot and pulled through the boot. To remove the spine I had to use pliers, because the barbs were so efficient. In areas favoured by this cactus, many people will not walk at night.

High Ground
People tend to go to high ground. There is no statistical information on this, but I have experimented with people on courses to see if there is any set rule. Depending on the terrain, most people *will* go to high ground, although a small percentage will go to low ground. If there is a social influencer within a group who favours high ground they will follow that person. Even trained evaders will go to high ground to enhance their view of the landscape.

In terms of being a strategically based decision, high ground is easier to defend, and indeed it is easier to attack from, so most trained people will go high.

Lights
People are attracted to lights, with the exception of those who are evading capture. Where there is a high tower in the wilderness, possibly with an aerial warning beacon, this will draw lost people in. If there are other

sources of light, including a camp fire, this will also attract people. Tactically, this is also likely to attract attention, so if the tracking team is operating covertly then they should restrict themselves to cold cooking or a Dakota Fire pit. (This is where a small hole is dug into the ground, with an adjacent hole and small tunnel interconnecting them. This allows the fire to burn below ground level and very little light can be seen.)

Camp fires are such a strong influencer that the tracker should always be on his guard around a fire. The light around the fire will illuminate the people and equipment nearby. Where the light gives way to darkness, it is very difficult to see anything. An enemy has merely to linger in the darkness very close by to remain hidden but still be able to observe and listen to the conversation. The finest example of this is in the behaviour of hyenas. They linger on the edge and, as the firelight shrinks, they get closer. Every tracker should take lighting a fire very seriously and must check tracks around the fire area in the morning.

Water and Food
Both water and food will influence people's movements. Depending on their state of mind and survival skills, they will be drawn to water sources. Humans can only survive three days without water. The desire to eat is another route influencer.

Habit and Knowledge of the Area
People often choose their route because of habit, or their knowledge of the area. In many cases, this is not surprising, but there can be some less obvious aspects to this.

For example, for some people there are certain areas where sacred sites are off limits, and locals will not go there and will not allow others into the area. These include ancestral burial grounds and other prominent features. On the other hand, some places with religious connotations will attract people. Scattered among deserts on the American border with Mexico there are shrines, usually under a rock or ledge. These are established for the predominantly Catholic drug and people smugglers to visit on Sundays as they make their way over the border. They are well established, with pictures of patron saints, crosses and candles.

Brightness, Lightness, Darkness and Contrast
Often novice trackers will only see the most obvious and dominant tracks. This can cause problems if the track is next to another which is more obvious. A common example is where a horse's hoof is either next to or on top of the target's track. The eye will naturally be drawn to the darker, more prominent track of the horse. The eye has registered all the information, including the track that is more difficult to see, but because it is not instantly recognizable as a human track, the brain will filter it out.

This shrine in the remote border area of Arizona is used by drug smugglers to pray and make offerings to their patron saint. The makeshift altar is stained with oil and wax from candles. It is extremely remote and took several hours to hike to.

Neural 'Aha'

After a few hours the novice tracker will reach a moment when, suddenly, they will see the most difficult track within the frame. This is often called the 'eureka moment'. The neural 'aha' moment has happened, and their brain begins to recognize the faintest of tracks.

Binocular Rivalry

The eye only looks at what demands its attention. In the modern age, advertisers know how to ensure that our eyes pay attention to their products. They use flashing lights and bright primary colours arranged in such a way that they out-compete other products. Easily recognizable features also compete for the eye's attention, e.g. the face of a human, or body outline of a human, and straight lines.

The phenomenon of objects competing for visual attention is known as binocular rivalry. The principle aim of camouflage is to mitigate and reduce rivalry between shades, colours and outlines.

We are used to responding to the flash of a red brake light on a car, or someone wearing high-visibility clothing to make them stand out, but what happens when muted colours of grey, brown and green are the only colours in the landscape? Rivalry between objects continues but in a more subtle way. Dark objects with straight lines will be easier to see than light objects with a curved or random outline.

As trackers we need to be able to filter out some of the rivalry. When a darker, brighter or lighter object stands out from the surroundings, then it is checked. If it doesn't correspond to what we are looking for we must develop a technique to look in the frame without it drawing the eye back.

With dirt-time and in the company of colleagues and instructors to provide reassurance, the novice tracker will soon learn the technique.

The ability to look *through* vegetation and shadows is a very important skill to develop. At this point the specialist skills being applied by members of the tracking team is important. It is a complex function.

In a way similar to chess, where each piece has a highly specialized method of attack, the tracking team need to adopt specialist skills, pertaining to their functions. The tracker is on point and looking for specific spoor. The flankers and controller need to be on the lookout, not only for tracks, but also for objects out of context and looking through foreground vegetation to objects behind.

In an earlier chapter, I mentioned how well an elephant can hide itself. Elephants are usually grey, although sometimes red, depending on the soil. They hide behind vegetation, so that in the competition for our eyes, we see the vegetation in the foreground first and not the elephant. Hard to believe, but they can be very difficult to find even when you know they are close by.

A good exercise to practise is to look at the leaves on a tree. You will notice how the branches and leaves in the foreground grab your attention. Now filter the foreground out and focus on the objects behind. You will be amazed what you will start to see.

Short Eye, Long Eye

Short Eye – the Tracker
The tracker needs to pay attention to the furthest away object for a small percentage of time. He will find spoor at the furthest away point at which it is visible and draw his eyes back, remaining focused on the spoor. Depending on the individual tracker's eyesight, the most efficient distance for human eyesight is between two and six metres. Most spoor will be found in this zone.

There will be occasions when he will need to track close to his feet, but never directly above the feet. Doing this will cause disconnection from the surroundings and slow the follow-up. This is usually done only when light conditions are poor, or when he is seeking to corroborate that he is following the correct track. Tracking is cadence- and rhythm-influenced. When the tracker is zoned in to the track and has got some rhythm he will move quickly, thus increasing the cadence. As he approaches the 'red zone' and is tracked-out, or is in difficult terrain, the cadence and rhythm will drop.

Long Eye and Short Eye – the Flankers
The primary function of the flankers is to provide security to the tracker. (This is not usually necessary for search and rescue.) The flankers will be casting out and scanning the horizon, scanning back to the mid-ground, then back to the near-ground. They are looking for outlines in vegetation, dark or light areas which are out of context, and for tracks that may have changed direction.

Long Eye – the Controller
The controller is in charge of the tracking team tactics, but one of his most important attributes is the ability to look into the distance. Using his long eye, he may be able to see fleeing suspects or other targets. He sees the bigger picture, and must carry a set of binoculars, so that he can see into the distance.

WHAT TO LOOK FOR – SPOOR

Any time someone or something moves they will leave behind tell-tale signs of their actions. The passage of humans, machinery, or animals will inflict a change on the environment.

These tell-tale signs are also referred to as spoor and it is the aim of every tracker to find and identify them. They are not always easy to find but, having found spoor, the tracker should be able reconstruct the events that produced it in a systematic and logical manner. It is akin to starting with a letter of the alphabet, then constructing a word, which then grows into sentences and then paragraphs, eventually becoming either a complete or incomplete story derived from the spoor.

To identify spoor, we have to be on the lookout for features that are broadly categorized by what gives them away. No matter where in the world I track, the following characteristics are evident in identifying spoor.

Absence of the normal: presence of the abnormal: This is a broad spectrum of spoor and can often be the first factor that a tracker might be aware of, which will lead him to the presence of other spoor.

Colour change and contrast: This is where the baseline colour changes. An example is where dry autumnal leaves on the ground are turned over. They are light on top and when something passes through and they get turned they reveal a wetter side which is dark.

Regularity and shape: This is usually straight lines and geometric patterns pressed into the ground. Off-road quad bikes leave a distinct pattern of arches and straight lines.

Flattening and compression: This is the generalized flattening of an area caused by pressure on it. This forms part of our compression shape analysis. By interpreting this we can draw some conclusions. An example would be where a rucksack has been put down and flattened the grass underneath.

Transfer: This is where a deposit of a substance is picked up and conveyed to another area, where it wouldn't normally be present. This is an very powerful tool for trackers. Examples are where fractions of mud collected on boots fall off while crossing a road. A very useful technique for tracking near water is be on the lookout for tracks that have been created by footwear or clothing that has picked up water and then left some water spoor on rocks or vegetation.

Disturbance: This is any other change from the baseline caused by the target. This can range from causing a change in bird dynamics, to disturbing insects, or a mixture of all of the above.

Disposables: These are articles that have been left behind intentionally or unintentionally by the target. Examples of this are cartridge cases and water bottles.

By using the above indicators the tracker will soon be finding spoor. In the landscape a tracker will be able to identify spoor from humans, animals or machines. Often this could be mixed with other spoor, or very difficult to distinguish because of lack of corroborating evidence. The tracker needs to follow the spoor that belongs to the quarry, which is not always easy. Spoor is also a very effective method of intelligence gathering. It is commonly used to find mass graves.

The ability to exclude the wrong tracks and follow the correct tracks improves with experience. A novice tracker will want more features to corroborate that he is following the correct tracks. However, an experienced tracker will take less time to confirm the spoor and need fewer features, thus the follow-up will be quicker.

Following a line of spoor that belongs to a person or animal can be viewed like a rope. A rope is made up of hundreds of strands, each strand adding strength. When the strands are twisted together, they make a strong rope.

When establishing the quality of the evidence, spoor is classified into two areas:

Conclusive is where there is no doubt that the spoor belongs directly to the target. This could be footprints, confirmed identifiable signature track (CIST), or disposables with name or ID. (Conclusive can also be used in the context of whether the spoor was caused by humans, animals or machines.)

Inconclusive is where there is no direct link to indicate that the spoor belongs to the target. However, several inconclusive strands could eventually convert the spoor to being conclusive.

The indicators of spoor are described in two zones and one category: ground spoor, aerial spoor and auxiliary/supplementary spoor.

Ground Spoor

Ground spoor is the result of anything which has changed the baseline of the ground or low-lying features, including vegetation. It ceases to be ground spoor at a height above the ankle. A great deal of forensic-quality evidence can be established from ground spoor. The following are key examples of ground spoor.

Flattening/Compression of the Substrate

Many people believe that this can only be caused by humans or animals with hooves. Depending on the ability of the tracker, he will also see flattening caused by animals with paws. This flattening is an excellent giveaway, even on the most difficult substrates including pine needles, granite and stone-chip road.

Flattening can also be very difficult to spot in certain areas. This is caused by a heavy-duty utility boot or hiking boot with a stiff sole and aggressive treads. One of the protruding treads could land on a very small

This stone has been kicked out of its socket. It is crucial that trackers can spot these invaluable clues. The stone usually goes in the direction of travel.

protruding stone. Most, if not all, of the sole pattern is raised off the ground and not visible, thus making rigid boots very difficult to track in dry conditions. The opposite applies moccasins, bare feet and flip flops. Because they are so soft, they mould intimately with the substrate, flattening everything that they step on. Whilst they may be good for stalking in, they are an easy giveaway compression shape, which is conclusively human.

Stones and Twigs out of Their Sockets

These can be vital clues, and many a follow-up has relied on this spoor to corroborate the direction of travel. If a stone or twig is kicked, by the forward motion of a foot, it will usually come out from its socket. If it comes out all the way, then it will always go in the direction of travel. It may travel a few millimetres and it is worth trying to match it back to the socket for corroboration. Also, examine the socket to see if it is still damp. (This spoor is not conclusively human.)

Broken/Creased Twigs on the Ground

These are often a result of a human standing on them. It is actually rare for the twigs to break, because the ground will have a degree of cushioning and, although twigs might look dry, they may still be flexible. The average speed at which a human walks does not exert enough downward force to break most twigs, even if they are dry and brittle. Most footwear is now made to mitigate the downward shock of the foot, with soft, spongy soles. However, if someone is running, carrying a heavy backpack or wearing military-style boots, it is likely that at least a crease line will be visible, or even perhaps a partial break. This could also be caused by animals with hooves. However, if the crease or break is the width of a boot then it is conclusively human.

Note that *creased leaves* can only be caused by animals with hooves, or humans.

Short Mown Grass

This can be one of the most difficult substances to track on. If it is mown regularly or grazed by sheep, then it is very hard tracking. The moment someone steps out of their track, grass will mostly spring back within seconds. To detect a compression shape, the tracker relies on good light conditions being maximized, and speed of tracking. However, if it has been raining, or there are residual drops of water on the grass, anyone walking over it will push the water off or pick it up on their footwear, which can provide useful information.

Worm casts are commonly seen on short grass. These are the result of worms surfacing during or just after rainfall and leaving behind small piles of soil. If a human stands on these the results are easily visible.

Spring and Early Summer Soft Vegetation

In spring and early summer, the plants that have been hibernating through the winter start to shoot up. These are very tender and prone to damage from the slightest contact. As the ferns, wild garlic and other shoots come up, they can cover an entire area, thus making it impossible to pass through without damaging them. Some plants, like wild garlic, give off a pungent, easy to smell odour when trodden on.

Compression Shapes

Compression shapes are the generalized shapes of objects. It is rare to find complete tracks, so it pays to learn the variation of compression shapes for mantracking. Once the tracker knows what they look like he will be able to spot them on virtually any substrate. The most important shapes are:

- Adult male: complete outline, including the arch, in-step and out-step sole.
- Adult female
- Child compression (the reason why we do not need to learn the teen-age compression shape is that, without additional features, it could be female adult)

To a tracker this area will give lots of information, in particular the compression shapes in the sand formed by rangers leaning on their rifles with the butt in the sand. It is possible to identify specific weapons by the compression shapes.

- Human lying down on front
- Human buttocks compression shape
- Rifle butt compression shapes, bi-pod shapes (i.e. small compression shapes from the two supporting legs at the front of a sniper's rifle)
- Rucksack compression shapes

A compression shape can be caused by anything, so the above list is by no means exhaustive.

Burial sites

Shallow graves sites can be distinguished by a number of features. Because the baseline of the ground has been disturbed, the overburden will naturally expand. When the body is placed in the hole, its volume, plus the expanded volume of the overburden, will cause a mound to be present. This mound will remain in place, and eventually, as the body decomposes and the overburden settles, the mound will shrink in size, and in some cases it will sink and appear to be a sump.

Within a very quick brief time the disturbed overburden will cause a change in vegetation. New flowers may appear quickly. As time goes on, the additional nutrients will cause a further change in vegetation. It is reported that nettles are a quick colonizer of shallow graves.

Transfer

This is where a substance, such as grass, mud, water or sand, is carried over from one medium to the other. This is the mantracker's ace card! Transfer is virtually impossible to hide from a tracker. The most common occurrence of transfer is where debris, including mud, is picked up on footwear. As the target moves from a muddy area to another medium, perhaps a road, car park or building, the mud will start to fall off the footwear. In areas where the substrate is clay-like in consistency and wet, the boot will become laden with thick mud. Once the covering is heavy, a wad will break off and often leave a clear imprint of the sole pattern. One of my personal favourite mediums is sand. Often sand contains sufficiently sharp grains that they will attach themselves to footwear while in a low-impact area and will only start to drop off when the target moves to a high-impact area, such as a road or building.

Disposables

This term covers anything someone has thrown out or left behind. On patrol in Arizona we came across a group of Mexicans in the desert. They scattered, and a long manhunt ensued. Several hours later I found a fresh garlic bulb on the ground. Garlic does not grow in the desert and it was out of context. When we eventually caught up with the Mexicans I noticed that one man had tucked a bulb of garlic into his socks. The reason for this is that many Mexicans believe that garlic tucked into their socks will protect them from snakes. Before they leave the desert they remove the garlic from their socks so that, if they are stopped, it is not obvious they had crossed the desert.

It amazes me that people on the run, or trying to conceal their presence, leave so much manmade debris behind. The addictive properties of tobacco ensure that smokers leave behind cigarette butts, matches and even lighters. Only the most cunning are able to hide the remains.

I have come across the tear-off ears of cyalumes (light sticks), alerting me to the fact that there are friendly forces in the area, but what is virtually criminal is that I also found the cyalume packaging, that clearly indicated that it was an infrared cyalume, which, to the enemy, is a very big clue. A tracker can deduce that it was used for communication, perhaps to a helicopter for a pick-up, or to other personnel using infrared detectors. If the enemy were on the offensive then their hunter force would probably know that an extraction of personnel was imminent.

The mantracker will be interpreting anything that is found. Discarded ammunition cases, and weapons paraphernalia, including cleaning and oiling items, will provide useful information about the assets of the enemy.

The following are some other disposable items that can provide specific information about the quarry.

Water receptacles can give an indication of possible welfare.

Clothing may indicate where someone has a pre-arranged location for changing clothing so that they can hide their identity. This is common on the Mexican border with the USA. Gulleys that run along roadsides where pick-ups are made are strewn with cowboy boots and other clothing that would identify the former wearer with Mexico.

Clothing is also discarded when people become hypothermic. For some unknown reason, it is quite common for hypothermic people to remove all their clothing, usually just before they die.

Ammunition, if found live, should be examined carefully. If it is still shiny, then maximum caution must be taken. It only takes two days (sometimes less) for the case to start dulling down. This means that the quarry has just re-armed and reloaded the magazine. Usually, if live ammunition is found on the ground, it is a good indication that the magazine was loaded, or the bullets, were handled at night, but it could also indicate a badly trained enemy.

I was with an African fire force and, in the rush to get into the vehicle and load magazines in transit, four rounds fell out and dropped onto the floor of the vehicle, and were swept underfoot. In the chaos to

This round of ammunition was found among used cartridges. It was either a
mis-fire and removed from the barrel or dropped accidentally. It may be that the
weapon was re-loaded under pressure, or by a person who is under the influence of
alcohol or drugs. The most likely reason for this was that the weapon was being
loaded in the dark.

de-bus from the vehicle at the destination, the rounds were trodden on
and fell out of the vehicle onto the ground, whereupon they were trodden on again, quickly becoming partially buried in the sand. When
the vehicle departed and the return ammunition tally did not add up, I
went back to the position of the vehicle and quickly recovered the missing ammunition.

Rations may give an indication of the nationality and diet. If discarded
rations are found then it should be determined whether they were
locally supplied (possibly identified by a price tag), whether they
require water for rehydration, or consist of heavy tinned food.

Bloodstained bandages or other medical paraphernalia should be closely
examined as a great deal of information could be gained.

In addition to objects such as these, there are categories of human waste
that can be considered as spoor: these are dealt with at the end of this
chapter.

Camp fires
Camp fires deserve a special mention, because there is lots of information that can be gleaned from a fire site. First, they must be approached

with extreme caution, since they are favourite places for a range of booby traps. There are signs to be looked for and the tracker's senses should be ramped up to maximum. Tactically, most people will have an escape route and an agreed rendezvous should the camp become threatened. In the jungle, some poachers will have established raised platforms to shoot from. It is also very important to realize that, at any time, the quarry could come wandering back into camp.

Tactical patience is therefore required when approaching a camp fire, and it should be reconnoitred thoroughly before approaching, checking for dogs, booby traps and people who may not be around the fire but sleeping or resting a short distance away. Also, be aware of latrines in the vicinity..

Once the area in the vicinity of fire has been declared clear, it can be approached, and following checked:

- Has the fire been in recent use? Check the temperature with the back of the hand.
- The fire may be cold but still recently used. The method of ageing a fire is to examine the ash. Light grey ash carries easily in the wind and may blow away. The light grey ash will quickly absorb moisture from the atmosphere and turn dark within twenty-four hours (or sooner, if it rains).

A tracker checks the temperature of the camp fire place using the back of his hand.

Aerial Spoor

Aerial spoor refers to clues in the environment which are above ankle height. In certain circumstances, it can be seen by damage done to flora and fauna.

Smoke

The need to approach camp fires with caution, and some notes about what may be learnt from them, was mentioned earlier. However, observed from a distance, smoke constitutes a form of aerial spore. Smoke from a hot fire will billow and spiral upwards. If it contains synthetic materials, especially plastics, it will be very dark, almost black. If the fuel is clean and dry, there may be very little smoke.

If the wood is wet, there will be a grey and bluish hue to the smoke and it could well hang just above vegetation owing to a lack of convection. This indicates an inefficient fire, or one that has just been started.

Colour change and contrast

Silvering

Often when a person moves through vegetation they will cause the leaves on plants to turn over. Usually, the upper side of a leaf which is exposed to the sun is dark green. The underneath is lighter in colour, with a silver tint. It is very rare, except in very high winds, for a plant to silver. This effect is not conclusively caused by humans on the ground. However, at the height above the tallest mammal (excluding monkeys and apes), any silvering is conclusively human.

Reflection/Shine

Where the quarry has walked through vegetation, especially grass, they will have pushed it over in the direction of travel. This is initially seen because the pushed down vegetation reflects light back into the atmosphere at a different angle from the vegetation which is still vertical. This is very helpful when tracking over fields with cultivated crops, especially wheat. The shine from the vegetation and flagging can sometimes be seen for several kilometres. If there is air support in the area, the crew will be able to adjust their flying altitude to see the shine better.

Flagging

This is where the vegetation has been pushed aside by the quarry as they pass through. The vegetation to the left and right will be pushed forward, sometimes interlocking. This is called flagging because the vegetation has the look of a flag in the wind. Where the vegetation points is where the quarry was heading. Flagging can also be caused by animals, and is not conclusive unless the flagging is above the height of the tallest

This track shows good shine and flagging. The direction of travel is indicated by the grass. This was taken with the track between the tracker and the sun.

animal resident in the area. It is very important to find and exploit flagging early on, as it cannot be guaranteed that no one else has walked in the opposite direction since the quarry passed through.

Stripped and cut vegetation
This can occur naturally or be caused by humans. Usually, when the bark of a tree is damaged, it will exude sap and expose the lighter wood underneath. This is a fairly common sight in the wilderness, where herbivores strip bark off trees to eat, or use it as territorial markers. Usually, where herbivores have eaten or rubbed the bark there is evidence of fraying. Where a machete or other cutting device has been used, the light colour of the wood is very visible. The cutting instrument will have penetrated through to

This track is exactly the same, but was taken with the sun behind the tracker. As a result the shine and track is much harder to spot.

the wood, and will be in clean, straight lines. Cutting with an axe will reveal deeper cuts than from a machete; both will reveal chippings where a campsite may have been.

Where a machete has been used to cut through vegetation, given that the majority of people are right-handed, it can be deduced that keeping the bottom of the slice on the right side you will be travelling in the correct direction.

A very common practice in the wilderness is for people to pull part of a plant off and then strip small parts of the bark and drop them along the trail as they walk. There is no obvious reason why people do this. Frequently, this will coincide with the vegetation being formed into a shape, usually woven into a circle, and then dropped.

Disturbance

Crushed and bruised vegetation
Soft leaf vegetation will show crush and bruising damage very quickly. If any leaves are seen to be drooping that could have been trodden on and sprung back, they should be inspected for damage. This is done by first examining the top and stem and then turning the leaf over. If it has been stepped on, it is likely to have cuts and bruising. Very often the tread pattern of a boot can be seen on the underside. This will also provide a valuable indicator to ageing the track.

Dragged vegetation
In many parts of the world there are vines and thorny growing plants that bind together in their natural state of growth. They are usually impenetrable and to get through them you either have to cut through or bash through, dragging them with you. These are obvious giveaways.

Where the vegetation is thorny it should be carefully inspected for broken off thorns, hair and fabric fibres. If the target has been wearing a burlap ghillie suit then it will have left some fibres on the thorns.

Supplementary Spoor
The term supplementary spoor takes into consideration any other spoor which is present. It serves to corroborate the presence, direction and well-being of the quarry. Here, it is categorized into signs produced by insect, bird and animal behaviour, and waste materials produced by the human body.

Insect Activity

Spiders' webs
These are very useful spoor. Spiders that spin the classical webs are active

at night, when most of their hunting takes place. The spiral part of the web is supported by frame threads, which consist of a bridge thread over the top, and anchor threads. Several anchor threads may be above the head height of a human, which means a human can walk through the web only destroying one anchor thread, which will give the appearance that no one has passed. However, if a person walks through the spiral section of a web this will destroy it, and parts of the web will become floppy and lack tension. This is a clear indication that a human or large animal has passed through, and broken the web. However, if the web is damaged at night, what happens if the spider has repaired it by dawn? The initial indication would be that no one passed through, but on closer inspection broken threads might be visible.

Fly and beetle activity

Tracking lions can be easy when they are on dirt roads, but they become masters of camouflage and stealth when they are in the tall grass and vegetation. I was tracking a lion that had been involved in a fight and had a limp on its rear leg. When it went off-road the cadence of tracking had to slow down in case I was walking into a trap. I noticed a plume of flies hovering above the grass ten metres away. On investigating, I saw that the flies were in a frenzy to get to an open wound that had been caused by another lion.

Sexton beetles are able to detect a dead body from some three kilometres away. They will pick up the scent and then hone in on the source. When there is an increased number of sexton beetles on vegetation or flying around you can be sure that there is something dead nearby. They are voracious feeders. They dig a pit underneath the decaying flesh and lay their eggs. When they cooperate they can easily bury an object the size of a rabbit.

Bird Dynamics

The behaviour of birds may not leave tangible spoor, but it can provide a great deal of information. A good understanding of bird dynamics is therefore essential for trackers. Birds can be our best friend or worst enemy: they can tell us where the quarry is and in what direction they are travelling, but they can also give the tracker's position and direction of travel away to the enemy.

You don't have to be a bird expert to recognize the behaviour, although some birds do have specific behaviour that can be useful. For example, ravens have a habit of following humans and may over-fly in a criss-cross pattern to investigate. Ravens also like to follow a patrol, usually a few hundred metres back from the last man. I don't know exactly why they behave like this, but it may be that they associate humans with food that has been discarded.

In Africa, birds are my eyes in the sky. Interpretation of their behaviour could save your life. The oxpecker can let you know that there are Cape buffalo nearby. Vultures circling at altitude are looking for a kill; vultures with a direct flight line indicate that there has been a kill. Vultures in the trees can indicate that there is a kill, but the primary predator is still feeding.

Alarm dynamics

All bird alarm dynamics are caused by a threat or perceived threat. It could be anything, including natural predators of birds, or humans. There is no real difference between the alarms triggered by humans or animals, apart from tree-climbing predators like snakes and weasels, when the alarms and actions will be frantic.

There are many kinds of alarms, but we will concentrate on those that are relevant to humans.

Bird plough: When birds are concerned about a serious threat, they will fly from the ground or roost upwards and away from the threat. The pattern resembles a snow plough, as it ploughs snow away from itself upwards and away. This is a reactive response to a threat that is moving fast enough to force the birds to move before they can assess the threat level. There are either fast or slow ploughs. If a bird plough is coming towards you at speed, then it is likely that a fast-moving predator is active, or a motorized unit is coming towards you.

If the plough is slow, again it could be a predator, or a foot patrol coming towards you.

Birds flying away at a *low* angle in plough formation indicate slow-moving people, vehicle or predator.

As a tracker you don't want to alert the quarry by bird dynamics, so you will concentrate on moving a little more slowly, giving the birds the opportunity to assess you as a threat. Once the skill of reading bird ploughs has been learnt, it is possible to estimate with some accuracy when and where the quarry will appear.

Sentinel: This is a bird, usually a corvid, perched on a high point. It is on the lookout for threats. If there is a threat, it will look directly at the threat. You just follow the line of the beak and the threat will be there.

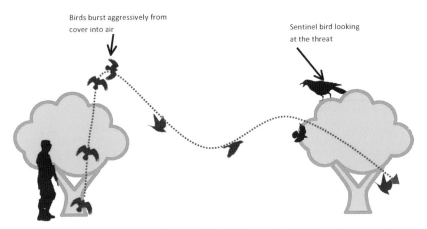

Birds flying away at a *steep* angle in a plough formation, indicate fast-moving people, vehicles or hunting predator.

Burst: This behaviour is a defensive mechanism to startle a potential predator. It is commonly done by pheasants and other fowl. The bird will wait until the predator is close by, in the hope that, by being still, it will remain concealed. If the predator continues to approach, it will make a frenzied dash for the sky, while squawking. It always comes as a surprise and it does have the desired effect of startling even humans. The squawk can be heard from a hundred metres away. If this occurs with pigeons, they will continue to fly through the canopy in a frenzy. This is easily spotted.

Vocalization: Birds communicate about food and territories amongst other maintenance issues, but we must be able to recognize the difference between an alarm call and other calls. Different species alarm in different ways, but as a general rule, compared to the baseline maintenance calls, the intensity and urgency will increase. Even if you don't see the threat you will hear the alarm calls.

Animal Behaviour

As with birds, we can use the actions of animals to tell us if there are humans nearby.

Sheep will go to the furthest part of field, away from the threat. They will be in a huddle, with two or three vigilant sentry sheep keeping an eye on the humans. They are likely to react very quickly to movement and will run in a frenzied manner.

Cattle will, at first, wheel away from the threat and then curiosity will overcome them. If the human remains still, they will approach. A sudden movement will cause the cattle to jolt backwards.

Deer, when startled by approaching humans (or predators) are likely to freeze and then run, crashing through vegetation.

Human waste products

Oral projectiles

A great deal of information can be gained about the quarry from oral projectiles. There are cultural and geographical links with some of them. Coming across the following will give the tracker a good idea of who put it there. It is categorically human.

Betel/areca nut: This is a mild stimulant and is associated with South-east Asia, India and Pakistan. Although it is associated with these areas, I have come across it in East Africa and the UK, perhaps because of the immigrant Asians. The nut is chewed, which gives the teeth a characteristic blood-red colour. When the nut is ejected from the mouth, it tends to be dribbled into a small pile of spit and nut; it looks like blood spoor or animal scat.

Khat: This is associated with the Horn of Africa, but has moved into East Africa, the UK and United States. It is popular among Somalis. It is a tender plant with a limited shelf-life. It is commonly used by poachers, pirates, smugglers and soldiers in Africa. It is a stimulant and thus it is of particular use to people crossing frontiers to poach and rustle cattle and head back to their territory without sleep. It is usually eaten but it is likely that someone who eats it will leave piles of green spit on the ground.

Chewing tobacco: This is very closely connected to the USA. In fact there were so many American Forces personnel chewing tobacco that, in certain areas of the world, if you found a pile of spit with chewing tobacco you could be sure that Americans had passed through. There has been a lot of pressure from within the army to reduce the number of tobacco chewers.

Spittle: Spitting can be culturally associated. During the Muslim time of Ramadan there are strict rules about swallowing saliva. During the day, a Muslim is not allowed to collect saliva in the mouth and swallow. Therefore, many Muslims will spit the saliva out.

If spit contains green mucus this indicates that the quarry has a respiratory infection.

Vomit: This is a bodily defence system. Depending on the health of the quarry, it can vary from contents of the principal cause of the reflex, to green bile. Note that some animals regurgitate matter which they cannot digest; it looks like human vomit, but regurgitation is different from vomiting.

Blood spoor

When injury occurs to a human or animal, blood spoor is extremely useful. It comes in many forms. I have successfully tracked poachers, not by their own blood, but by the blood of the animal they killed to eat. They went to great lengths to take anti-tracking procedures: they cut the animal up and threw all the remains into the nearby fast-flowing river. The boundary of the river was boulders, pebbles and rocks. It is very difficult, but not impossible, to track on rocks.

I noticed that a small (10 cm) piece of brown grass had been flattened, but had partially sprung back. At that point it looked like flagging, which is not conclusive, but on further investigation I found an exact imprint of the grass, in blood, pressed onto a flat pebble. This was conclusive evidence that they had been there, and all that we had to do was cast around for tracks.

The physiology to blood and clotting is a complex subject. As trackers we need to know what to look for and the impact it is having on the quarry.

The type of blood spoor will depend on the nature of the wound. Some wounds, whether arterial or venous, will take longer to clot. A long, clean slash will take longer than an open wound, because it is contact with oxygen that causes it to clot.

Arterial blood is under pressure, therefore an arterial wound will have a characteristic spurting pattern.

Venous blood is under less pressure and will seep out into one area, perhaps causing pooling.

Not all blood spoor is the result of a wound. In many cultures, women have been used in combat and reconnaissance, so finding menstrual blood is a possibility.

Human excrement

At some point, your target will need to relieve themselves, and this detritus can give you clues as to your target's health and location.

Faeces: The appearance and consistency of faeces varies according to culture and geographical location. The contents and the location will be good indicators. In many areas, where the ground is too hard, it will simply be left in the open, but most of the time a rock will be placed on top. Western cultures are likely to use some kind of paper, while other cultures don't use anything, and clean their hands.

Faeces can be aged, but this is dependent on the environment and insect activity. Flies will be attracted when it is fresh but, as a crust forms, the number of flies will diminish.

Examination of the latrine area may give an indication of the target's well-being. Be on the lookout for evidence of diarrhoea and dysentery.

Urine: Depending on location, signs of urination can be very easy to see. In areas with snow or dry dust it is very apparent. I have tracked someone in a location where there were lots of contaminating footprints. It was a suspected abduction, and I was quickly able to corroborate the remains of a joint of hashish with an area where they had urinated.

We can tell the difference between the spoor from a male and female area of urination. The male tends to eject urine in a forward motion, which is generally in a linear pattern. Female spoor will be in a concentrated area, forming more of a circular pattern.

CHAPTER 9

Elements of a Track
– the Footprint

Every footprint has a story to tell. Experienced trackers will be able to assess a track very quickly, looking at and analysing the track in a glimpse – although sometimes it might need a close-up look.

When a person pushes off from the ground while walking they exert a force upwards on the shoe that is greater than the downward force of gravity, so the foot accelerates upward to start the step. When the foot hits the ground, the ground exerts an upward force on the foot, causing it to decelerate to a stop. The faster the foot comes to a stop, the greater the deceleration and the larger the impact force. When running on a surface such as sand, the deceleration is significantly less than when running on concrete, so the impact force that the foot feels at every step is less for sand than for concrete.

BASIC FOOT ANATOMY

The foot is a very complex part of the anatomy. It takes mechanical care of balance and locomotion. As I mentioned in Chapter 2, I broke an ankle in New Mexico. I was due to train combat rangers in Kenya and so, although diagnosed with a broken ankle, I chose not to have it placed in plaster. It would have been impossible to travel through the bush on a foot in plaster and conduct field exercises, so I chose to strap it with duct tape. The result was that the ankle pitched severely to the right and, when running, I was propelled by the right foot and the left foot dragged. It's only when you are harbouring an injury to the foot that you realize how crucial it is to everyday life. I had difficulty balancing and could fall over at the slightest movement. My body was not adapting very well, so I had to completely retrain the ankle and the brain over several months to work together.

The human foot is made of 26 bones and 100 muscles and tendons. It is divided into three different parts: the fore-foot, which is compromised of the toes and the ball of the foot, the mid-foot, which is made up of the arch, and the rear-foot, which consists of the heel. The major tendon in the foot is the plantar fasciitis, which stretches from the ball of the foot to the heel. When the foot first impacts on the ground during the stride, the plantar fasciitis acts as a shock-absorber and then tightens during the take-off phase of the stride, causing the foot to act as a lever.

WALKING MECHANICS

The walking gait is divided into two parts: the first, when the foot is on the ground, called the stance phase, and the second when the foot is in the air. During an average stride, the foot spends 60 per cent of the time in the stance phase, with each full cycle of a step taking approximately one second.

The stance phase is further divided into three distinct sections: heel strike, mid-stance and heel lift. During the heel strike, the outside of the heel hits the ground first and the foot begins to pronate inwards. During pronation, the arch of the foot drops and the ankle turns inward. Because the outside of the heel impacts first, the outer edge of the heel of a shoe tends to wear faster than the rest of the shoe. Generally, this is the part of the gait when the foot experiences the highest impact forces and pressures. During the mid-stance, weight is evenly distributed over the foot, and the plantar fasciitis acts as a shock-absorber. The foot is maximally pronated during this phase and the pressures experienced by the sole of the foot are at a minimum. During the heel lift phase, weight is shifted to the ball of the foot and the foot supinates (rotates outwards) as the toes bend, and the plantar fasciitis is elongated. This causes a transition of the foot from a soft shock-absorber to a rigid lever necessary for propulsion. The pressure under the ball of the foot increases again but the force is still less than what the heel experiences during the heel-strike phase.

RUNNING MECHANICS

In a way similar to the walking gait, running is divided into the stance phase and the airborne phase. For the average person, 40 per cent of the time is spent in the stance phase and each full cycle takes approximately 0.6 seconds. While most people's walking gaits are similar, two distinct types of runners exist: heel strikers, and mid-foot strikers. More than 80 per cent of the human population are heel strikers, meaning that the heel is the first part of the foot to impact on the ground during the running gait. The other 20 per cent of the population are mid-foot strikers; either landing on their mid-foot, or even their fore-foot, while running.

Unlike walking, when running the maximum forces felt by the foot are during the lift-off phase rather than the heel-strike phase. This distribution is true regardless of the running surface, but the absolute value of the force varies depending on whether the surface is hard or soft. Because of this, running on a hard surface, such as concrete, creates higher stresses on the foot than running on a soft surface, such as sand or grass.

During the stance phase, when the foot is placed down and pressure is exerted on the substrate, the matter will either compress or be pushed out. This is what causes a track to be formed. The amount of information that we can acquire from that track will be dictated by the substrate, the amount of pressure exerted and weathering.

FOOTPRINT DYNAMICS AND TRACKING

For the purposes of tracking, where the physiology and dynamics of the foot are manifested in the ground they are described as follows:

Primary impact point/ heel strike (PIP): This is where the foot controls the fall as it lands on the ground, resulting in the maximum energy being pushed into the ground. Often it is the PIP that will attract the attention of a tracker, with its characteristic deep imprint.

Terminal impact point (TIP): This is where the foot becomes the lever and propels itself forward. This is called the terminal impact point because this is usually the point at which the track finishes.

The evidence left in the substrate is the construction of a track, which is as follows:

Track horizon: This is the natural level of the substrate on a horizontal or near horizontal plane.

Primary Impact Point is where the heel strikes the ground, but sometimes this can be other parts of the foot if a person runs. Nothingness is a feature of the track between the heel and sole and is the roll-over phase of a footprint. The Terminal Impact Point is where the foot pushes off to propel the body forward and then loses contact with the ground.

Track wall: This is the impression of the foot as it pushes down through the substrate on the vertical or near vertical plane. The track walls at the PIP and TIP is unlikely to be vertical because, as the foot descends into the track, it does so at an angle and as it is lifted out it will also be at an angle. However, the track wall at the side of the foot *could* be vertical.

Track floor: This is where the stance phase comes to a stop. It is where the substrate can no longer be compressed and is at the bottom of the track on a horizontal or near horizontal plane.

Track crest: This can be seen in very soft substrates. This is where the track horizon is interrupted by a crest with a junction at the track wall. It is a very good feature to look for when ageing a track.

Track features: In addition to the construction of the track there will be other features that will be useful. We will be able to determine sex by the size and style of footwear, approximate height and weight by comparing the depth with someone who makes a track next to the target track. We may also be able to determine any physical abnormalities or injuries.

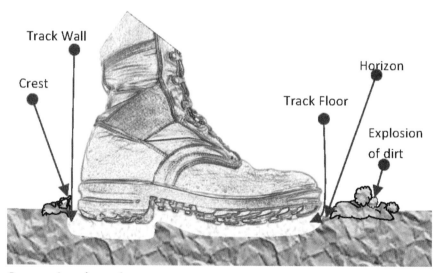

Construction of a track.

CHAPTER 10

Track Analysis and Gait Analysis

Gait analysis is one of the most difficult skills for a tracker to acquire. Some of the information will be science-based, but unless the tracker actually sees the target foot coming out of the track then a high percentage of analysis will be based on interpretation of the track. Sometimes the odds are that the tracker will be right; on the other hand, the odds could be stacked against him because of the lack of corroboration.

To analyse a track, it is necessary to create a virtual picture of the target, using skills described in other chapters and the hard facts within the track. Only then are we able to analyse a track to the best of the tracker's ability.

WHAT THE DYNAMICS OF THE FOOT REVEAL

The dynamics and physiology of the foot are limited and, in some cases, enhanced by footwear. Unlike a mechanical piston that goes up and down, the human foot can change its form at any stage during the stance, when the foot is in contact with the ground, or in the airborne phase, when the foot is off the ground. This could be directly linked to propelling ourselves forwards, backwards, upwards or sideways; it could be the result of something unrelated to walking. The brain can send out a message to pick something up, look left, right, down or up, and the foot will have to compensate. The brain may send a message out that the body is going into a particular stance, perhaps stalking, climbing a hill or coming to a dead stop from a sprint. The feet will automatically react and compensate accordingly. This reaction is recorded in the tracks left behind.

The Sphere
The sphere is the environment that causes the brain to send messages of the type described that would influence the actions of the foot. We cannot look at a track in isolation; we need to look for the external factors and circumstances that caused the dynamics. We should repeat the tracker's mantra: 'Who, what, why, where and how?' Sometimes the stimulus may still be there, for example a hill. It may be a temporary feature that has

since moved, like a tent or mobile caravan. It may even be that the quarry was carrying the stimulus, like a rucksack. There is also the possibility that the stimulus simply no longer exists, like a dog barking or sudden illumination from a flare, security light or torch beam.

The influence that something may have on the quarry is literally limitless. He could have a leg injury, coupled with dehydration and then be influenced by something which no longer exists, yet the track in the ground will reflect the dynamics.

Action Indicators

The reactions recorded and evidenced by the track are called action indicators. These action indicators can be very small and yet give an enormous amount of information, but they are reliant on an easy-to-read substrate and on not being influenced by the landscape. Most mantrackers do not have the luxury of time to study these micro action indicators.

If we zoom out, even the bigger action indicators can give an insight to the target's mentality and physicality just before the foot strikes the ground and while in the stance. The manifestation of the target's intention is left behind in the tracks, without their knowing. This is the basis for forensic tracking. We can piece together, not just the presence of someone, but what they were thinking.

I have given evidence on this subject during criminal proceedings. One case involved someone being shot through a window, in a pre-planned, meditated manner. I was looking for a variation from a normal walking gait pattern to one that may have reflected a nervous disposition prior to the defendant raising the gun and aiming at the window. Had the gait shortened, stopped, doubled back, perhaps more than once and come to a stop where he took aim and fired? It was possible to ascertain that the defendant had acted in a furtive manner by pacing around the perimeter of the garden, although he had made an attempt to conceal his final tracks in the snow by using crutches to get into position before taking aim with the rifle. The tracks he left behind gave away the whole story.

The ability to interpret action indicators can only be acquired from practice and experience.

I know from experience that, where the eyes look, at least one foot is likely to point in that direction, even if the quarry is walking at speed. If someone is acting in a furtive or suspicious manner, they may look over their left or right shoulder. The action indicators would show a short stride. The foot on the same side as the shoulder they looked over would pitch outwards, precisely when they looked over their shoulder. It may be that the person is pacing up and down, waiting for an opportunity to pounce on an unsuspecting victim. The action indicators would be a short stride, which would increase, perhaps even into a jog or sprint, when they have committed to a predatory stalk or pounce.

If a struggle ensued between assailant and the victim, then this would also be reflected in the action indicators, which could be a concentration of scuffs, and footprints on top of footprints, indicating where the struggle took place. Dependent on the outcome of the pounce, there could be drag marks and a short stride or, if the victim escaped, we would expect long strides during their escape.

Under different circumstances, we might see tracks that indicate that two people were close to each other, inside an individual's personal space, which is normally reserved only for friends and loved ones. The tracks may indicate a male and female walking next to each other. If they are relaxed, the stride will be short and the pitch (see later this chapter) will be increased.

Every tracker must use action indicators continually to patch together individual facts so that he can decipher what has happened at the scene. Successful interpretation of action indicators is the most important skill a tracker can have. It is the skill that gives trackers the tactical edge in a manhunt.

It is useful to be able to see a line of tracks, so that the baseline of the gait can be established. Imagine that you are watching an adult human on the beach. When he turns left the deepest indentations inside the track will be on the left; likewise for turning right, the deepest indentations will be on the right. This is because the lever of the foot is pushing in that direction and exerting most downward pressure on the substrate, and the same is true for any variation during forward motion, with the proportional amount of depth for the speed and direction.

Where a person is walking and suddenly accelerates we will see a pronounced indentation on the fore-foot, where maximum force has been exerted to propel himself into accelerating in the minimum amount of time.

To turn left, his brain will send a message to make the levers point in the direction of travel. This is likely to take place during the airborne phase and so we won't see a twisting of the track because the foot will have landed already pointing in the direction of travel.

Now we need to think not just of the role of the foot for locomotion, but also as a compensator for various actions the person will make.

If he turns to the left, most of the weight will be redistributed to the left side and vice versa for the right. If he drops his head to pick up a stick, the weight will be distributed to the front of the feet. (Exactly the same general principles apply to animals.)

BAREFOOT/SHOD FOOT

Barefoot Tracks
There are vast cultural differences when it comes to bare feet. In some

cultures, where people are always barefoot, they are likely to have wider feet. Typically, people from Western cultures who wear shoes are prone to having thinner, less muscular feet. This is very evident when they walk barefoot. Whereas people who are used to walking barefoot will spread the load and leave a wider track, Westerners tend to claw with their toes, their feet are narrower and they leave a thinner track.

When checking barefoot tracks, always count the toes. We have had one person on a course who had six toes and the Wadoma tribe in Zimbabwe have a tendency to have two toes.

Check the following:

- Size and shape of the foot
- Length of toes, short or long (and is the second toe longer than the first)?
- Any distinguishing marks, injuries, blisters, creases, cracks or scars

Footwear Tracks

Footwear is the bread and butter for mantrackers, and on courses a large amount of time is given over to the subject.

When analysing a track, the first thing to look for is association. Who made the track, and is it any way indicative of the owner of the footwear?

In areas of conflict, it may well be that the locals only wear a certain

This set of trainers left a unique track, not only because of its tread, but also the imprint of the big toe, which could be seen in the tracks.

type of shoe and the guerrillas another type. If the tracker arrives in an area where the tread pattern is associated with foreign troops or special forces, then immediately the presence of the tracker will become conspicuous. An example of this is the Adidas GSG 9 boot. This is associated with special forces, because it is basically a trainer in boot form, with a highly distinctive nipple-effect tread pattern. It was originally designed for the German GSG special forces as a 'high-grip boot'.

If working in an area where you don't want to become conspicuous it is always worth acquiring and wearing the same footwear as locals. Shortly before writing this book I was in Borneo. In the jungle the locals wear a flimsy plastic shoe made from PVC, known locally as Kampong Adidas. The sole pattern resembles a football boot, hence the name. They are very effective at gripping the slippery jungle mud and do not absorb moisture and are thus rot-free. I visited the local market and bought a pair for myself.

Another time, I was on an operation in Brazil and detected a Hunter Wellington boot pattern in the jungle. The only people who possessed these boots were the kitchen porters in a hotel several miles away. There was a significant amount of poaching going on and it was traced back to the hotel staff being involved in the transportation of bush meat out of the area.

In Mexico, the drug mules are provided with high-quality walking boots that can easily be distinguished from the normal cowboy or hiking boot.

Tracking teams can distinguish themselves by cutting a nick into one of the lugs on the sole, this being easily identified by other trackers.

The following should be noted from a footwear track:

- The tread pattern
- Length of footwear
- Width of sole and heel
- Length of sole and heel
- Distinctive marks or wear patterns
- Style of shoe

GAIT PATTERNS

Having a good understanding of gait patterns is essential to mantrackers as, not only does it give a good insight to the target, it will also help when tracks suddenly become difficult to spot.

As the body moves forward, one limb typically provides support while the other limb is advanced in preparation for its role as the support limb. The gait cycle is comprised of stance and swing or airborne phase. This process is the basis on which a gait pattern is established. As trackers we

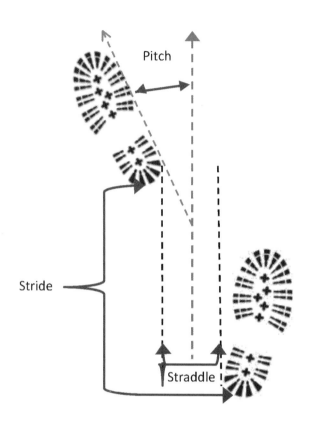

The *median line* is drawn mid-way between the left and right track. The pitch is measured from the median line. *Stride* is measured from heel to heel. *Straddle* is measured across from the left foot print to the right.

are unlikely to see the swing or airborne phase, when the foot is changing position, so we can only examine the stance phase.

Analysing track and gait patterns will give us a good idea of what the person was doing when they made the track. By reading the tracks there will be set of action indicators that, if interpreted correctly, will give a three-dimensional picture.

To interpret the gait pattern we need to look at the median line, which is the line that is drawn midway between the left and right track, and then at the following factors.

Pitch

This is the angle at which the foot slews off-centre from the median line. It is measured by drawing a line from the median along either the in-step or out-step of the track. The angle of the pitch can indicate the following:

- Injury to any part of the body, especially the back, foot and legs
- Birth abnormalities
- Male or female (females tend to pitch more)
- Speed of travel

- Physicality: fit and healthy people tend to have a reduced pitch; people who are very heavy will have an increased pitch
- Mentality: indicates if the person is mentally tired, nervous, depressed, or aggressive. For example, someone who is lost or nervous will keep looking behind themselves, which action will reveal a pitch to one side or the other, whereas someone who is relaxed (perhaps walking their dog) will stop at intervals and in the spot where they are standing, they will rotate their body 360 degrees while they look at the landscape, resulting in footprints that resemble the hands of a clock as they rotate. This pattern is caused by the person lifting each foot and putting it down at a slightly difficult angle until they have completed their rotation. Lost and disoriented people will behave in the same manner, as they stop and rotate trying to get their bearings.
- Military training: someone who is tactically trained will have a reduced pitch most of the time, but they will turn either to the left or right to look behind themselves. At the point where they look behind, the pitch will be pronounced. They may even carry out a tactical turn, where they will do a full circle while continuing along the median line.
- Walking backwards: the pitch will be reduced

Step Length

This is the distance from the primary impact point on the left or right to the opposite primary impact point. It is measured by drawing a line behind the PIP of the left or right and another line behind the next PIP. The following can be interpreted from the step length.

- Height of person
- Injury will show in a step length in one or both legs being variable
- Birth abnormalities
- Male or female: females have a smaller step length
- Whether walking in a normal, relaxed way: if so, the step length will be a regular distance
- Speed of travel
- Whether jogging: the step length will widen, the pitch and straddle will reduce. The track will be deeper, probably showing the complete foot
- Whether running fast: the step length will be considerably longer, the pitch will be reduced and the track will probably only show part of the track from the fore-foot
- Physicality: a regular step length indicates someone who is fit and healthy whereas an irregular step length may indicate someone who is old or unwell, and one or both feet could indicate being dragged
- Mentality: a varying step length in a normal walking phase could indicate someone who is nervous; where the step length in a jog or normal

walking phase suddenly increases, this indicates that the quarry has seen the trackers or others and taken off
- Reduced step length: means the target is carrying weight and/or walking backwards

Straddle

Straddle is the width between the left foot and right foot. To obtain this we draw a line down the in-step of both tracks and measure the distance to the median line. The following can be interpreted from straddle:

- Height of person
- Injury
- Birth abnormality
- Carrying a heavy load: the straddle will increase with a load on the back
- Walking backwards
- Male or female

Male/Female Variations

It will be noted from the criteria listed above that they may indicate whether a target is male or female. The following is an indication of likely differences between the two sexes:

	Male	Female
Step Length (cm)	79	66
Stride Length (cm)	158	132
Cadence (steps/min)	117 (60–132)	117 (60 132)
Velocity (m/sec)	1.54	1.31

It will be seen from this that there are some generalizations we can make.

Female adult tracks are smaller than male adults (but be aware of the adolescent male track resembling an adult female).

The female stride is also smaller than that of men. However, some women walk faster than men to keep up, thus increasing their cadence and velocity of the push-off, which results in more pronounced tracks.

Also, the female stance, depending on footwear type (and not the person) will reveal more of a pitch and less straddle. The fact that the straddle is smaller than for men is surprising, since the pelvic girdle is wider, and in any animals the straddle on a female is wider than the male.

Often we can extract a great deal of information from the gait pattern and analysis of the track but we must always be aware of the interaction of other people in the sphere. Analysing and knowing the gait pattern will help to eliminate spoor from others that are not related the target.

CHAPTER 11

Ageing

THE TIMESTAMP OF TRACKING

Once the tracker has found spoor, he will go through a process of sifting information to establish that he is following the correct spoor. It is a complex process, with many factors to consider. Sometimes everything can fall into place easily, but it can also involve trying to identify the active spoor from a trail that has been used several times a day for many months by the target. It could be a route that the target uses to walk to work, collect water or go hunting. Distinguishing the active spoor from the passive spoor is difficult, even for experienced trackers.

From the very moment that spoor is created it will begin to break down. The amount of degradation is dependent on how fragile the substrate is, the weather conditions and location. For example a grit gouge on basalt rock in the bush will last significantly longer than a footprint in the sand on the beach.

It can be surprising how long spoor can remain. In Poland some 250 million years ago an animal smaller than a house cat walked across fine mud and left tracks, which have remained preserved. In the Lake District of England, glacial scars are evident on many of the rocks.

Time gathering information is not time wasted! Speak to people: it may be that the security light went on at a certain time, perhaps the dog barked, they heard the sound of human voices, saw car lights going past, or heard a gunshot.

Technology is also a good way of establishing a time bracket. Modern technology spreads its tentacles far and wide. There is CCTV, which is operated by several organizations, including the police, town and city councils, private shops and individuals.

I was once called to track someone in an urban environment. He had taken public transport into town, and had then held up a jewellery shop and made his getaway in a car he had parked several days earlier. At the time the car park had unmanned security cameras but with several blind spots. When he made his getaway, it seemed as though he had disappeared into thin air and I tried every tracking trick I use for urban tracking, but drew a blank each time. It turned out he was very cunning. He had parked his car where there was no camera coverage. When he made his getaway, he simply went to the car, opened the boot and climbed in, locking it behind him. He stayed in the boot overnight until the next morning and calmly made his getaway.

CCTV was checked for all routes in and out for a bracket of time of three hours surrounding the robbery, but didn't show his car.

I returned the next day and found a banana skin that had been peeled about six hours earlier, and a chocolate bar wrapper. They were at the back of the car space, in a central position, which was unusual. Based on that small snippet of information, the police were able to look at a wider timescale to cover the time that he drove off from the car park and trace the driver.

In some frontier areas geophones are placed in the ground and they record accurately the time of passage.

TIME BRACKETING

Track ageing is caused by either biological or mechanical factors such as:

- Wind
- Rain
- Sun
- Human causation (for example, helicopter downwash can obliterate fragile tracks)
- Temperature

While they can cause a track to age, they can also help us to obtain a bracket of time.

Day/Night Factors
There are various factors that offer clues as to when tracks were caused.

Daylight/Sun
Where there are human sitting compression shapes grouped into one area under a tree, assuming that they would have sat under the tree for the shade and that the sun has moved from east to west, we can estimate the time that there was shadow over the people. Using this rough calculation we can estimate the time that the people were sitting there.

Spider's webs are usually repaired at night, so damage to a web will probably have occurred during the day.

Night Time

Superimposed tracks
Superimposed tracks are a very good indicator of time. Where there is an established trail, path of least resistance or funnel, then it is likely that

This shows several tracks of varying age. The most significant feature is that one track is on top of a recent motorcycle track. If a motorcycle had been seen or heard, then this would provide an accurate timescale.

any track put down will be stood on, cycled over, or cattle or sheep will have been driven over it, or wildlife will have walked through. Although these tracks do not necessarily have to have been made at night time, if the target's track has a nocturnal animal track superimposed on top of it, then we can be sure that he travelled before sunrise.

This technique is especially useful in rural areas where livestock is usually moved at routine times. For instance, in Africa the cattle are moved into thorny enclosures before sunset to keep predators out. The daily movement of the livestock changes the baseline on the ground at least twice a day. Any tracks on top of the cattle tracks would have been made since they were herded.

In parts of the world where sheep and cattle are moved from field to field, then checking the entrance to the field at the gate will pay dividends. It is an excellent track-trap that will also assist in ageing the track.

Dew

As an indicator, dew bridges the gap between night time and early morning. First light and dawn are good times to track, not just for the low angle of light, but also for the dew. Dew is formed during the night. It can form several times a night, sometimes soon after sunset, and come and go through the night. Typically, dew will form between 2–3.00 a.m., when the land mass is at its coldest. It will remain on the grass first thing in the morning for a very short time. As soon as the sun rises, or a warm, dry wind comes through it will disappear.

Tracking on dew is fast, reliable and easy. However it does not last long and can literally disappear in front of your eyes. Therefore, wherever possible, a tracking team must exploit this resource to the maximum. This is not the time to take a break or prepare for the follow-up. The tracking team must be ready and prepared to start on the trail without delay.

Direct Comparison

Where there is spoor left behind in a soft substrate we can carry out a direct comparison. This is done by placing a foot alongside the target track and making an impression. When the ground is saturated with water, the target track will have back-filled with a varying amount of water. If the track is more than two hours old it will have become full of water. If the ground is not saturated, and is perhaps clay, there will be a sheen that will only remain visible for a short time before it dries out.

Insect Activity

Ants

There are some insects that react very quickly to the passage of humans. Ant trails are a significantly useful method of ageing. Ants follow other ants by their chemical trail. Usually, the line is single file, but some ant trails might be 25 mm wide. When the delicate chemical trail is broken, the ants become disorientated and rapidly disperse, looking to pick up their trail again. The behaviour of the ants is somewhat frantic. If the tracker finds this, he will know that he is not far behind the target. He must, however, be on the lookout for ant trails himself, because the last thing a tracking team will want to do is give the quarry similar information about themselves.

Forensic entomology/Decomposition

This is where the lifecycle of insects that feed on decomposing flesh is used to obtain a timeframe. It helps to work out how long someone or something has been dead, and how long since faeces was deposited. I have observed this in the desert, bush and northern climates. I noticed that there is a vast difference in how quickly insects will deposit eggs in the flesh. I also noticed there is a difference between urban areas and rural areas. In urban areas the blow flies seem to arrive within a few minutes, whereas in rural areas they can take several hours. It is difficult to judge the age of the larvae, since different species hatch at different times, and it is a factor that we, as trackers, can only guess at.

Dependent on the ambient temperature, the fly eggs will hatch into larvae within twenty-four hours. The larvae will go through several stages of development and hatch into flies in approximately fifteen days.

There are also a number of beetles and moths that will feed and lay eggs in decaying flesh. The sexton beetle is a flying beetle that can pick up the scent of decomposition from some three kilometres away. They start arriving very quickly, and can be seen in flight looking for the source of decomposition. In the vicinity of the decomposition there may be several sexton beetles resting up in the vegetation.

In the wild I noticed that literally hundreds of butterflies would descend on any area that had been urinated on. Some minerals are rare in the jungle and the butterflies are quick to detect the presence of the minerals in urine that they require. They are attracted to both animal and human urine. However, in many areas where I have tracked there are very few, if any, animals. So in these locations a collection of butterflies on the ground is a sure sign that a human has urinated in the area. (In areas where there are animals, then there is a chance it could be human, but it might be animal.) It is very hard to estimate how long the urine remains attractive to the butterflies, but from personal observation they seemed to have lost interest within approximately four hours. Continuing interest gives a good indication on ageing a trail, and could also be valuable corroborative evidence that the quarry passed through the area.

AGEING TEST STAND

Ageing tracks is a localized skill and, as such, each tracker should get to know his local substrates, flora and fauna.

An ageing stand is created by locating and observing objects to see how they age over a given time. It will vary dramatically, even in similar climates. Exposure to the elements, especially rain and wind, or if the object is primarily in the sun or shade, will have the most significant influence. Not only will temperature and humidity affect the breaking down of an object, but so will bacteria, fungus and insects.

To begin ageing stands, break some vegetation, split a stem and crush a leaf. Study how long it takes for the vegetation to stop giving off a scent, repair itself and what it does when it is damaged beyond repair.

The objects that can be studied are wide and varied. Never miss an opportunity to study something as it ages. One of my trackers has established a system for studying the ageing process of discarded beer cans and bottles found in the wilderness. He purchased and experimented with a large range of beers. He created an ageing stand where he could record the different smells given off from the beer over a period of time.

At first this might seem a little strange, but he sniffs the cans and bottles for the smell of alcohol, which would disappear with twenty-four hours or less. If there is no smell of alcohol, he checks to see how strong the smell of beer is. If the smell of beer is strong but the alcohol has evaporated then he can age the can at over twenty-four hours, but within fifty-six hours.

He has used his specialist skills in operational tracking, where he can ascertain old cans from new by utilizing the experience learnt from his ageing stand. It is by no means a science, but it could be very useful in getting a timeframe for a track.

Experiment with the substrate in the local area. Make a series of 25 mm holes, about 10 mm deep. Observe every half-hour how quickly the track wall and crest start falling into the track floor.

Ageing needs to be categorized by the tracker. As he becomes more experienced, by using an ageing stand and operational tracking he will soon be able to make reasonably accurate estimates.

In the absence of specific information, there are several zones that the tracks should be classified into:

Hot: This is for tracks that are anything under one hour old.

> 1–2 hours
> 2–4 hours
> 4–8 hours
> 8–12 hours
> 12–24 hours
> 24–48 hours

Thereafter units of days are used.

CHAPTER 12

Camouflage and Stalking

MASKIROVKA: THE ART OF DECEPTION

If any trackers have had to get in close to their target, or lie in wait, they will have asked themselves how well they are camouflaged and, figuratively speaking, will have wanted to cut their buttons off to get flatter. The importance of camouflage is crucial; get it wrong and the enemy will see you: get it right and you will be invisible to them. Camouflage is an extension of the tracker's body; if it gets spotted, so does the tracker.

We are constantly attracting attention to ourselves through sound, smell, movement, colour and contrast. For trackers, avoiding this advertisement is the aim of concealment by stealth and confusion and, with well-designed camouflage, we can remain hidden.

The word 'camouflage' comes from the French word, *camoufler*, meaning 'to blind or veil'. The Russians adopted a system which became known as *Maskirovka*. The word simply means to deceive, however it became more of a doctrine and was applied to everything. I grew up in an area where the Russians were fostering tactical relationships in Africa and they were very serious about *Maskirovka*. The bush was littered with military decoys, including decoy street lights to counter night aerial reconnaissance, and the installations themselves were extremely well camouflaged.

I believe the doctrine and camouflage ethic of *Maskirovka* is an ideal technique for mantrackers to adopt.

Most people assume that camouflage only occurs when a figure blends in with a background. On the contrary, it is most likely to result from a high-difference strategy that consists of blending with dazzle, in what is called coincident disruption. In cognitive psychology, shapes that are encrypted by coincident disruption are known as embedded figures. Fracturing the subject figure's outline by using varied patterns of spots and stripes, irregular angles and contrasting tones will confuse the edge-detection algorithms that the brain uses in visual processing. This makes the shape, size and orientation of the subject difficult to determine and creates false edges across the surface of the figure, rather than at its real edge.

Recognition Factors when Using Camouflage

A small mistake in camouflage could cost your life. The tracker may think he is well camouflaged, and perhaps have a false sense of security that he has got it right, until a camouflage error gives his position away.

To camouflage effectively he must continuously visualize himself from the enemy's viewpoint and prevent enemy detection by applying the following recognition factors to tactical situations.

Reflectance

Reflectance is the amount of light returned from a target's surface as compared to the light striking the surface.

Visual reflectance is characterized by the colour of a target. Colour contrast can be important, particularly at close range and in homogeneous background environments such as snow or desert terrain. The longer the range, the less important colour becomes. At very long ranges, all colours tend to merge into a uniform tone. Also, the human eye cannot discriminate between colours in poor light. For this reason black is the worst colour to wear in rural environments. It 'blobs out' at both close and long range and makes for a very effective target.

When adopting a camouflage policy, it should be applied one hundred per cent to all equipment and clothing. Shiny carabiners, belt buckles or anything else should be camouflaged either with green sniper tape or other camouflage tape.

I make sure that everything is camouflaged, including the lenses of my binoculars. In bright sunlight early in the morning or late afternoon it is very easy for the lens to reflect light several kilometres away. I have spotted covert observation points (OPs), high up in *kopjes*. The people in the OP gave their position away by the reflection of the sun in the binocular lens. To avoid this I place nylon tights over the lens. They are still easy to see through, but they stop the reflection.

Shape

Natural background is random. An enemy can easily see silhouetted targets and can detect targets against any background unless their shape is disguised or disrupted. Humans easily recognize straight lines and the shape of another human, especially the face. We can distinguish them from the general background. Therefore, to hide the face and straight lines effectively, the lines should be disrupted with vegetation or camouflage colouring, and the face should either be camouflaged, or a face veil worn.

Shape is also relevant in the form of patterns left by auxiliary equipment. If vehicles are used, careful attention must be given to vehicle tracks and their effect on the local terrain during operations. The tyre marks of a vehicle are easily spotted on most substrates, but especially on grass, sand and mud.

Shadow

Shadow can be divided into two types:

A cast shadow is a silhouette of an object projected against a background. It is the more familiar type and can be highly conspicuous. In desert environments, a shadow cast by a target can be more conspicuous than the target himself. The tracker must be conscious of a cast shadow, as it could provide an early warning of the target, especially when going around corners, and breaking into the open to cross a road.

A contained shadow is the dark pool that forms in a permanently shaded area. An example is the shadow underneath a vehicle. Contained shadows show up much darker than their surroundings. Although they are easily detected, natural contained shadows like those of vegetation and rocks make for an ideal place to lie-up.

Movement

The human eye is hard-wired with the brain to detect the slightest movement. The tracker must make every effort to move slowly wherever possible. Slow, regular movement is usually less obvious than fast, erratic movement. If the tracker needs to make a movement, perhaps to look through binoculars, or swat a biting insect, he should do so very slowly.

Noise

Noise and acoustic signatures produced by vehicles and humans are easily detectable. There are very few sounds that carry as far as radios crackling away. If trackers need to communicate they should do so by silent hand signals or whispers to each other close to the ground, to avoid the sound travelling too far.

Clothing

A certain amount of attention should be paid to clothing principles.

Noisy clothing

To continue the theme of noise, some garments make a continuous distinctive rustling sound. I have found that calf-high gaiters can be one of the worst offenders as the gaiters rub against each other continuously.

The other noise factor to avoid is clinking of metallic objects and, where pouches and pockets are concerned, buttons and pop studs are superior to Velcro because of the characteristic sound of tearing when opening an item.

Texture/Shine

A rough surface appears darker than a smooth surface, even if both surfaces are the same colour. For example, human tracks can change the texture of the ground by leaving clearly visible track marks. This is particularly true in undisturbed or homogeneous environments, such as a desert or virgin snow, where tracks are highly detectable. Similarly, the texture of glass or other very smooth surfaces causes a shine that can act as a beacon.

Animals have evolved very effective camouflage in their fur, because it absorbs light. Hairy type clothing, like tweed and some woollen garments, absorbs light and reflects it at different angles. Ghillies, gamekeepers and some hunters still wear tweed, which makes excellent camouflage.

Many modern-day fabrics may perform well in wet weather, but, because of the waterproof repellent, they have a reflective sheen.

Smell

This is very high up on the mantracker's list of detection. As discussed in the senses (Chapter 3), trackers usually have a good sense of smell, and when they smell something, they will visualize what the cause is. Trackers will not give up until they can find the source of the smell.

Manufacturers go to great lengths to mask natural smells and produce volatile smells like toothpaste, detergents, soaps, shampoo and deodorants. Unknowingly we can create highly distinctive smells. Polished boots and belts can be detected from a few hundred metres away. Gun oil and insect repellent are amongst the most easily detectable smells.

There are products that are manufactured to remove human scent and some suits that claim to lock scent in. These are of little use, because the suits themselves smell and scent remover simply creates another smell.

So, given that we are going to create smells, whatever happens, how do we mitigate and camouflage scent to the best of our ability?

Clothing should be washed in detergents as little as possible. Often, washing in running water, utilizing a small amount of ash and sand, will clean clothes adequately. They could be stored outside, or placed in an airtight bag along with local vegetation for a few days.

The best method is to take a smoke bath. This is done where field expediency allows, and is safe. Light a very small fire, no more than a handful of twigs. Place some leaves onto the twigs and waft the smoke all over the body, paying special attention to the hair. Rotate the body, so that the back also gets smoke. A smoke bath would usually last less than a minute.

While it still creates a smell, it will remove some of the more volatile smells and is a scent that is not easily detected in the wilderness. It also has the benefit of creating a mild insect repellent.

Preparation for Camouflage Operations

Change the outline of weapons and equipment by tying vegetation or strips of cloth onto them. Many weapons are handled every day for several years. The friction of the hand polishes parts of the weapon, especially the magazine, upper latch area and rail of guns. This can become highly reflective and can be the weakest point in camouflage. If this has happened it is worth re-bluing the weapon. The bluing chemical can be bought from most gun dealers.

Make sure the camouflage does not hinder the equipment's operation. When hiding, cover yourself and your equipment with leaves, grass, or other local debris, but make sure that by gathering vegetation you don't create ground or aerial spoor that could be spotted by an enemy. Conceal any signalling devices you have prepared, but keep them ready for use. Be prepared to change any vegetation that you have used for fresh, so that it doesn't show signs of being stripped.

Many biomes of the world have different characteristics, with a variation in colour patterns and textures that are natural for that area and season. For example, in the bush just before the rainy season, it is hard to believe that the dry, desolate scrub can become green and dense overnight. During the dry season, muted khaki and grey and brown work well. Virtually overnight, everything is green and the best background colour would be green or grey.

While colour is self-explanatory, texture defines the surface characteristics of something when looking at it. For example, surface textures may be smooth, rough, rocky, leafy, or many other possible combinations. Use colour and texture together to camouflage yourself effectively. Ensure that your chosen camouflage is in context; it would be futile to camouflage yourself with green grass in the middle of a desert or rocky area.

Adding a three-dimensional feel to yourself is a very good idea. Sewing patches of frayed garments onto an existing jacket makes for excellent camouflage. Perhaps consider a ghillie or leaf-cut suit, but be aware these are made for stationary observations and are unsuitable for movement. They are heavy, and the tracker can become snarled in thorny vegetation, restricting movement and sometimes coming to a dead halt. The other problem is that ghillie suits and, to a lesser extent, leaf-cut suits leave identifiable and conspicuous fibres and spoor.

The Body and Background

No matter how much effort has gone into personal camouflage, it must merge with the background. To hide and camouflage movement in any specific area of the world, you must take on the colour and texture of the immediate surroundings.

Human skin is naturally oily and highly reflective so cover all areas, including face, hands, neck, and ears. Use camouflage paint or, where this is not available, you can make excellent camouflage from natural products.

First, a base coat needs to be applied to take away the shine. Use cold ash and apply to all exposed areas. You have to be careful, because when ash mixes with water it forms an alkaline solution that can burn the skin. After the base coat is applied, charcoal, which has been rubbed between the fingers to soften it, is applied to the skin.

Cover with a darker colour areas that stick out more and catch more light (forehead, nose, cheekbones, chin, and ears). Cover other areas, particularly recessed or shaded areas (around the eyes and under the chin), with lighter colours. Be sure to use an irregular pattern. Attach vegetation from the area, or strips of cloth of the appropriate colour to clothing and equipment. If you use vegetation, replace it as it wilts. As you move through an area, be alert to the colour changes and modify your camouflage colours as necessary.

It is a good idea to fuzz up, which means you roll vigorously on the ground so that your clothing picks up vegetation. This will create spoor that a tracker will spot. Experienced trackers will know that it was used to fuzz up. Less experienced trackers will assume that the spoor was caused by animals rolling in the ground. It is important that the spoor is then camouflaged as best as possible.

When aircraft fly over, never look up: the easiest method of recognition for observers is the human face looking up.

Specifics of Camouflage Clothing

With the ongoing conflict in the Middle East, there has been a great deal of time and money spent on research on various types of patterns. No camouflage pattern will do all jobs.

I have collected numerous patterns over the years and found that whichever pattern I have it needs at least six or seven washes before the edges become more effectively muted.

When choosing a personal camouflage system, the tracker must be aware of the associations with the given pattern. In a military environment, some of the civilian patterns have a negative association with hunting. Conversely, in civilian use, people dressed in military camouflage can be misunderstood.

On operations, I am likely to wear a mix of camouflage, including different patterns for the top and bottom. Because the legs move more than the upper body, I find a lighter pair of trousers works best, because it can pick up shadows, especially under trees. To a certain extent they can match a tree trunk, while the top is slightly darker to match the foliage.

The Multicam pattern is very effective, but as a personal choice, I still favour the Canadian Disruptive Pattern (CADPAT) system. I use CADPAT Arid trousers with either a Multicam or CADPAT Temperate pattern top.

Footwear is often overlooked for camouflage. Often, a shiny black boot will be obvious. Some desert-coloured boots also stand out. It is now becoming easier to find boots that are made of camouflage material. I have worked with snipers who spray-painted their boots with blotches of green, which was very effective.

One of the biggest giveaways, apart from the human face, is the hands. People tend to move them fast, and will reach out to support themselves on trees and posts as they go along. Gloves add the final touch to a well-camouflaged body. If they are patterned, then all the better.

A lightweight face veil can also be very useful. Make sure it is loose fitting, so that it does not block your hearing.

STALKING

Slow is fast, and fast is dead. Stalking is closely connected with camouflage. It is the method by which a tracker moves in to the enemy in a silent and undetected manner, and thus a time to be camouflaged and to camouflage movements by concealment. Not only is it used to get in close; it is also used to slip away undetected. The enemy will be looking for target indicators, which are features that will attract attention and give your position away.

Inherent in the process of stalking is the likelihood that the tracker will leave an area of relative safety and move to a location which may be unsafe. The object of stalking is therefore to move completely undetected. While being camouflaged is not a guarantee of remaining undetected, close attention to all the features of camouflage mentioned earlier is clearly essential. Special attention should be paid to wearing clothes that don't rustle, changing the outline of the body, and choice of footwear.

It is essential to be able to feel the ground through footwear and thus, heavy Vibram-type soles are not ideal. It is personal choice, but I find that the average walking and hiking boots are too heavy, so I use desert boots. Some say that moccasins are best. They probably are for silence, but they leave a very obvious track, and are not ideal in wet or muddy areas with inclines or when load carrying is required.

While stalking it is worth considering wearing a ghillie poncho or hood. The biggest giveaway of the human frame is the head and shoulders. For this purpose I have a custom-made neck wrap and partial hood, which changes the shape of the upper body, but does not infringe on awareness. It packs away into a small space when not in use.

Movement when Stalking

Assuming that all the requirements of good camouflage and conceal-ment have been achieved, we will look at how best to move. It is best to come in from a deep position and approach the enemy head-on. This reduces your personal target indicator index by not having to turn. It is much easier for a person to spot something going across their vision than coming straight at them.

The following rules apply to this movement:

1. Break up your outline and match your surroundings at all times.
2. Try not to look at the ground, and keep your eyes on the target.
3. Choose your route in advance and take your time.
4. Do not take the most direct route. Exploit every bit of cover. Choose that which gives the most cover for the longest time, and will get you closer to the target without exposing yourself.
5. Remove as much equipment as possible. Slip out of your backpack (if it's safe to do so) and be aware of the snag potential of your equip-ment.
6. Don't make the mistake of going in too close if it will increase your chances of being spotted. It is very easy to be tempted to go in too close, but that is worse than being too far away.

When stalking, there are several modes of movement that can be adopted.

Upright Position
The fastest method for stalking is the upright position. The stride should be about half of the normal length. This position means we can cover more territory while stalking, but we also expose more of our shape and risk being detected by our movement and stepping on twigs that might snap and give our position away.

In an effort to change body shape, the arms and elbows should be tucked in. The feet will now change from the usual walking position of landing on the heel to being placed down gently on the ground. Start by dropping the back leg a small amount so that there is a bend in the supporting leg. Move one leg slowly forward, in a smooth continuous motion, lifting the foot in a horizontal plane. You should be able to freeze at any point and hold your position. Place the outer edge of the foot on the ground and roll the foot inwards. If you stand on something that is going to snap or break, lift the foot up and move it to another position, checking it is safe before transferring weight on to it. Don't step too far forward or narrow your straddle too much, because you will lose balance and fall over. There are several people who maintain that there is a set time in which to complete one cycle but, in reality, the tracker will be making the judgement to move fast, medium or slow.

Crawling

This is very effective when exploiting irrigation canals or gullies. It is also useful if approaching a ridge, where a standing human would be silhouetted.

This is an easy skill to get wrong. The body is supported by hands, knees and feet. As you move forward, move your hand into an outstretched position, then move the same-side leg so that the knee goes to where the hand was. Repeat for the other side. The most common fault is that people unconsciously tend to stick their backside in the air, so extra care should be taken to keep it down.

The crawl has been used successfully in guerrilla warfare and by poachers, where there is a quick strike. They then drop to the ground and crawl at speed for the first few hundred metres. They know that any returned fire will be aimed at body height, and reactive fire will be aimed at the shape of a standing human. Having gained ground they return to standing position and make their getaway.

Leopard crawl

Sometimes misnamed, this crawl has a resemblance to a leopard stalking, as the name would suggest. Still remaining on the hands, knees and toes, the body is lowered very close to the ground. The stomach area should not touch the ground. The body is stretched out. This is a strenuous stalk and takes a good deal of core strength. It is ideal for very close-quarter stalking or crossing areas of low cover.

Belly crawl

This can be done very fast. The body lies on the ground. The movement of propelling with the feet, knees and elbows alternately means that a weapon is easily carried across the forearms and relatively long distances can be covered in a short time. The advantage of this position is that it does not cause twigs to break. The disadvantage is that it does not easily allow a change of directions and, because the tracker is low down, it restricts his view of the target.

It may be that it is necessary to go into a belly crawl at very short notice. This is a dangerous move, because it requires a forward dive onto the ground, and should only be done if it is not possible to lower yourself in a controlled way. The dive is done from the existing position and the aim is to land on the stomach and not the hands. The risk is that it will damage front-mounted equipment and injure the back.

Slow low

This is the slowest of all stalking techniques, and offers limited visibility and manoeuvrability. The tracker's awareness in this stalking technique will be very poor.

It is done by having the complete body flat on the ground. The feet should be flat with the ground; the heels should not be in the air. The head is either laid to one side or lifted up. The hands are crossed, with palms touching the ground. To move, the tracker will push with the toes and pivot on the forearm. It is only possible to move a few centimetres at a time.

Freeze
As soon as the tracker feels that he has been compromised, he must freeze. By doing this he neutralizes the strongest human sense of seeing movement. Sometimes he may think that he has been seen because the enemy are looking straight at him. More often than not they will not have a seen a well-camouflaged person.

CHAPTER 13

Communication

A tracking team must be able to move fast to close the time-distance gap. To do this there could be three to five trackers in each team, two or three teams and command and control. Communication is the key to a successful tracking team.

Not all communications are electronic and the best communication between trackers is done silently, using hand signals. Sometimes trackers will attract the attention of other team members verbally, by tapping on a weapon, or by using devices such as whistles, torches and chemical light sticks.

There are some signals that are essential to any tracking team which include those relating to the quarry, danger and success.

HAND SIGNALS

The advantage of hand signals is that they are silent and they do not waste valuable radio battery life. A tracking team needs to adopt a set of pre-arranged signals, so that they can silently describe an action to the controller or other trackers, sometimes from a few hundred metres away.

The disadvantage of hand signals is that they have a limited vocabulary and are restricted to being used within visual distance of other trackers, with the result that at night and in bad weather conditions they have limited use. Hand signals are also easily misunderstood.

To avoid alerting the enemy, hand signals should be kept below shoulder height, if possible, and must be slow and deliberate.

NON-VERBAL DEVICES

Tapping on a weapon, or using clickers, are good ways to attract the attention of other trackers but unfortunately the weapon tap is a universally recognized method of attracting a colleague's attention and will, if overheard, instantly be recognized by the quarry. Some people are able to recognize the high pitch of a dog whistle but unfortunately most people can't hear in that range until they are taught to recognize the sound. It is ideal, because the enemy are unlikely to hear it.

Clickers can be useful, because the sound is very sharp. If used once, even if the quarry overhears them, they will not recognize the sound.

However, if used more than once, they can become a danger to the tracker because the quarry will know it is a foreign sound second time round.

There is a multitude of other ways to communicate information. One common method that may be used by the quarry is to leave some kind of natural sign. These signs are rarely recognized, apart from by trackers. It may be a pile of small stones, indicating distance and route, or cut vegetation.

Torches can be used to pass signals, especially if there is confusion about positions. In a covert role the use of torches for signals must be carefully considered so that it doesn't give your position away. In a SAR role using torches to signal to another group can be very useful. Often at night it can be hard to describe a location by radio to another group. A good method to establish a group's position is to request over the radio that they flash their lights, say, three times. To acknowledge their light signal you would then flash back three times.

A very good method of silent communication is writing detail on a small slate or notepad.

VERBAL (NON-RADIO COMMUNICATION)

Non-radio verbal communication is best because it can describe information in much more detail. The disadvantage is that voices could alert the quarry and too much talking will distract the tracker and damage his rhythm. To attract the attention of other trackers, use a tongue click or bird call that is local to the area. A tongue click doesn't travel very far and a bird call will not alert the quarry.

RADIOS

Radios can be the making of a successful tracker, but they have also been the downfall of many trackers.

I have used a radio scanner to listen to people we were tracking at night. Their first message to each other was a broadcast to say that we were following them. They then decided to lie low in the hope that we would walk past them. During their broadcasts, the closer we got to them the quieter their voice became until it became a whisper. We knew at that point that we were within a few metres of them and had the advantage on the pounce (i.e. where the tracking team simultaneously spring on the quarry).

The advantage of radios is that lots of information can be transmitted. While this is useful, it is easy to talk too much, to the extent that the radio batteries can become flat. There is always a tendency to do this when radios are available and, in addition to flattening the batteries, this is a distraction for a tracking team.

When radios are used:

- Conversations should be very short and succinct
- Correct radio procedure and protocols must be used
- Since radio broadcasts can be intercepted, no personal names should be used
- Wherever possible, pre-arranged codes or nicknames given to features such as rivers or mountains (and sometimes, the target) should be used
- Where an operation is given a code name, aggressive-sounding names like Venom, Talon, Cobra, etc. should be avoided; aggressive names can attract unwanted attention

Where there is the possibility of transmissions being listened to, encrypted radios would be best or, if possible, mobile phones. Other good practice is to change to a pre-arranged frequency at pre-arranged times.

When using radios to which the quarry could be listening, it can be prudent to make use of a click code. This is a pre-arranged code where the PTT (press to talk') is pressed to communicate a message. It is usually done where the receiver is unable to speak. This could be the result of being in a compromised position, batteries running low or on the outer limit of range. The transmitting tracker will request the information and the receiver will click-code the answer.

Radio protocols vary around the world and from unit to unit. Within Shadowhawk tracking teams our procedure is outlined as follows (this is where Tango 1 – using the phonetic alphabet, 'T' assigned to trackers – is wanting to talk to Tango 2).

Ensure that the radio PTT button is pressed for about a second before attempting to broadcast. This opens the frequency, and ensures that the full message is transmitted. It is common for people using radios to press the PTT simultaneously with speaking. This will only transmit part of the message.

Tango 2 is called twice, followed by one call Tango 1. This is done so that, at the first call to Tango 2, his ears will prick up and he will locate his radio, by which time he will hear his call sign confirmation. This is simply followed by the person calling up, in this case Tango 1.

'Tango 2, Tango 2, Tango 1.'

Tango 2 will reply, 'This is Tango 2, go ahead Tango 1.'

Tango 1 will then go ahead with the message.

Do not make the mistake of transmitting too much information in one go. It is better to transmit at the rate of about one sentence at a time for factual information. If too much information is transmitted in one go, it is unlikely that the tracker will retain all the information and the person transmitting will not know if everything he thought was being transmitted had in fact been received.

It is common for earpieces to be used with radios coupled with VOX (voice-operated). Under most tracking conditions an earpiece is a hindrance, since it cuts down the ability to hear other sounds and reduces awareness. VOX is very useful but it can also transmit at the worst possible time.

Where radios are used in a tactical or combat role, if safe to do so, they should be turned off, and silent hand signals used for the pounce. When trackers switch radios off, they must inform the controller by the statement 'Off comms'.

RECORDING AND DESCRIBING TRACKS

Footwear patterns can be very hard to describe over a radio. It can be time-consuming and confusing. The best method of communicating tracks is to use the Easy Id Guide. It contains a range of tread patterns which are described by a horizontal number and vertical letter. Every tracker should carry an Easy Id Guide.

Once the track has been identified and described from the Easy Id Guide, then a more detailed description should follow, which will include any obvious wear marks or other distinguishing features. During the follow-up, any distinguishing features of the gait pattern should be recorded and communicated to the controller. This is done by dividing the tread into six segments: two for the ball of the foot, two for the in-step and two for the heel. Each distinguishing mark should be allocated to a segment which is numbered from 1 to 6 on the Easy Id Guide.

The track should be recorded on a spoor card.

There is always a clash of interest in describing and recording tracks and closing the time-distance gap. Time spent recording information can give the quarry a significant start, so wherever possible it should be done quickly or, if there are two teams, one team will record the tracks while the other team commences the follow-up. The follow-up should never be stalled by taking too much time to record a track.

Modern technology with the ability to take good-quality photographs on phones means that this process can be speeded up. However, I still prefer to photograph a track on a Polaroid camera and pass hard copies to the trackers. This way, if batteries run out on phones there is always a hard copy.

Once the follow-up has started, the tracks should be given a nickname. For some unknown reason trackers find it easy to remember a nickname and associate it with a track. When giving a track a nickname, it should bear some resemblance to the track and usually the best names come from a snap judgement. The nickname should then be passed to all members of the team and the controller.

CHAPTER 14

Team Formations

Team formation is one of the most 'safety to life factors' in tracking. This is where a misjudgement could cause injury or death to the tracker and tracking team. There are a number of formations, all with a specific application, depending on the landscape, the quarry, the mission objective, experience and manpower. The correct formation must be used and everyone in the team should understand their specialist role. If the formation is correct, then there will be a safe follow-up. Get the formation wrong and the tracker and entire tracking team is at risk.

I have found that, despite teaching tracking formations that consist of a minimum of a tracker and two flankers, the majority of operational tracking is conducted by one tracker accompanied by other officers. This is mainly through a lack of manpower, resources, or a misunderstanding of the tracking role.

I have trained thousands of trackers, out of whom fewer than a hundred or so have kept an interest and are able to identify basic spoor. From those hundred or so trackers, very few are at the required skill level to form a specialist tracking unit. Tracking is a degradable skill; keep getting dirt-time in and the tracker improves. No-dirt time and no practice means that the tracker's ability to work at the peak of his performance will degrade, and maintaining his skill will be impossible. However, it is not essential to be tracking at peak performance to spot the lucky track, which could be all that is needed to locate the quarry.

There is a misconception that all follow-ups go on for hours or days and cover long distances. The reality is that sometimes they can be extended for days, but the majority are resolved in a matter of hours. The mission objective may be intelligence-gathering and therefore a full complement formation of trackers is not required.

Where there is a culture of tracking and sufficient resources then a tracker unit should be established. This may be a cadre assembled from other units or it may be a dedicated tracker-hunter force. On the other hand, if a culture of tracking does not exist, or if there are insufficient resources, then tracking may fall to one individual. With safety being paramount, the tracker should consider whether an unconventional formation should be used.

A conventional tracking team would consist of four people, all of whom are interchangeable when the tracker gets into the 'red zone' and is tracked-out.

At all times the tracking team must stay within visual contact of each other or, under certain circumstances, the effective firing range of any weapon carried. This can vary from just a few metres to 800 metres. Flankers should resist the temptation to come in to the tracker.

COMPOSITION OF TRACKING OPERATIONS

The following are the conventional components of a tracking operation:

Command element: Command is usually remote from the tracking on the ground; he or she will be coordinating tracking and other resources and disseminating information to the teams.

Tracking Controller: Has localized management of the team, usually on the ground with the trackers.

Tracker: Follows spoor, but is interchangeable with flankers and controller.

Flankers: Have responsibility for tracker safety, flanks and change in spoor direction.

Conventional Tracking Formations

Conventional Y Formation

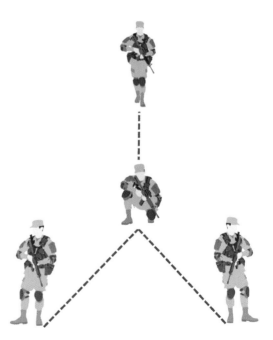

- One controller is three to four metres behind the tracker
- One tracker
- Two flankers

The flankers are the tracker's protection and should always be ahead of the tracker in a Y formation, looking outwards. This formation

In the 'Y' team formation the controller is behind the tracker and two flankers are ahead of the tracker on both sides, thus forming a 'Y' shape.

is the conventional system. However, it does vary dependent on terrain. Only when their attention is required should flankers look inwards. The purpose of the flankers is primarily the safety of the tracker, whose sphere of awareness may be reduced, because his eyes are working in the short range and he is in the zone.

Conventional X Formation

This formation is ideal where there is a surplus of trackers and where there is a possibility of group targets who may bombshell or 'skip the horns', which means they will have carried out anti-tracking techniques with the intention of looping back on to their old tracks and back-tracking out of the area. This is a complex formation and should only be used with an experienced team.

- One controller
- One tracker
- Four flankers: two up front and two at the rear

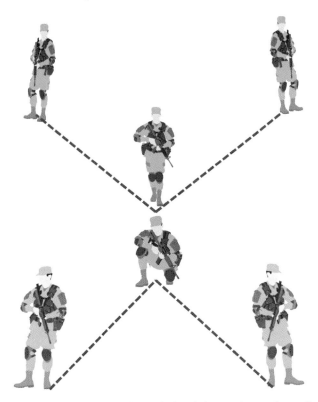

In the X team formation the controller is behind the tracker and two flankers are ahead of the tracker on both sides and two flankers are behind on both sides, thus forming an 'X' shape.

Variations on Conventional Formations

Half-Y or half-X formation; barriers on the flank

Where there is a barrier on one of the flanks and it is impractical or unsafe to place a flanker in that position, the flanker will fall in behind the controller. Although he will be in single file behind the tracker and controller, he will still have responsibility for the flank where he should be. This could be alongside a valley, where he can still keep an eye on the other side, or a river, where he should be observing the opposite bank. The formation would resemble a half-Y.

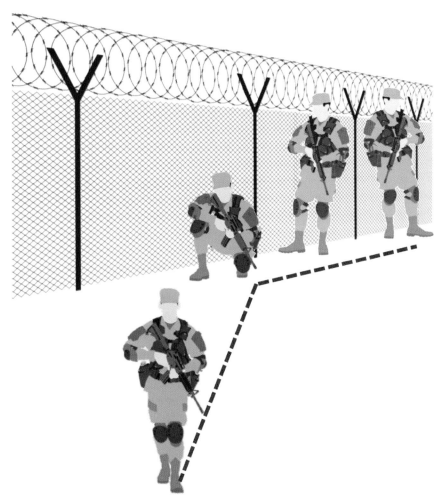

In a half-'Y' formation the team is constricted on one side. A flanker is ahead of the tracker; the controller is behind the tracker; a second flanker takes up the rear, behind the controller.

Single file

Barriers on both flanks, such as dense vegetation and rough ground.

This is a very dangerous formation, because it exposes the tracker who is up front. When the flankers are not able to work on the side because of barriers, or the going is too tough because of rough and broken ground and their progress is slow, the controller will bring them in to fall behind the tracker. This is judged by whether the flankers are safe and if they are slowing the follow-up.

The formation will be tracker up front, flanker, controller, flanker. Where the risk element escalates, the controller may move both flankers up behind the tracker so that they can still observe their respective flanks. Teamwork, discipline and experience are required by the flankers in this role. There may be occasions where the tracker will be stooped as the flanker has his weapon 'in the low' ready over the tracker's shoulder.

In single file formation there are factors constricting the tracking team on both sides, forcing the team to form a single line. Here the tracker leads the formation, with one flanker in position behind him, followed by the controller, and a second flanker taking up the rear.

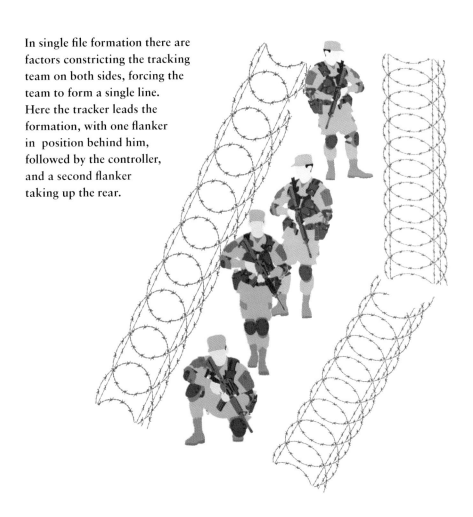

Unconventional Formations

Sometimes it is not possible to have conventional formations because of available manpower, skills, or the mantracker accidentally happens across spoor and supplementary trackers are not available. The question will always be: should the tracker wait for back-up or should he proceed and follow the spoor?

Under ideal conditions he would wait for back-up, but often this is not available. I have been in these circumstances in the bush where I radioed for back-up but, because it was a weekend, it was unlikely that anyone could join me until Monday at the earliest.

The first consideration is always the tracker's safety. If there is the slightest risk of being injured or being compromised then the tracker should mark the last known spoor and extract himself to a safe area.

Sometimes the tracker's curiosity can override safety and he will continue to track.

Where the target is known not to be dangerous, or in the detection of IEDS, it may be that one tracker will be deployed.

One Man

As mentioned, this can be a dangerous procedure, so should be avoided if possible.

The location of the tracker must be communicated to control so that a vigil can be maintained on his progress. Wherever possible, he should be in visual contact with another person, perhaps another law enforcement officer or searcher (not necessarily a tracker).

The lone tracker must move very slowly (wherever safe to do so) and stop for safety regularly. He must make an extra effort to use his awareness.

Two Man

The two-man formation, although not without risk, is significantly better than tracking alone. However, it should only be undertaken when risk is considered minimal.

In this formation, the tracker will be able to concentrate more on the spoor. The second man will be the 'long eye' and his awareness will probably be better than that of the tracker. He will be the tracker's protection.

In this formation, usually the tracker will be up front and the second man will be three paces behind. In areas with dense vegetation or blind corners, the second man will have his weapon in the 'low ready' position and will be very close to the tracker. The agreed procedure between the tracker and second may vary if their security is compromised.

Running on the Spoor

This is the classic perception of trackers and is similar to the Bushmen of the Kalahari running down their prey.

It is actually very rare for trackers to run on the spoor. However, it can be done and I have certainly run on the spoor for short periods. It has risks:

- Injury, e.g. sprained ankles and pulled muscles
- Noise, e.g. clattering equipment and footfalls on the ground
- Missing vital spoor
- Increased fatigue and water consumption
- Booby traps and IEDs
- Ambush
- Adrenalin drop

So there are some guidelines for running on the spoor. When the decision is made to run on the spoor, it is not just a free-for-all run: Formations will be maintained. The best time to run on the spoor is when the terrain is open and visibility is good, so that booby traps and spoor are easily spotted. I like to run when there is flat terrain or slightly downhill, lessening fatigue. It would be rare to consider running uphill.

WORKING WITH CANINE TEAMS

There is usually good-humoured rivalry between dog handlers and trackers and often the dog handlers are also good trackers. It may be that a tracker will be attached to a canine team, or that the canine team is deployed alongside trackers.

There are hazards attached to working with canine units. If the dog is a war or attack type dog, it will go for anything that it feels is a target. Bites to dog handlers and innocent people have occurred in error.

There is the possibility that the dog will attract attention to the tracking team by its movements and barking.

If working with bloodhounds, they are likely to be scent-specific, whereas other dogs are not scent-specific, so any spoor that the tracking team leave will be picked up by dogs.

I have worked with a range of dogs. When I was with the US Border Patrol, the canine team were considering deploying a dog alongside us. It was very hot and the desert floor was littered with jumping cactus spines, so the dog required protection for its pads. It was kept in an air-conditioned vehicle, so it is not surprising that when the dog handler attempted to deploy the dog it did not want to leave the vehicle and kept going back to it to get out of the heat. On the other hand, I have worked with bloodhounds in Africa who continued on the trail throughout the heat of the day, narrowly avoiding Cape buffalo and lions.

Bloodhounds can be very useful for trackers because they will follow the specific scent trail on the ground as opposed to lifting their nose to scent air. The advantage is that they can lead the handler to caches of weapons, illicit goods and hideouts.

There are occasions when it is not practical to deploy dogs, because of contamination or adverse conditions.

Tracking teams and canine teams can work in a number of arrangements.

Dogs attached to trackers, but not in use: In these conditions the dog handler will keep the dog on a short lead and remain behind the controller.

Dogs supporting the tracking team, and dog takes over the lead: This is usually where a dog handler is attached to a tracking team, initially in a passive role. Where and when conditions are suitable the dog may take up the lead trail. This is usually an agreed tactic but can only be done with the permission of the controller. Most of the time the handlers will put forward their reasons for releasing the dog on a long lead or allowing it to roam. The controllers usually agree and the dog will get precedence. Depending on the dog handler's advice, the tracking team may withdraw and leave a supporting tracker with the handler, or continue tracking.

Dog casting for scent in the area already occupied by trackers: Trackers have commenced the follow-up before dogs have been deployed. The dog handler should be informed of the tracker's whereabouts and keep the dog on a long lead, until tactics can be agreed.

Dogs already working an area: Where dogs are already working an area, under no circumstances should the tracker enter, without the permission of the dog handlers and command and control. The trackers could easily destroy scent or put themselves in harm's way by being bitten.

WORKING WITH OTHER SUPPORTING UNITS

This can often be a difficult task for tracking teams. Trackers prefer to travel light and fast, and my trackers go to great lengths to customize their already specialized equipment. They make sure that they can access most things without removing packs and remove any unnecessary weight. They also give a great deal of thought to their boots, clothing and equipment so that they are in 100 per cent camouflage mode. They are also in 100 per cent silent communication mode.

Often supplementary units can be cumbersome and noisy, stumbling and clanking along, which is contrary to the tracker's ethos.

When tracking in a tactical mode, it is good to have a support unit within one tactical leap, if required. This could be a helicopter deployed from nearby, or a unit nearby but laying up in cover.

THE ADVANCE

Cadence of the Advance

Tracking teams will have to consider the advantage of a speedy advance over the need for stealth and safety. This will depend on such factors as the difficulty of finding spoor, terrain and team morale. The reality of mantracking is that the cadence will start off slowly, then gain speed, before dropping off and picking up three to four times a day. This is typically when spoor has been lost or the team is in the 'red zone'.

Crossing Obstacles and Open Ground

In pursuit mode this is where a tracking team will get very nervous. It is the time that they are at their most vulnerable, because they are engrossed in tracking, and still have to make a potentially hazardous crossing. The terrain will dictate the actions, but rivers, marshes, high ground on sides, pinch points, barriers and moving into open ground require maximum vigilance from the team. In areas where IEDs are used, consideration must be given to route attractants so that the team do not unwittingly make a decision to go into a gully and find that it has been booby-trapped.

As soon as an obstacle is spotted, the controller will be notified. The X formation is ideal for this operation. The obstacle will be approached to within a safe distance. The controller will call out for a TOS (time out for safety) and go into a listening halt. The tracking team will hold fast.

Once the controller is satisfied that there is no threat, the two forward flankers will advance to cross the obstacle. The two rear flankers will move up to take their cover positions.

The tracker and controller will continue on the spoor, ensuring that the exit point is confirmed to the other team members. They will then hold fast in an area of limited visibility until the rear flankers have crossed the obstacle. Once this is completed the follow-up will continue.

Halting the Follow-up

A temporary halt to the follow-up must be done to set guidelines so that spoor contamination does not happen. This could be done when the team requires a rest or a briefing, or prior to moving to a lie-up position.

The tracker will mark the last-known spoor and back-track for a few metres before breaking from the spoor.

If the team is going into a lie-up position for the night, they must remain vigilant just before dark and just after dark, and the same just before first and after first light, because that is the most likely time of an attack, or an enemy being on the move.

During the lie-up position at night, light discipline is crucial. In an area of high risk, no lights are used. In areas of medium risk, light can be used, but only green or red, and lights should be never be held above the waist or shone upwards. Obviously, in a SAR role, light discipline is not necessary unless the trackers want to preserve night vision, in which case they should use green torches.

Changing the Tracker

If the tracker gets into the 'red zone' or gets tracked-out, he will need to be changed out for another tracker. This can also happen if one of the flankers picks up the spoor before the tracker. There is no set time for a tracker to remain on the spoor.

I have noticed that once a tracker gets tracked-out and rotated back in, the periods for which he can sustain tracking diminish. It may be that, at one point in the day, he was able to track for three hours. By the time he has rotated back in a couple of times it could be as little as five to ten minutes.

The Tracker gets Tracked-out

The tracker will communicate to the controller that he is tracked-out. The controller will give the signal to stop the advance to the other team members, who will stand fast. He will call in one of the flankers, who will be shown the last known spoor and the furthest away spoor by the tracker. If the replacement tracker is able to confirm that he can see the spoor and that it is the correct spoor then he will take over as tracker and the retired tracker will go onto a flanking position.

The Flanker Comes Across Spoor before the Tracker

The flanker can sometimes come across spoor before the tracker does. This is because the flanker is ahead of the tracker and the quarry may have changed direction.

When the flanker comes across spoor, he will communicate this with the controller. The controller will halt the advance and send the tracker to confirm the results of the flanker's find. If it is confirmed as the correct spoor, the flanker will take over as tracker, and the retired tracker will take up the flanking position.

CHAPTER 15

Lost Spoor Procedure

Never give up, never give in. Lost spoor procedure is the bread and butter of any tracking operation. No matter how expert they are, the tracks will become hard to see at some point because of the environment, the tracker being in the 'red zone' or the quarry using anti-tracking techniques.

It is the sign of a good tracker when he recognizes that he has lost the spoor. Tracking teams are measured by the way that they carry out the procedure. Very often pride, ego and pressure will influence the inexperienced tracker and frequently he will start to force his mind to see spoor that isn't there. It's called seeing faces in the clouds!

Admitting that the spoor has been lost can be hard, but it is better to carry out the lost spoor procedure and pick up the right tracks rather than continue following the wrong trail. Sometimes it just needs a fresh set of eyes, change of position to get the right angle, or a cloud to blow over.

For some reason people tend to rush the lost spoor procedure. Unless there is undue stress, the tracker must take his time. Expect to spend half an hour to one hour looking for confirmed spoor.

When the spoor is lost, the hand is raised with the palm facing upwards. The arm should be slightly out to the side, so that the controller and other trackers can see it.

As soon as the tracker loses the spoor he should give the lost spoor signal, which is a hand raised in the air, palm facing upwards and fingers curved as if holding a football on the hand. The rest of the tracking team will then take appropriate action. The flankers will move to cover and provide security for the tracker.

The controller will be expecting the tracker to take the following action.

INITIAL PROCEDURE

1. Continue for no more than four metres and conduct a segmented quick scan from the furthest viewpoint, using binoculars if required, and check 360 degrees, in case of a change of direction. Ensure that the optimum angle of tracking and light is being achieved.
2. If no spoor is found, give the lost spoor signal, as described above.
3. Mark the LKS and investigate the likely lines of travel, paths of least resistance or route influencers for no more than approximately ten metres. This could be repeated several times, depending on how many likely trails there are.
4. At this point the controller and tracker will consider changing out, because the tracker may be in the 'red zone'.

In the lost spoor procedure, the tracker gives a quick scan. The tracker continues no more than 4 m from the last track and scans the area to the front and left to right for spoor.

What is the likely direction of travel? The last known track is marked, and the tracker investigates the likely direction of travel for no more than 10 m.

When searching for lost spoor, the controller issues an instruction to the tracker to conduct a 360-degree search. The last known track is marked, then the tracker takes two steps back. From this position he conducts a 360-degree search.

5. If no spoor is seen, mark LKS and the controller moves up to the LKS.
6. The tracker takes two steps behind the LKS and conducts a complete circle heading forwards. The size of the circle is dependent on the landscape. This can be repeated several times in ever-increasing circles (*see* p. 155, below).

ENHANCED PROCEDURE

If the tracker is not able to locate spoor after the initial check, then the controller can draw upon the flankers to enhance the tracker's search. If, at any point during the enhanced lost spoor procedure tracks are found, then the person making the find will give the found spoor hand signal, which is the hand outstretched, palm facing the ground and fingers curved as if holding a football from the top.

Unless or until this happens, the procedure continues as follows.

1. Flanker 360-degree

The controller will communicate to one or both of the flankers to conduct a full circle from their positions. This is done by a circular motion of the index finger held upwards. The flankers will then conduct their search,

When the spoor is found, the hand should be facing downwards with the palm facing the ground. The arm should be out to the side so that others can see it.

Another technique for looking for lost spoor has the controller issuing instructions for the flankers to conduct a 360-degree search. Each flanker will move to a suitable radius and at some point they should intersect.

part of which should intersect. The size of the circle depends on terrain, and should be done cautiously as they could be exposed to danger while out of formation. The controller will be watching both flankers for hand signals to indicate if they have found spoor.

If the flankers find the spoor they will give the hand signal and the tracker will move up and make an examination. If it is confirmed, then either the flanker or tracker can pick the spoor up. If it is not confirmed then the tracking team will consider the quality, and whether or not it is the best option available. It is worth marking and returning to after more lost spoor procedures have been carried out without finding confirmed spoor.

2. Flanker Cross-over

This technique is especially useful if the tracking team is approaching a natural or manmade barrier. The flankers will be instructed to cross over by the controller using the appropriate hand signal, which is pointing to both flankers and making an arm movement going from left to right followed by another arm movement going from right to left. They will turn inwards and make their way to the opposite flanking position. In doing so, they are likely to come across the target spoor before the tracker.

The controller issues instructions for the flankers to cross over. At this point they will turn inwards and make their way towards the previous position of the opposite flanker.

The cross-over technique is efficient where the barrier is a river or stream with muddy banks. The flankers will follow the bank, checking track-traps. If the banks are too steep or treacherous, the flankers should be checking the opposite bank with optics.

3. Box Search

This is used where a field or pasture is contaminated by livestock or where there is a clear boundary formed by hedges, stones or fences. It is very effective if there are wildlife trails or breaks through the border.

The last-known spoor will be marked and the tracker will have carried out all the initial lost spoor procedures, and the first enhanced lost spoor one.

It may be that while the tracker is carrying out lost spoor procedures the controller will give a hand signal to the flankers to carry out the box search. This procedure is very effective and the flankers will simply follow the boundary all the way round, until either they locate the spoor or arrive back at their original position. While the flankers carry out the procedure the tracker will extend his initial lost spoor procedure to further than normal.

A box search for lost spoor can be carried out by the tracker or flankers, who will make their way round the perimeter of the allocated area. This technique is also effective to find spoor at the beginning of a follow-up.

4. Flanker Alley Way, or Path Of Least Resistance

The controller will give the appropriate signal, at which point the flankers will explore 'alley ways', or the path of least resistance. Extreme caution must be taken by the flankers because the paths of least resistance are the natural choice for trail guard booby traps. The alleyway must be scanned before entering.

The controller gives the flankers instructions to investigate alleyways and paths of least resistance. The approach must be cautious because alleyways and paths of least resistance are ideal locations for booby traps.

A flanker may have observed a track-trap a distance away from the tracking team. He would then give the appropriate signal to the controller, which is all four fingers brought up to the thumb and repeated twice. The controller would then take action to despatch the flanker, or for him to hold fast and despatch the tracker or other flanker to check the track-trap.

5. Over Vector

Where all other lost spoor procedures have not found tracks, then this technique can be used prior to an intentional pull back.

The results will depend on the experience of the tracking team. The trackers can either take a compass reading of the general direction of travel of the target and follow that in the hope that the target will continue on that bearing, or make deductions about the direction of travel. The team will re-form and vector the area as though they were on spoor. The distance and time spent on the vector depends on the terrain and time of day.

It may be that, by using a map or liaising with mission control, there are features ahead that will force the target to react.

I have used this technique in Africa. At a distance there were two hills on the left and right. Within two hours of walking, I could see that the hills were the tail end of a mountain range on both sides and that there was a pass between the hills. On this occasion the vector technique established a number of different features: natural barriers and funnelling.

Everything, including elephants, would either be faced with a difficult and dangerous climb up the hills or would take the easy and quickest route through the pass. The quarry would be influenced by such a feature. If they were in good physical condition and on foot they might be tempted to take the least obvious but more treacherous route over the hills, which would take more time and risk injury, or take the quickest route through the pass. Most people would opt for the quickest and easiest route. The pass was vectored into our follow-up and we headed directly to the entrance, as though we were following tracks, where we were able to find the well-worn game trail and quickly picked up spoor from the quarry.

6. Intentional Pull Back

This will happen either because command and control have decided to pull the team, or because the tracking team have run out of options.

The intentional pull back is rarely done, because it feels like a defeat, but by pulling back more information may come to light. It may also be the catalyst to the target getting on the move again because he thinks that the tracking team have pulled out and thus it is safe for him to do so.

Use of Technology

Depending on the target's value, it may be possible to use other resources.

Aircraft, either fixed-wing or helicopters, can be very successful in picking up lost spoor. Often the pilot and observers can position themselves so that they are maximizing the angle of light reflecting from the ground. I have been deployed as a tracking team by helicopter on several occasions because tracks had been spotted.

Fixed-wing, including drones, are highly effective, but have limitations on establishing a direction of travel for the tracks.

In certain parts of the world geophones, which detect size and direction of travel, have been placed in the ground; the information is then fed back to the tracking team.

CHAPTER 16

Starting the Follow-up

PREPARING TO START THE MISSION

Preparation for tracking and the follow-up are two different disciplines. The tracker should arrive at the follow-up prepared. Physicality and mentality should have been acquired through training and experience, equipment should be in good working order and he should thus be prepared in all areas to start the job.

Every professional tracker needs to be prepared for immediate deployment. My Maxpedition pack and duty belt contains everything that I need for a two- to three-day follow-up anywhere in the world, including survival equipment.

Although sometimes there is time to plan, more often there is no time to scrabble around to find equipment. By being prepared it is less likely that the tracker will leave something crucial behind. Something as simple as leaving without water could have catastrophic consequences further down the line.

Avoiding the 'Incident Pit'

'Incident pits' can occur during an operation and must be avoided at all costs. Something like forgetting to fill the vehicle with sufficient fuel, may result in the vehicle going out of commission. This may have a knock-on effect in numerous ways. It may be that you have to wait to be picked up and miss the commencement of the follow-up. In the rush a vital piece of equipment may be forgotten, such as a flashlight. That night you might be bitten by something in camp, but cannot see what it was in the dark. It could have been an insect, but turns out to be a venomous snake. As the venom starts to work, you cannot inspect the wound and could end up dead. The message is that the incident pit may start off with a gentle fall on the slippery slopes, which quickly steepens until catastrophe becomes inevitable.

Dress

A professional appearance is important in the view of other units or members of the public. However, while on a follow-up in the bush, it may be that a relaxed dress code is appropriate. This allows for individuals to customize their own clothing and kit configurations.

On some occasions camouflage may be appropriate, while on other occasions a non-camouflage uniform will be required. Only wear high-visibility clothing when required. The reason for this is that, when wearing high visibility clothing, trackers will attract attention from members of the public, which will lead to questions about what they are looking for. This distracts the trackers and will disrupt the follow-up. On one occasion when I was required to wear a high-visibility vest, a crowd of children gathered, asking if I was looking for snakes. They hung around me like a cloud of flies and could have contaminated spoor.

Some form of identification is essential, both a photo ID and a patch.

IMPLICATIONS OF THE FOLLOW-UP

The follow-up commences as the result of an operation where it is deemed that using trackers will enhance the prospect of finding the target, or where intelligence will be improved.

The term follow-up implies that there will be a pursuit and that there will be a person, or people, at the end of the trail. On many occasions, especially in the world of counter-IED operations, it is unlikely that the priority will be to follow someone in a pursuit, as this may be outside the skill level and objectives of an explosive ordnance disposal (EOD) team. The pursuit of the bomb-maker and accomplices will form a separate mission, in which tracking will prove to be invaluable.

For counter-IED and surveillance tracking, the primary skills require the tracker to be extremely mindful of changes in their environment Contextual awareness will alert them to a change in the baseline. This could be the fact that usually an area is active, with people going about their daily business, but on this specific occasion people start to leave an area, or people are behaving in abnormal manner.

It is likely that tracking will be called upon as part of a planned operation; however, there will be occasions where different levels of tracking will be reactive to unexpected factors. Example of this could be that, while conducting a routine patrol, suspicious tracks are detected; law enforcement officers are called to an incident, which results in the suspect fleeing the area; or combat and tactical trackers come across booby traps or an ambush, in which pursuit is deemed a valid tactic.

BRIEFING

The command element of the tracking teams will probably be responsible for other operations simultaneously with the tracking mission. This could be air operations or other disciplines, including maritime and ground operations. The command element will give a briefing, which may be either formal or informal:

Heavily armed New Mexico State Troopers gather and prepare for a briefing before commencing a follow-up.

A **formal** briefing will be given either to the controller for passing on, or to the assembled tracking team. At this point the tracking team must obtain the maximum amount of information. It may be that the command element has not worked with trackers previously and thus questions regarding footwear patterns and other information may not have been previously raised. Time spent gathering information is not time wasted, and it is much easier to obtain information in the briefing than over radios.

An **informal** briefing is the most common type of briefing and can often be the most informative. There is no checklist. However, while an informal briefing may have benefits there is a possibility that vital information could be missed out and that individual members of the tracking team might not be present during the briefing.

I have conducted informal briefings from my motor vehicle while en route to the follow-up.

Information Required
The following basic information is required for any mission:

- Mission objective: this includes the anticipated duration

- Location: grid reference or physical location
- Type of terrain: risk areas, fast-flowing rivers, dangerous wildlife

Information about the Target

In order for the tracker to have an advantage over his target, he must, among other things, have as much information about him as he can get. The more information he has the better. Research has shown that, just after a briefing, the tracker is at one of the highest degrees of awareness of the target.

Information could come from:

- Informers
- Law enforcement agencies
- Historical patrols
- Intelligence networks
- Evidence found

Background information about any of the following characteristics could be helpful.

Personal drivers, i.e. motivation:

- money
- martyrdom
- fame
- revenge

Known interests:

- martial arts
- firearms and weapons
- recreational survivalist/professional survivalist

Relevant military/law enforcement skills:

- existing member or ex-officer
- regiment, unit and specialist skills
- engineer or special forces, including a pioneer troop who are accomplished booby trap specialists
- weapons carried by the target – knowledge, proficiency and ability to use weapons

Nationality/loyalty/political affiliations:

- tribal

- gang
- family
- colleagues
- cause

Religion/beliefs/customs:

- a Catholic may have a shrine in a remote area and patron saint tattoo
- a Muslim will take breaks to pray in the direction of Mecca
- known superstitions, traditions or customs may influence behaviour

Diet:

- details related to nationality and/or religion may influence diet

Physicality:

- gender
- height
- weight
- age
- build
- fitness
- hair
- facial features
- distinguishing marks, including tattoos
- clothing and footwear

Mentality:

- mental illness
- devious and cunning
- weak-willed or strong-minded
- aggressive or passive

Habitat:

- level of ability to survive in a rural environment or urban areas

Profiling

Once information has been obtained, it may be possible to profile the target. However, this should be done with caution, because research has shown that profiling can be inaccurate, especially if based on someone else's interpretation of information.

The data is relative to the profiler and is highly subjective. For example, a profiler who has little or no knowledge of certain conditions could either under- or overestimate the target. Luckily, trackers are able to interpret tracks and spoor, thus building their own and often more accurate profile of the target.

Statistical Information
There are several very good databases from around the world, including the Catchem Database and several lost person behavioural patterns. These databases are usually crunched and instigated at the command element of a follow-up. Detail of the databases would require another publication but the information relative to how quickly people move in various terrain can help trackers to estimate the time-distance gap.

THE TIME-DISTANCE GAP

The time-distance gap can either be theoretical or actual, and can change at any time during the follow-up. For the purposes of this book, the theoretical TDG is calculated for foot patrols and does not take into consideration the ability to drop trackers in by aircraft or vehicles.

Where the tracking mission is pursuit, we can calculate using statistics and knowledge how far the target has travelled and how long it will take us to catch up. In covert operations, including snipers and reconnaissance roles, the time-distance gap to the target is just as crucial. While they will strive to avoid detection by the target, they will be keeping a critical gap between them and the target.

Theoretical Time-Distance Gap
There are several methods for calculating the speed at which people travel. One of them is Naismith's Rule.

Naismith's Rule is a rule of thumb that helps in the planning of a walking or hiking expedition by calculating how long it will take to walk the route, including ascents. The rule was devised by William W. Naismith, a Scottish mountaineer, in 1892.

The basic rule is:

- Allow 1 hour for every 3 miles (5 km) forward, plus ½ hour for every 330 yards (300 metres) of ascent
- When walking in groups, calculate for the speed of the slowest person
- The basic rule assumes hikers of reasonable fitness on typical terrain under normal conditions
- It does not account for delays, such as extended breaks for rest or sightseeing, or for navigational obstacles

- For planning expeditions or walks a party leader may use the rule in putting together a route card

The timings produced by applying Naismith's Rule are usually considered the minimum time necessary to complete a route. This is because of the huge variety of factors that can influence the total route time such as:

- the number of stops taken
- weight carried
- fitness level
- weather conditions
- many other factors

We are able to extrapolate target speed in various landscapes combined with load and night factors.

Target Landscape/Speed Table for Foot Calculations

Vegetation and Terrain	Foot running Km/h	Light gear Km/h	Heavy Load Km/h	Night No load Medium Moon Km/h
Open/Flat Terrain	8–12	4–6	2–3	2–3
Open/Broken Terrain	6–9	3–4	1–2	2
Non-Dense Bush or Forest/Flat Terrain	5	3	2	1–2
Non-Dense Bush or Forest/Broken Terrain	4–5	2	1–2	1
Jungle/Medium Bush Flat Terrain	2–3	1–2	0.2–0.4	0.2–0.4
Jungle/Medium Bush Broken terrain	1–2	0.5–1	0.1–0.2	0.1–0.3
Dense Bush, Woodland, Jungle, Swamp or Bog	0.1–0.5	0.1	0.1	

Other Modes of Transport

	Bad Road Condition Km/h	Good Road Condition Km/h
Bicycle	15–35	
Small Motorcycle	25–45	40–70
Vehicles	40–60	70
Canoe 3–4Kmh		

Given that the speed at which people walk is dependent on numerous factors including load, physicality, mentality and terrain, and coupled with a means by which we can age their tracks from the initial commencement point, we may be able to calculate a theoretical TDG.

This is dependent on detecting spoor in a given area.

PRESERVATION OF THE INITIAL COMMENCEMENT POINT AND SPOOR

Preservation of spoor at the ICP is crucial; however it is a rare occurrence. Before trackers arrive at the scene, it will have been trampled by people who are not necessarily trackers, and the last place they will look at is the ground.

There may also be conflicting interests, whereby the ICP is kept sterile for scene of crime investigation, thus excluding trackers.

If trackers are first on the scene, they should establish a no-cross line. This does not mean that people cannot cross the line; it just means that people will be more aware when crossing. There should also be a no-cross line for vehicles. Frequently vehicles will drive straight up to get closer to the ICP and in doing so destroy crucial tracks.

A vehicular barrier should be established that is realistic for the landscape, convenience and safety of the vehicle and passengers. There is little point in making the vehicular barrier several kilometres away, because the passengers are likely to ignore it. Dependent on conditions, one hundred metres is a realistic distance.

In the event of an abandoned vehicle forming part of the follow-up, there are some prime spoor areas that should be protected. If trackers are en route, prior to their arrival they should request that these areas are protected.

Humans are creatures of habit. The way in which they exit a vehicle is predictable, as is the way in which they place or remove goods from the boot. The method by which they exit the vehicle guarantees that there will be tracks in a very specific area between the vehicle and the ark of the door. If the boot has been used and goods stored or removed, tracks will be found within a metre arc of the latch.

I have used this technique with success on several occasions. I always watch out for footwear changes at the rear arc. This is because people will often exit the vehicle with one kind of footwear and change into another at the rear.

Very few people exit cars and go to the front, unless there is a route influencer, for example a scenic view, or where they have backed the vehicle into a spot. Even if someone does not use the boot it is still likely that they will move to the rear.

When a confirmed identifiable track is found, it must be preserved at all costs. It should have a circle drawn around it, either with a stick or chalk dust. Consider marking with trail tape.

Cutting for Spoor

In an ideal world, while information is being gathered by one tracking team, the other tracking team is out cutting for spoor and will await information to be communicated.

The reality can be very different. Often the ICP is a confused area, with various people coming and going, including trained and untrained searchers.

It may well be that the ICP is so badly contaminated and confusing that cutting for spoor in the immediate area will be a fruitless exercise.

One of the things I do when ramping-up a follow-up, is to remove myself from the confusion of the search at the ICP, and take a nose around the proximity. It may be that I am waiting for other trackers, other resources, or the go-ahead from the command element. I don't waste time waiting for them. This has several benefits. It helps me to zone in and there is always a chance that the crucial track might be found in the loose proximity of the ICP.

Perimeter Cutting

The trackers need to perimeter-cut any features in the landscape. This is generally an area that has boundaries. Examples are agricultural fields,

The US Border Patrol drags old tyres behind their vehicles to get rid of old tracks on dirt roads. Later in the shift, they re-visit the drags to see if anyone has crossed over.

woods, forests, or fenced and walled areas. Other areas that are ideal for boundary cuts are lakes or ponds. Efficient perimeter cutting can be done quickly and give the tracking team a significant advantage if tracks are found. This can be done on a large scale, covering several kilometres.

One of my instructors, who tracks alone as part of his job, commences every job with an external perimeter-cut of the area to gain intelligence and if he finds a trail he then works his way inward.

In Africa we use drag lines and the US Border Patrol drag the perimeter of the US/Mexico border every day. This is where the gravel road is dragged with old tyres behind a vehicle, thus obliterating any old tracks. If a target crosses the road, his tracks will be picked up, even if he uses anti-tracking techniques. This is a very fast and efficient method of perimeter cutting and works extremely well at night.

Many of the Border Patrol vehicles have a halogen light permanently mounted on the driver's side, low down and behind the rear wheel. The location works well, because it casts a low beam across the tracks and, because the headlights are turned off, the vehicle is operating in as covert a mode as possible.

However, I found that permanently mounted tracking lights are prone to damage and, to avoid the vehicle being identified as a tracking vehicle during the day, I use a magnetically mounted halogen spot in the same place, with excellent results.

Well-preserved ICP

If the ICP is reasonably well preserved, then the trackers should have first bite at the cherry. This may conflict with dog handlers and forensic teams: it is for the tracker to liaise with them as to the best way to maintain all protocols. It would be foolish to damage evidence which is crucial to a prosecution and, indeed, if bloodhounds are being used, they should have early access to the ICP. However, it is not always essential that dogs are required at the ICP. They may have been given a sample of clothing to use for scenting, and air-scenting dogs don't discriminate between their targets.

Trackers should be able to identify the direction of travel of the target. As soon as this is known and six consecutive identifiable signature tracks are found, it becomes a full blown follow-up. This should be reported to command and control.

From this information, they will be able to decide where and when to deploy additional resources, including air support units and cut-off teams.

I was the tracker deployed in a cut-off team in Arizona. We were guided to the ICP, where among the rugged ground was a sleeping area, and a confirmed identifiable signature track (CIST). I was taken by helicopter and dropped into some rocky hills that had a path leading along the ridge, which dropped into a gully for several kilometres. We knew the direction of travel of the Mexican drug smuggler, and the route influencers ensured that he would be coming in my direction.

My job was to pick up his tracks, and follow him at the same time as another tracker headed in from the opposite direction in the hope that he would locate the target or back-track him.

Shortly after being dropped off, the trail was clear for about 1.5 kilometres, but then I found his tracks, on the path, and heading off into a rocky outcrop. I was tracking on my own and we were both surprised when we nearly walked into each other as he was making his way back to the trail. He had been making his way back to Mexico when he heard the helicopter that dropped me off and decided to take cover. Hearing the helicopter pass over, he thought it was all clear to break cover and re-commence his journey. This cut-off by a tracker saved several hours of the Border Patrol time. However, as I was not a sworn officer of the law, I was not allowed to arrest the Mexican, or lay hands on him, except to provide medical assistance. Every arrested Mexican is interviewed by their consul in the holding areas and the US Border Patrol has to avoid any allegations of vigilante groups operating in the area.

Medium Contaminated ICP

This is likely to occur as the result of officers attending a scene. They will have moved around the area, attempting to gain information and do their duty. However, there is a degree of preservation of spoor.

The tracker should investigate the ICP to see if there is any suitable spoor and to see if he is able to salvage some tracks. If a partially identifiable signature track is found and the direction of travel determined, then information should be passed to control and a follow-up should commence.

If there are sufficient trackers, it may be worth considering using a micro-skilled tracker at the ICP, and deploying experienced macro-trackers to carry out perimeter-cuts and examine track-traps.

Heavily Contaminated Potential ICP

An area may have been heavily contaminated for several reasons, however it is still worth checking. An experienced tracker may be able to gain some information, despite several tracks being in the area. He will also be able to assess whether or not the trackers should invest time at the ICP. If there is sufficient information, the procedure for medium and well-preserved ICP should be adopted.

The most important thing in a heavily contaminated ICP is not to assume that spoor will not be found. I have attended scenes where non-trackers made assumptions that tracking would be a futile exercise.

A number of years ago, the police requested that I attend the scene of a missing person with the possibility that the person had been abducted from the scene. They had told me that several hundred people had passed along the sand dunes, which were a short distance from a busy camp. They said that they had only considered trackers as a last hope as other resources such as dogs, SAR land searchers and a helicopter had failed to locate the subject.

Trackers look for segments of information, or parts of the puzzle, knowing that, as more parts become available, the puzzle will become clearer. They do not need the whole picture to carry out a follow-up. Because of this, trackers are extremely useful in a heavily contaminated area

On attending, I found the longest stride length of any person I have ever tracked, coupled with a very big partial print of a shoe. The description of the subject was given to me and it indicated that he was 2.06 m (6 ft 9 in) tall. This being the case, I was able to find his tracks by stride length, which appeared every few hundred metres. The tracks were faint, yet nevertheless confirmed his presence in the area. This goes to show that tracks can be found even when there is a strong likelihood that they have been obliterated.

Casting for Spoor
If there is not sufficient spoor at the scene, then the trackers need to start casting out for spoor. The techniques used would resemble ripples, emanating from the ICP, spreading to the nearest track-traps, barriers, funnels and other route influencers. Every piece of land with boundaries must be perimeter-cut.

Real teamwork is required. The command element needs to be feeding as much information through to the trackers as possible. The controller will need experience and to be able to count upon his trackers to deliver results, especially as they may be casting for spoor several hundred metres or even kilometres away.

More than One ICP
Although, in theory, it is impossible to have more than one initial commencement point, it is quite possible that the trackers will leap-frog to close the time-distance gap, to a point where what is, in effect, a new ICP will be discovered. For the purposes of tracking operations, every time the team relocate to spoor on the same target it will acquire a new ICP number. ICP 1 could become redundant in the follow-up as the trackers translocate to pick up spoor. This will become ICP 2, and so on.

It is important that the communications and data clearly state **Tracker** ICP 1, 2 or 3. Otherwise, other resources may get confused by the number of ICPs.

As soon as the follow-up commences, a tracker should be sent to high ground, if it is safe to do so. They will prove invaluable if they can get a visual on the target.

What if there is no Spoor?

Ask any tracker his worst nightmare and he will say 'Losing the spoor'. For me, the worst nightmare is knowing that the target was in the area but spoor cannot be found. If the target had passed through, he will have left spoor. It could have been washed away, been obliterated by livestock, be beyond the skill level of the tracker to discern, or the target may have used anti-tracking techniques.

Clearly, if he has not been in the area, then no spoor will be found, but often this information is not known until trackers have made an investigation, or further information comes to light.

Different trackers have different views on this matter. As far as I am concerned, until the trackers are 100 per cent convinced that the target has not been in the area, then they will remain in the area, as long as they are not required elsewhere for further operations. We simply don't call it a day without very good reason.

UNPLANNED, REACTIVE PURSUIT TRACKING

Reactive pursuit tracking is where something has simply happened; it may have been a contact with poachers or renegades. It is the most intense type of tracking and requires the maximum amount of training and discipline. It is also the last resort, as hot pursuit can easily cause the table to turn on the trackers. The chase instinct, especially in trackers, will be very powerful. It must be subdued at all costs, at least until they can take stock of the situation. (This does not necessarily apply to apply to SAR tracking.)

Immediately the trackers come under attack, they have three options. They are likely to be outnumbered and possibly outgunned. They could take cover and withhold fire in the hope that fire was not aimed at them, they could take defensive positions and open fire, or they could run through the lines laying down a large amount of fire.

The tactic deployed is very dependent on experience, training and knowing who is opening fire. I have been on the border with Somalia, where people carry automatic weapons to protect their cattle from other tribes. Bursts of automatic weapons could be heard regularly, but they were not aimed at us. Therefore taking defensive cover was the appropriate reaction.

Once there has been a catalyst for a reactive pursuit, the tracking team must stop and slow everything down. The quarry is likely to flee the scene and for the next few minutes he will be driven by adrenalin, which will give him either the fight or flight reaction. During those crucial minutes, it is very dangerous to pursue the target. He will feel stronger and perhaps invincible. If he is armed, as trackers we must give him room for flight. Before long, because of the adrenalin drop-off, he will need to rest. It is possible that he could continue walking, but the ability to run will be very difficult.

By interpretation of bird and livestock dynamics we may be able to locate the target. Only when the tracking team have made arrangement for back-up, or they feel that they have the upper hand, should the pursuit start.

PLANNED PURSUIT TRACKING

In terms of pursuit tracking this is the best option. It gives time for intelligence-gathering, and for the deployment of assistance. This could be in the form of air support or non-tracking units based within a tactical leap of the tracking teams. The trackers can influence the outcome by choosing the time of day and sometimes location. In South America I was involved in a follow-up where there was the option of making the arrests deep in the jungle or waiting for the poachers to emerge closer to the road. Obviously closer to the road is the best option for the trackers, because the poachers were tired from their trek through the jungle with their wares. Support, including paramedics, was available at the roadside and the journey to the vehicles was only ten minutes, instead of seven hours.

When the Target is Spotted

As ever, the trackers should always try to avoid direct conflict and only deal with the target when the odds of a successful outcome are stacked in the trackers' favour. Often the job of arrest is best left to others, so that the tracking teams are not wrapped up in the bureaucracy that will follow.

The action on seeing the target is governed by the powers and rights of the trackers, and they must follow their standard operating procedures. (There are different procedures for various circumstances.)

When the tracking team are prepared for the pounce there are certain silent signals that are given. If a weapon is carried, the weapon will be in the low-ready position. Once the target is identified, the tracker who has seen him will raise his weapon to the firing position and he will raise the fingers on the non-trigger hand (one finger for one target; two fingers for two and so on). The other trackers will follow the direction of the weapon and know where to look. If they can see the target they will follow the same procedure. Special attention must be paid to target fixation and cross-fire.

When tactical advantage has been obtained, the tracker who makes the first sighting will shout loudly the number of subjects he has seen, in the words ' I have' one, two, or three (depending on how many subjects he can see). Immediately other trackers in the unit will shout out how many people they can see. This is done, because each tracker may have seen a different number of people, because of the direction that they approached. The trackers will then pounce and give the target appropriate instructions.

This technique also works extremely well with sticks rather than weapons, because of the ability of other trackers to follow the line of the stick.

In addition to following established procedures, the trackers' response when the target is spotted may also be influenced by the way in which visual contact is established – see Forms of Visual Contact below.

More Than One Target

Often there will be several targets, and it is important to be able to assess the number in a group from the tracks or other sources. Sometimes this can be very difficult. On virgin ground with a good substrate it may be easy to establish the numbers accurately, however, in well-trodden areas it can be difficult.

Trackers should be able to estimate if there was more than one person, or if it was perhaps one person who had walked through the area twice.

To estimate numbers, look in track-traps, preferably where the target would have been funnelled into paths of least resistance.

One method is the direct count method. To do this, draw two lines about 1.5 metres apart. It is not important to be exact, but it is important that the distance would be sufficient to capture all the tracks. Then count the number of tracks in the space between the lines. Divide the number by two. This will give an approximate number of people. This is sufficient information to make a rough estimate.

Forms of Initial Visual Contact

Initial visual contact can take more than one form, and will have an influence on how to proceed.

When the Target is Seen by the Trackers First

The tracking team should immediately consider the landscape, cover and distance from the target. For example, they could be very close to the target; however, a fast-flowing river, international border, frontiers or high fence could be between them, or the target may have the tactically superior terrain. For example, the target could be high up on a mountain or about to enter dense cover. Under these circumstances, issuing instructions to stop would be useless.

I have encountered many of such contacts, especially on country borders. The target will knowingly move into the neighbouring country and in some cases has opened fire.

In Tanzania and Kenya, where there has been a contact with poachers, the rangers, police and army have a ten-kilometre zone in which they are permitted to carry out a 'hot' pursuit.

If the tracking team have time on their side, for example if the target is sitting down or sleeping, than there may be sufficient time to prepare for the pounce. However, if the target is on the move, then they will have to keep up.

A spotter despatched to high ground would be very useful. Consider a high cut-off team.

When the Target Sees the Tracking Team First

When this becomes apparent, the tracking team should freeze. Sometimes people can be looking in your direction but can no longer see you.

Of course, it may be that, unbeknown to the trackers, the target has spotted them. There is no additional action under these conditions, unless the visual contact details have come to light from intercepted radio communications or an observation post.

It may be that the target only picked up a glint of a reflection, or is able to interpret wildlife and bird dynamics, which has led them to believe that someone else is in the area. In these circumstances, they are unlikely to know the full details of the tracking team.

On the other hand, the target may well have had a good chance to observe the trackers, and know everything about them, including weapons. There have been several occasions in Africa when the quarry has been so close to the trackers that they were able to listen into conversations. This is a very dangerous situation because the quarry will know the strengths and weaknesses of the tracking team and could easily have laid ambush positions and booby traps.

Ultimately, if either the trackers come across the point from where they were spotted, or they have been advised that they were spotted, they must increase their camouflage index and take appropriate action to avoid ambush or making contact. Taking cover with effective camouflage can deceive the target. They will have spotted you, but you then disappear from view.

A period of zone-in is recommended for most tracking operations; however, if the tracking is part of a pursuit then the trackers must take into consideration the delay in taking cover and the effect on closing the time-distance gap.

The other consideration is to ensure that the quarry does not get the impression that they are tactically superior. The danger of this is that the quarry could turn and become the aggressor; the hunter becomes the hunted.

Close scrutiny of the action indicators will provide the necessary information for the trackers when deciding on tactics. Is the quarry tactically aware, well-trained and well-fed, or are they hungry, tired and have little or no training?

The Target is Coming Towards the Tracking Team

Where the target is coming towards the tracker there are numerous factors that will dictate the action to be taken.

If the target is spotted before he sees the tracking team, it gives the trackers significant advantage. The options are to call for back-up or change location to provide tactical advantage by using the landscape.

It may be that immediate action is required to close the time-distance gap. However, even under these circumstances stealth is crucial. The closer the trackers can get to the target before making themselves known, the better. There is always a likelihood that the adrenalin-fuelled target will take flight, running faster and jumping higher than they could do normally.

There are occasions when, unbeknown to the trackers, the target is aware of them, but has not been able to locate their exact location. It may that the target has slipped through the net, lying low or has doubled back. If the tracking team become suspicious that the target is aware of them (perhaps because of bird dynamics, animal behaviour or other indicators), the best configuration is to use the X formation and preferably despatch a spotter to high ground. The spotter should be able identify what is causing the birds and other animals to alarm. They may be able to see the target, and report their findings back to the tracking team.

CHAPTER 17

Counter- and Anti-tracking

DEFEAT THE MIND, DEFEAT THE TRACKER

Without doubt the most effective tool of counter-tracking and anti-tracking is the mind. All the techniques in this chapter are designed to influence, confuse, harm and disrupt the tracker.

I have defeated trackers, to the point where they could not go on, by the simple use of psychology and a mixture of dummy and live booby traps. Likewise, a group of targets attempted to defeat my tracking team by the use of a written message in the sand using their nicknames. The message read: 'Soon it will be dark, you cannot find us. Tonight we will find and attack you! Mick Jagger.'

The message had a devastating effect on the already fatigued trackers, and left a number of questions in their minds. The quarry was feeling confident enough to leave a message and threaten an attack. They had the element of darkness on their side and had anticipated our route. Should the tracking team continue the follow-up, retreat or make a defensive camp.

Legitimate organizations around the world have adopted skilled tracking techniques, so it follows that they will also adopt counter- and anti-tracking skills. They will be used for surveillance, reconnaissance, general patrols and special forces, including sniper teams.

Tracking is a powerful weapon for legitimate purposes, but is an equally powerful tool used for illegal purposes. For this reason, some anti-tracking and counter-tracking skills have been intentionally omitted.

COUNTER-TRACKING

Counter-tracking is where a deliberate attempt is made to hinder the tracker or tracking team directly by injury or death. This includes primitive and modern-day booby traps and conventional anti-personnel mines. Counter-tracking is limited only by the imagination and the ingenuity of those who use it.

Some booby traps are set as a guard against an installation, perhaps a drug factory, cannabis farm or cache of illicit goods. These are usually aimed at keeping competitors out or preventing other people from interfering. It is not unusual for windows and door handles to be wired into mains voltage. However, some techniques are designed to attract the tracker into the trap, whereupon the devices will be activated. This could be discarded weapons, items of evidence or other materials.

Like a fish hook with an attractive bait, once the tracker has bitten and the barb is engaged, there is no getting off. It can be a specific tactic to attempt to draw a tracking team into a follow-up, during which they could be ambushed or drawn into an area strewn with counter-tracking booby traps.

Counter-tracking can include psychological techniques. Some primitive booby traps are not very effective in their operation, but look menacing. On the other hand, improvised explosive devices (IEDs) can be either basic in construction or sophisticated and highly efficient.

A good tracker has to be able to use anti-tracking tricks of the trade and also be able to construct counter-tracker devices and techniques. This is easier said than done. Take, for example, the construction of a simple booby trap, where a trip-wire is laid below knee height and then connected to either a primitive spear or explosive device, such as a hand grenade, detonator or shotgun cartridge. The mechanisms themselves are quite difficult to construct. Where a primitive weapon has been prepared there is likelihood of wood shavings nearby.

The choice of trip-wire is essential. Some people think that fishing line is ideal but it catches the light and is quite easy to see. In addition it

A Brazilian policeman holds up a spear used in a booby trap. This spear, which was made from construction steel, was recovered from a booby-trapped trail. It was intended to kill large animals, but could have easily been triggered by a human.

stretches, especially when it is hot, and may not have sufficient tension to activate the trap. It also snaps very easily when it is hot. The best material for a trip-wire is a thin ready-tensioned steel cable 2 mm or maximum 3 mm in thickness. Para chord is a poor substitute.

In many areas the simple trip-line is not used for anti-tracking but is laid by hunters. In South-east Asia and parts of South America sprung spears designed to kill wild pigs are ready and cocked waiting to spear anything that activates the mechanism, including trackers. In many parts of the world large spring-jawed traps are readily available. These are capable of severing a limb. In Africa, large stabber dead-fall traps are commonplace near areas where hippos are present. These large stabbers are designed to kill a hippo, and are equally dangerous to humans.

Although they are aimed at wildlife, if a hunter is capable of preparing these traps, and he turns them to human counter-tracking, the threat level becomes so high that it may not be worth deploying a tracking team, but rather to consider other resources – but in no circumstances should the follow-up be conducted in poor light conditions.

The construction of traps takes time and it is a risky business. At any time during the laying and preparation, the trap could be activated accidently, risking not only injury but, if it is an explosive device, giving the position away.

The positioning of a booby trap is crucial. For example, a booby trap placed on the vast salt pans of Namibia and Botswana is less likely to be as effective as one placed on a narrow game path in thick jungle.

Likewise, knowledge of human behaviour will add to efficiency. People are social beings; they generally group together, and when something out of the ordinary is presented their curiosity will draw them in to look. Common sense dictates where to place a booby trap, but always consider the least common-sense location when attempting to defeat trackers, because they are less likely to fall in with the norms of human behaviour.

On my mantracking courses, I use returning students and instructors to lay trails and, on some occasions, to lay booby traps. I will have informed them before the course that they need to devise and construct a booby trap mechanism before they arrive.

On every course, the booby traps have been too complex to be relied upon, or have simply failed to function. Significantly, every instructor reported that they had underestimated the stress and pressure of having to lay effective booby traps. Follow the logic through and this gives a good idea of the pressure a real quarry is feeling as they prepare booby traps.

I overcome this by carrying a number of inert dummy but suspicious-looking devices to lay on a trail. It could just be trip-wire, not connected to anything. That way people will still approach with caution and the speed of the follow-up will stall and slow down as they search for more booby traps.

I have had a number of experiences with booby traps that could have had disastrous effects, because they could have been activated by the wrong people. On one occasion I laid a series of trip-wires connected to devices along a dried-up river bed. The positioning was ideal; there was an effective route influencer and I could observe the booby traps from a kilometre away from a perfect observation point at the top of the steep valley.

Shortly after settling in I noticed through my binoculars the smallest of movements coming up the valley. I could see a local fisherman was walking straight towards the traps. Without doubt he would have detonated at least one.

Four problems arose. I had to compromise my tactically dominant position. Would he get to the traps before me and detonate them? Would he spot me disarming the traps, or would I accidently detonate the devices while either disarming or re-arming them? Since there wasn't much time, I dropped straight down into the valley and disarmed the booby traps before he got there.

The other problem I have had is livestock getting tangled in the trip-wire and somehow dislodging the entire device without detonation, and then moving in my direction.

In areas where there is the likelihood of illegal activities, especially in the rural environment, it is likely that the target will be a tracker of some sort. If he is hunter and trapper then counter-tracking is to be expected. Likewise, if the target is operational in an area in which he resides, he is likely to have established a labyrinth of trails, with a discreet sign indicating whether the trail is safe to pass or not.

Some methods of counter-tracking can be very cunning. While I was in the Himalayas, tracking the legendary Yeti for a TV programme, we were operational in an area which was controlled by Maoist rebels. I noticed a faint trail that led off the main track. To get to it, I had to go down five metres and through some vegetation. There were some large rocks that looked like ideal stepping stones. As soon as I stepped onto one of the rocks I slid off at speed and landed in the undergrowth three metres below. Because the rock had looked good on initial examination I went back to examine it. To my amazement, it had a thick coating of a slippery substance. The substance appeared to have been smeared and taken on the appearance of the rock, with some growth and moss on the surface. After several weeks in the Himalayas I came into contact with the rebels and asked them about their counter-tracking techniques designed to slow government troops and tempt them to take shortcuts off trails. One of the techniques is to make a mixture of cow dung, a large percentage of animal fat and live yogurt. Strategic rocks were coated with this substance, creating well-camouflaged, potentially lethal rocks.

Some Types of Booby Traps

Primitive Traps
These can sometimes be common. They are inexpensive and rely on simple mechanisms; however, they are silent and can be deadly.

Stabbers
One type of booby trap to watch out for is formed of spikes or stakes that can stab. These can cause life-threatening injuries.

Nails in planks of wood: These on their own do not pose a lethal threat, however it is very rare for them not to have human faeces spread on them so that they inflict a wound that will become infected.

Punji: These come in a few variations. The basic construction requires a disguised pit that contains a range of stabbers. Generally a wild-life *punji* pit will contain upward-facing spikes. Tactical pits contain a range of upward-facing stabbers, along with downward-facing stabbers that are designed to puncture above boot level. Some variations contain nails.

Horizontal stabber: This is a fixed number of stabbers (although usually one) tensioned on bending branches, usually activated by a trip-wire mechanism. The stabber has to hit the target at the correct position and velocity to be effective. The longer the branch is under tension, the less effective the device is.

Spear: This, again, is tensioned by vegetation, and the spear is launched, sometimes at high speed. The mass of the spear, size of the shaft and sharpened spearhead can cause serious injuries.

Arrow: Similar mechanisms are used to launch an arrow, but arrows can be more difficult to spot. They are unlikely to kill immediately, but they will cause a serious wound.

Electrical and Electro-mechanical
Electro-mechanical devices are used in which a small electrical current is required to initiate a detonator. They can either be pressure plates or switches under tension connected to a trip or activation wire. These devices are all easy to make from everyday items available in general shops.

Other electrical devices are mainly those used to initiate an explosion. This can be either by remote operation or on-site. This is the primary method of inflicting damage and injury in certain regions of the world.

They can be very sophisticated. However, rangers and police in India report fatalities to poachers who have removed overhead high-voltage cables, exposed the conductors and camouflaged the deadly cables. They are aimed at killing livestock, but nevertheless a tracker could easily find himself faced with this kind of danger.

Avoidance

The best tactic to avoid injury from counter-tracker devices is to be in a heightened status of awareness. Although it is very difficult to maintain this level of awareness for long periods, the tracker should always not only be attuned to physical spoor, but able to interpret subtle messages of intent. This may be in an area that has previously had some human traffic, yet in which there are no humans present at a given time.

Countering Dogs and Dog Handlers

It is not easy to use anti-tracking techniques to evade dogs. Dogs have a great deal of stamina and their noses, ears and eyes are hard to defeat.

Since dogs have excellent hearing and can detect movement, good camouflage and stalking principles will help to minimize detection.

Dog and handler are a close-knit team and given a dog's agility and stamina it is best to attempt to defeat the handler. This can be done by crossing natural or manmade barriers. In disciplined organizations there will be health and safety factors to be considered by the dog handlers: they are unlikely to attempt to take the same risk as an evader, which could endanger their lives or that of their dog. For example, it is unlikely that a police handler would cross a fast-flowing river or abseil down a building unless he had been trained to do so – although the same cannot be said for handlers from some other organizations.

However, in an area where the dog handler is able to move easily it may be necessary to counter the dog, so that the handlers' organization will have to reconsider whether deploying dogs is safe for the dog.

There may be environmental factors such as wind direction or temperature that will affect the dog's performance. Some dogs can operate throughout the day and in high temperature with phenomenal success. In Kenya I did an exercise with bloodhounds. The objective was for me to move through the bush for several hours, including midday when temperatures can soar up to 40 degrees centigrade. As I did so, I was leaving notes in which valuable intelligence was described. I moved as fast as I could and used several anti-dog tracking techniques. I had run through dense bush, past herds of buffalo, elephant and a pride of lions. I crossed a lake with crocodiles and hippo. At 1330 hrs I needed a rest and a drink. By 1400 hrs, the dogs had found me within three hours. They had been relentless, and all tribute to the handlers who trusted the dogs and let them perform.

This bloodhound and his handler are a very efficient tracking team. They tracked me over several kilometres through highly dangerous and challenging terrain.

When being attacked by a trained attack dog, presenting a wrapped arm may be your best defence.

One technique to counter dogs silently is by use of a specialized line of devices. These are very successful. However, because they are so effective and their use would cause suffering to dogs, I cannot go into further detail. The technique would be easily spotted by a tracker, yet devastating to a dog.

There are some basic principles to be followed when detected by dogs. With search and rescue dogs or bloodhounds it is likely that you may be able to escape unbitten because these dogs are trained to bark and stay with you, or return to the handler and indicate your location to him. If you are detected by attack dogs, such as German Shepherd or Melanois, options are limited. It is unwise to run from these dogs because they will inflict several painful bites and they will not let go. The best action it to wrap one arm in clothing and present that to the dog. They are trained to go for the arms, so if you present one arm to the dog it is likely it will take hold of that arm. This is unlikely to prevent a bite but may reduce the injury. I have had a Melanois bite my arm during training. I was wearing the usual reinforced arm protection. The power of the bite was incredible and despite the substantial protection, I still had some bite marks on my arm.

Fire

This is one of the most extreme methods of counter-tracking. In parts of Africa it is common for poachers to set fire to the bush so that it will drive wildlife in their direction and drive the police and military out of the area. The poachers are usually knowledgeable about wind direction and areas of safe haven for them. They also know the ferocity at which the fire will burn. If there has not been a bushfire in that area for a number of years, they know that the head-fire and fire-line intensity will be far greater than if the bush had been burnt within a year.

I have been in bushfires, and they are ferocious. Sometimes the only escape is to defy logic and break through the fire-line to the already burnt and smouldering bush. This can only be done if the fire intensity at the fire-line is fast and low and the area behind the fire-line has been burnt out. Never set fire to an area that you are in if it consists of fir trees or other trees with inflammable resins.

The tree canopy will burn extremely fast, drawing oxygen from underneath. The result is that the area underneath the canopy is oxygen-depleted and will not support human life.

When fire is used for counter-tracking, it must be the last resort. The fire is lit and the quarry (i.e. the lighter) will travel upwind, leaving the fire catching behind him. In many areas the wind will change direction at different times of the day and the quarry could well find himself being chased by the fire he set.

Most bushfires are characterized only by the intensity of the hottest part of the perimeter – the head-fire. The fire intensity will vary around the total perimeter.

ANTI-TRACKING

Anti-tracking is the ability or attempt to lose the trackers by spoor reduction or by using a number of tricks to throw the trackers off the trail. Knowledge of anti-tracking skills should therefore be developed and maximized by the tracker.

In an area where I trained combat rangers, they used rocky outcrops otherwise known as *kopjes* for covert observation posts. The view is 360 degrees and for many kilometres. These are so valuable that they are manned permanently. Rangers will go into the *kopje* for three months. They are forbidden to leave, apart from when replenishing water or until relieved by incoming rangers. The incoming rangers bring with them two large drums filled with water, which is concealed at a secret location close to the observation post (OP). They are dropped several kilometres away and the incoming rangers make their way to the *kopje*. The closer they get to the OP, the more anti-tracking techniques they apply. It will start with conventional walking backwards, cutting corners, rock-hopping, and finishing with time-consuming re-setting of vegetation as they pass through. Some of the techniques used are extremely cunning. Even experienced trackers would have difficulty spotting the results and giving an accurate interpretation.

Some of these OPs are manned by only two people. With such small numbers, they would have difficulty defending their position from attack by a superior force. Therefore, their job is to remain undetected and report back any suspicious activities in the area. Their lives depend on being stealthy and using highly skilled anti-tracking techniques.

Most anti-tracking is learned from a book, internet or movies. The tricks are so commonly used that they are the tracker's first line of investigation. However, the lesser-known anti-tracking skills used by special forces and illegal operators can be far more devious and hard to detect. The general rule of thumb is that, if someone has had to use anti-tracking skills in real-life situations on several occasions they should be deemed as expert. They may be using techniques that have been learned and have been replicated elsewhere, or it may be a skill-set never seen before. There is a likelihood that they will have experimented and found techniques that are successful.

Anti-tracking can include the use of other humans. In the Sonora Desert I was working at night when we came across the fresh spoor of one individual. By the tracks we could tell that he was carrying a heavy pack, usually only carried by drug smugglers. As we followed his tracks other units were brought in to speed the follow-up. Quad bikes, helicopters and other personnel joined the search.

Eventually I spotted him by the shine on his forearm. He had concealed himself under a bush. When he was caught it was found that he was physically very fit and strong but had a severe learning disability. Over a period of three months, several more people were caught with a similar method of operation, and all had learning disabilities. It became clear that the drug smugglers were using people with learning disabilities as 'throw downs'. This technique meant that the decoys did exactly what they were told and, not understanding the implications of being caught, they were prepared to venture into the desert. The Border Patrol resources were concentrated on finding the 'throw downs' while, in another location, the real 'coyotes' made a swift and effective delivery of their drugs into the USA.

There is some interesting psychology going on when the target is anti-tracking. An experienced target may find some comfort in knowing that what he is doing will give him a significant chance of remaining undetected, and he will feel that he has the upper hand. On the other hand, a target may feel intimidated by the possibility of a tracking team and will use anti-tracking techniques in desperation. Under these latter circumstances the trackers have a significant advantage. The target will be taking up time to create anti-tracking, thus allowing the trackers to close the time-distance gap. The classic techniques of walking backwards, brushing out or crossing streams will only slow him down.

Spoor Reduction

The basic technique for all trackers to adopt, and be on the lookout for, is spoor reduction. None of my trackers will walk straight through a track-trap and, in most areas, they walk on the peripherals of tracks and rock-hop without thinking about it. They also follow a 100 per cent no-litter policy so as to not give any advantage to other trackers in the area.

By doing this they reduce the chance of detection, but on some occasions they will specifically place tracks in a track-trap or leave litter for training purposes, and also as a diversionary or deceptive tactic.

Spoor is any giveaway that a human or animal is present, and because we know that animals can give our position away, it is always a good idea to take steps to neutralize our scent by not using highly volatile deodorant or toothpaste. Some ointments, especially Savlon, have a very distinctive smell which carries far on the wind. Wherever possible, the tracker should smoke his clothing and hair.

Lying up points or overnight stops requires special attention. Consider cold meals or cooking devices that do not leave scorch marks on rocks and vegetation. If using an open fire, consider constructing a Dakota fire pit. This ingenious fire pit is buried below ground level so that the light does not carry far. It can be put out quickly and, when filled in, it is virtually impossible to see.

Trackers will spend a large amount of time analysing a campsite when found. They will be looking for any hints or clues about their target. Therefore it is important that no trace is left, so that they do not even notice the camp. If they do find it, as much detail as possible should have been obliterated. Individual lying-ups must be concealed by covering or brushing.

I was involved in tracking down some armed poachers in Africa that resulted in a fire-fight. The poachers fled the scene. However, where one of the armed poachers had lain-up he left a very clear imprint of his belt buckle, which was from a specific regiment.

As a follow-up commenced on blood spoor, another team deduced that the quarry would head for the military barracks nearby, and so cut ahead. The group were apprehended on a road. One was wearing trousers held up by the same military belt we had spotted previously. He had also sustained a minor flesh wound, which was enough evidence to place him at the scene.

Footwear

In the context of spoor reduction, this is where existing footwear is either temporarily or permanently adapted, manufactured specially, or carried with the intention of changing. It is a subject in which I have a keen interest, because it amazes me the length people will go to disguise or modify their tracks.

The easiest technique is simply to wrap something over the existing footwear. This could be a T-shirt, headscarf or any suitable material. The thickness of the wrapping will determine whether or not a sole pattern is identifiable. However, it will not disguise tracks; they will still be visible,

Left to right, the tracks show the compression shapes of string boot covers, an uncovered tread pattern and a track where a blanket cover was placed over the tread.

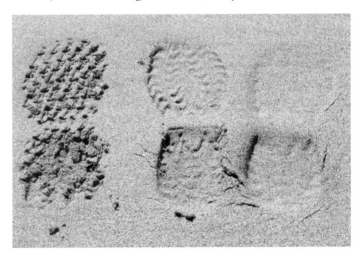

A blanket boot cover is a common method of deceiving a tracker. The tread pattern is still visible, but looks old.

and could well constitute a confirmed identifiable signature track (CIST). In the border towns of Mexico there are thriving industries making shoe covers out of blankets. They are made to fit over the footwear and then secured to the ankle using wire or string.

With these shoe covers there is only one thickness of blanket, so the sole pattern is visible. You might think that the covers are not doing their job if you can see the tracks. However, this concept is much more cunning than first thought, because although the tracks are visible (which any tracker would have discovered), the blanket takes away the edges of the track, giving the impression that they are old. Most trackers would fall for this and, having found these tracks, would probably classify them as aged and move on to find fresh tracks.

Tracking teams should do everything they can to blend their footwear with what the locals use. As I mentioned in Chapter 10, I wore military-style boots in the jungle of Malaysia and they were easily identified as imported boots. I then bought some locally made Kampong plastic Adidas boots. They were very effective in the jungle. I no longer slipped along the muddy trails and my tracks were indistinguishable from locals.

In Africa, shoes made from car tyres are commonplace (and, indeed, are worn by the Shifta, lawless bandits from the Horn of Africa, who ply their violent and illegal trade through East and Central Africa). Flip-flops are also commonplace and I have, in the past, attached flip-flops to the soles of my boots to disguise them and make the footprint look like a local person, rather than an easily identifiable boot worn by an outsider.

Modified footwear
This can be soles attached facing backwards, a different tread pattern on the left or right side, or attaching animal feet.

People go to great lengths to make footwear that have animal feet attached to the bottoms. One of the commonest is the attachment of cow's hooves to wood, which is then strapped to the footwear. The bene-fit of these is that they can be removed when required, and this will throw most lay people. To the trained tracker the opposite is true. Because the gait patterns are not consistent with a real cow, the shoes will also dig in on the cleave of the hoof and be very obvious (as a cow's hoof shoes have two sets on each foot, so when walking four hooves are seen). This tech-nique has been around for a long time and has been documented as being used by moonshiners smuggling their contraband in the USA in 1922.

Amongst the easiest tracks to follow are bare feet, flip-flops or mocca-sins. This is because the entire sole is in contact with the substrate. It follows that where flip-flops are attached to boots, they are easy to track.

Boot covers
Carpets or other material are used to cover the tread patterns of shoes. There are some boot muffs available from hunting suppliers, and waxed string covers from the Second World War, which have been reputed to be devised for anti-tracking, although they were developed for additional grip in snow and icy conditions.

A string boot cover was originally designed for walking on snow and ice, but can sometimes be used to change visible tread pattern in tracks.

Other Methods of Disguising/Obliterating Tracks

Rock-hopping
This is stepping or jumping from rock to rock, and can be highly effec-tive. Where this is done, tracks will not be visible; the gait pattern will be determined by the rock or stone. Tracks should, however, be visible in the area just before and after the rock-hopping stops. If the rocks are small, or in a soft substrate, any pressure exerted will cause a gap to be visible and this will be spotted by trackers. Although very difficult to spot, there may be some very hard grains of sand on the rocks. I have tracked elephants over rocky outcrops. Despite their size they tread very

Where track traps have been observed by a member of the team, they could elect to investigate these or be instructed by the controller to do so. The best track traps are areas where the subject would have been funnelled through a patch of wet mud or sand.

lightly and the only spoor was a few grains of rock that had slid against a large boulder, causing a small white scratch

Following a tarmac road

Although this will disguise tracks, it is a fairly obvious ploy and such a road will be considered a route influencer. However, there may be a high degree of speculation required as to where a target has abandoned the road and a tracking team will need to make good use of flankers to check for breakthroughs in vegetation on the edges of the road. If the road is bordered by fences or other barriers, trackers will move quickly through the area as it is less likely that the target will have left the road at that point.

There are areas on roads that should be checked. The gravel and dust in the middle can be very fine as the result of ground-up grit and tyre material. The edge where the road meets either dirt or the curb is also an excellent track-trap.

Tree-climbing

It is surprisingly rare for people, including many trackers, to look up. Tree climbing is only suitable in areas where there are good trees to climb, with sufficient foliage and density. A typical place for spoor reduction by climbing is a densely wooded area where branches of trees connect to other branches. I have experimented with this technique and was able to travel sixty metres from tree to tree.

Following rivers and streams

Sometimes this can be an effective method of spoor reduction, but it is also one of the most dangerous. Flowing water can be deceptive. Water which is heavy with sediment can easily wash someone downstream and very quickly any clothing or equipment will be stripped off.

The river bed can be littered with slippery stones and drop-offs. Consideration has to be given as to whether footwear is removed. If removed, the advantage is that the footwear will be dry when coming out of the water, making for a more comfortable experience. However, the river bed could contain dangerous debris, including protruding glass or metal. Overall, it is recommended that footwear is kept on. While I was in South America, among the piranha-infested rivers, there also lurked electric eels.

Following a river without local knowledge is extremely hazardous. In the mountain range between Zimbabwe and Mozambique, I dropped down into a steep and slippery gorge and followed the river. Before long the rocky bank was riddled with three-metre deep swirl holes and within a few hours the bank was too steep to climb out of and the unmistakeable sound of rapids and waterfalls lay ahead. When I got to the waterfalls, there was no way out and this forced me to return upstream. Neither the waterfall nor gully appeared on maps.

From the tracker's perspective, soft vegetation at the area of entrance will be crushed; moss may be scraped off rocks. Tracks can be left behind in the floor of the watercourse and sediment can go into suspension and be washed downstream, giving the position away. At the point of exit, carried over material including water or wet debris will be left on the bank.

Brushing out

This technique is used to contain an area by brushing track-traps, but it is also used to eliminate tracks. By breaking off some vegetation or using a clutch of sticks, the tracks are brushed over. It is mostly used on soft sand where a track would be obvious. It does have the advantage that it will destroy unique factors contained in the track and may fool non-trackers.

There are features associated with brushing out that a tracker will look for. Typically, a broken tree or bush nearby and the material discarded once it has been used. Using brushing, it is virtually impossible to re-create the original grain pattern in the substrate. A form of brushing out is used extensively by the US Border Patrol. A vehicle drives the frontier road, thus laying down tread marks. The patrol then returns to check the tracks. If someone has crossed over, this is quickly detected, even if they brushed their tracks crossing the trail. If brush-outs are used for containment, it is essential that these are checked regularly to see if any new tracks have appeared.

Resetting vegetation

This cunning trick is used close to an observation post or whenever it is felt necessary. It is very time-consuming but highly effective when used in conjunction with other anti-tracking skills. As you pass through vegetation, use a stick with a Y shape and push everything back up to the vertical position. This will conceal the spoor and will not be spotted except by very experienced trackers. It has to be done meticulously and cannot be rushed. It is also dependent on the environment and the vegetation. Most green-stemmed plants can be restored.

Walking Techniques

Some walking techniques can be used independently or in conjunction with other techniques.

Walking backwards

The most effective place to commence walking backwards is on a hard surface, so that the transitional mid-step gait will not be visible. Theoretically, this should be easy to spot, but it can be difficult unless spoor is in a straight line and in a soft substrate. The stride will reduce, the straddle may reduce, but the most important factor to look for is the primary impact point, which is the toe and fore-foot.

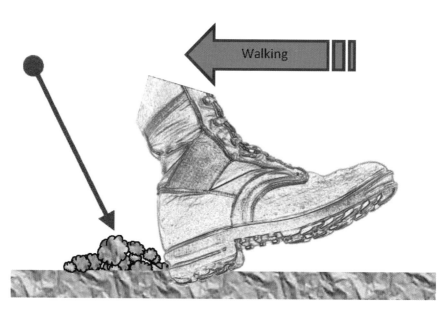

Where a target has been walking backwards to counter tracking, this is usually easy to spot due to the debris that is displaced in the direction of travel. The debris tends to appear near the heel area of the track.

Here are two separate tracks showing the direction of travel. The left track indicates forward travel. How can we tell? Debris has been pushed forward in the direction of travel and the terminal impact point is deeper at the toe end of the boot. The right track indicates walking backwards (debris has been pushed in the direction of travel and the terminal impact point is deeper at the heel end of the boot).

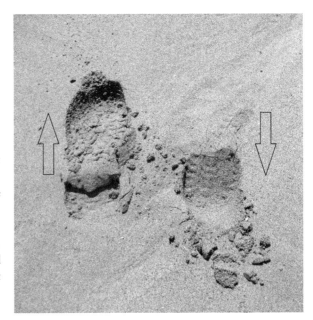

Back-track

A development of walking backwards. The idea is to continue along the trail normally until a suitable screen, like a boulder or fallen tree, is seen. Walk ten to fifteen paces past the screen and then walk backwards, ensuring that the feet go back exactly on top of the previous tracks. At the screen, change direction, usually at 90 degrees to the previous direction of travel.

Walking on the side of the feet

Although this may lose a non-tracker, the spoor is still visible and a good tracker will notice the change in tracks.

Join busy pedestrian, livestock and vehicular routes

This technique is very effective and is widely used in village areas in Africa. Many villagers move their goats and cattle into kraals at night. There is only one entrance and exit from the kraal, and it is busy not only with livestock, but also the herders.

Anyone walking on a livestock trail to the kraal, or to water, or along the main road to the village, will soon have their tracks obliterated. However, sometimes a complete or partial track may have survived and usually a busy trail will have some established track-traps and funnelling. By conducting micro-tracking on the path, trackers may identify a CIST or PIST. Two lines would then be drawn across the trail approximately one or two metres apart and the area between the lines checked carefully.

A previously laid trail could have been obliterated by livestock, either accidentally or deliberately to throw off the trackers.

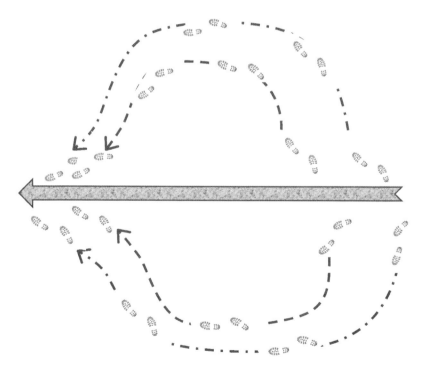

People peel off the trail at intervals and sometimes both sides of the trail. They may meet up further down the trail or at a pre-arranged rendezvous.

Peel and splice

This can be an effective method for groups of people. As the group move along, members will peel off either by jumping off the track or walking backwards. They may peel backwards into an ambush position, or splice back into the group further down the trail. This can be very difficult for a tracker to deal with. If he detects that a peel and splice has been done then obviously he cannot follow all the targets. If there are not sufficient trackers then the tracker would need to identify the most dominant track and follow that. Peel and splice can be very dangerous for trackers. The peelers could be going to get reinforcements, or lying in ambush positions.

Scatter and splice

This is also effective for groups of people. The difference from the peel is that the group scatters in a random manner. They may well regroup along the trail or at a pre-determined rendezvous point. As with the peel, trackers would follow the dominant tracks.

The scatter and splice could be the response to a surprise encounter and will be either an uncontrolled scatter or a planned scatter. In the bush in Africa, the Shifta would lie-up in small groups with other individuals scattered loosely in the undergrowth. If they are attacked there is not just one scatter, but trackers could easily find themselves surrounded by scattering groups. This is very dangerous, since the scatter will not last very long and the splice could be very close by.

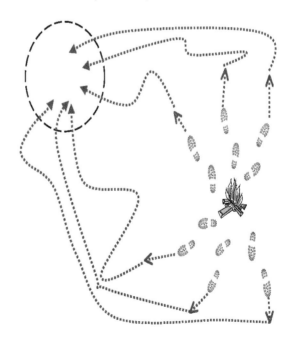

The scatter is a random movement of people from a location, usually due to an unexpected event. The splice could evolve naturally or could be at a pre-arranged rendezvous.

Cutting the corner

This is when, upon approaching a road or railway line at ninety degrees, the quarry veers off at 45 degree either left or right. This gives the trackers the impression that they are taking a short cut to the road and it will suggest to them a direction of travel.

When the quarry reaches the road, there is the option of laying a short false trail on the other side, or turning directly on to the road or railway line. They may use spoor reduction techniques to walk back up the road to the initial desired direction of travel. The greater the distance from the shortcut intersection and the desired trail, the more effective the ruse, with 100 metres being a practical minimum.

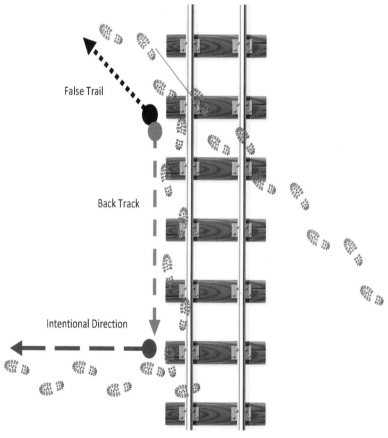

The team initially approaches a railway line or road at 90 degrees. As they get closer, they 'cut' the corner and veer off at 45 degrees. Once across the feature, a short false trail should be made. The feature should be re-joined and followed to the intentional direction of travel. Good spoor reduction will limit the chances of being detected.

Before coming to a temporary halt or approaching an observation point, a movement similar to a fishhook is deployed. The team change direction and loops around a feature. In this example the trail changed before reaching the lake to avoid mud track traps. Trackers can be seen on the edge of the lake looking for spoor. Meanwhile they are being observed from a high point established by the fishhook manoeuvre.

Fishhooking

This technique is used when coming to a temporary halt or observation point, when it would be unwise to make a trail directly to that feature. Therefore, a trail is continued past the feature before fishhooking back on this on the other side of the feature. It is extremely useful in conjunction with observation points as any trackers following will be observed.

Watercourses

It is a myth that crossing a river will lose a tracker: the entry and exit points are easy to establish. However, a few additional features will slow a tracker down. These include cutting the corner as described above, laying a false trail upstream, including an exit, then re-entering the stream and walking carefully downstream as far as possible, preferably beyond a turn in the stream. Finally exiting using spoor-reduction techniques will increase the degree of deception.

Big tree

This is a very effective anti-tracking skill. A large tree is identified, preferably with a large trunk. Skimming the tree, walk 15 to 20 paces past it, laying a false trail. Back-track to the tree and then commence the trail on the opposite, or blind, side of the tree. This works well, because the tracker's eyes will be drawn to look forward.

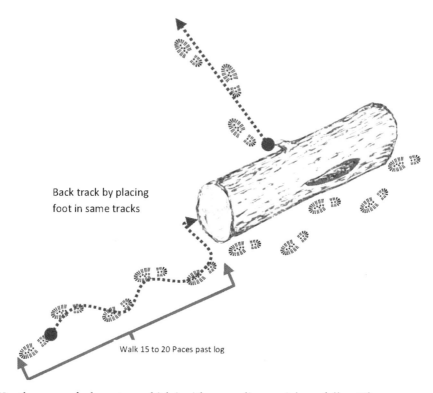

Back track by placing
foot in same tracks

Walk 15 to 20 Paces past log

Use the cover of a large tree which is either standing upright or fallen. The team passes close by and walks 15 to 20 paces past it. By using spoor reduction techniques they back-track and use the occluded side of the tree to continue the trail.

CHAPTER 18

Equipment

Better to take it and *not* use it than not take it and *need* it. A tracker will always struggle with the balance of how much kit to carry. On one hand there is the desire to be self-sufficient and carry technical equipment. On the other hand, a tracker will be hindered by a heavy load and must travel light to close the time-distance gap.

Some equipment is essential, but most is optional. When it comes to carrying equipment the tracker must be highly selective about both essential and optional equipment.

TRACKING STICK

This is my most useful piece of equipment. If a weapon is not being carried then a stick is a must.

The primary use of the tracking stick is to measure gait characteristics, including stride and track size as described in Chapter 10. Tracking sticks can be made of aluminium or wood; some are purpose-made and some are customized. I prefer wood, especially Irish blackthorn, because it is a dense, dark wood, which makes it ideal for its secondary purpose of defence. It is very rare to find a straight piece, and so other trees that provide straighter sticks can be used. My stick has a recessed compass and a join in the middle so that I can disassemble it for transits to follow-ups.

The tracking stick should be one metre long and about 25 mm diameter. One end should be sharpened, or a metal ferrule spike attached. This is important so that the tracker always knows which end of the stick he is using to measure.

At least two rubber or silicon 'O' rings should be threaded onto the stick.

In addition to measuring, use it for parting vegetation and testing the ground before stepping on to it, which is essential in snake-infested areas and sinking mud or sand. I have also trained to use my tracking stick both as a defensive weapon and a highly effective attack weapon.

I have used it on many occasions when confronted by dangerous animals including lions, elephants and bears. When raised above the head in a strike position it threatens the animals, causing them to move off.

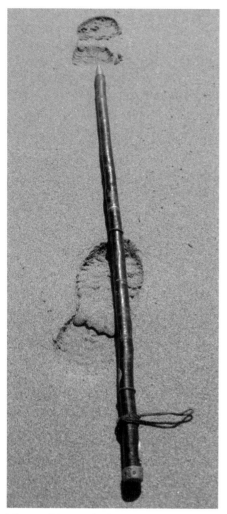

The tracking stick shows the 'O' ring marking the terminal impact point and primary impact point of the next track.

It is also useful when confronting humans. What appears to be an innocent tracking stick can quickly turn into an effective weapon. In most parts of the world it is illegal to carry firearms and ammunition, especially for a foreigner. The penalties for carrying a firearm are severe and, if it is used against a person, even more severe, so while a tracking stick may not be ideal, it might be the only way of legally protecting oneself.

CLOTHING

The pattern and colours of clothing has been covered in Chapter 12. Where camouflage is not appropriate, the best colours are olive drab, foliage green, khaki, brown and grey.

Clothing is highly specialized to the environment. Clothing that I have worn in sub-zero temperatures is very different from the clothing worn in the jungle, which is different from clothing worn in the desert. This applies to both the textiles and the design. An example of this occurred while in Poland during the winter. In principle, the garment was good, but it was only when I needed to do the buttons up that I found my frozen fingers were unable to access the buttonholes. The top pockets were mounted too high up on the chest to access with gloves on. In contrast, I wear lightweight, nylon combat trousers in the jungle. They are rot-proof and dry quickly. The pockets are well placed and well designed.

I have a multi-purpose multi-climate top that I have worn from the Arctic to the desert, which is a Ventile top. It is single-layer, and has been customized for my use. It is very robust and practical.

FOOTWEAR

Boots

I have several pairs of boots. No one boot will do all areas. I favour a heavy, rigid Vibram high boot for deep snow, and desert high boots for most other environments.

The desert high boots are extremely versatile, and are designed for first-fit comfort, thus avoiding having to wear them in. Generally this is the kind of boot that I use, but the trade-off is an over-technical boot, which contains foam padding and various linings. The foam padding absorbs water and takes a very long time to dry out, and these are useless in the jungle, because they start to rot. Generally, after a prolonged stint in the jungle, they have a strong odour. Ideally a jungle boot with single skin and drain holes would be better.

The only place where I don't always wear desert boots is in Africa. The Courtney boot range is designed for use in the African bush. They have evolved over many years of use on the *veldt* and perform extremely well.

I never wear a shoe or low boot when tracking. The advantages of a high boot are that it gives support and a degree of protection from snake bites. In South America some of the forces wear horse-riding calf-height protectors to protect them from snake bite.

Socks

Without doubt the best socks for all environments are the Merino wool socks from various suppliers. They are comfortable and wick sweat away, thus reducing the chances of blisters. They are good for both hot and cold environments. Where a tracker needs to reduce weight, these are ideal, as one pair can last more than a week. They wash quickly and dry easily.

In wet areas I prefer not to rely upon boot lining for waterproofing. Instead I wear Sealskins Merino waterproof socks. They do an excellent job of keeping the feet dry.

KNIVES

I have had a large range of knives and have used them in most terrains. There is a vast array of machetes, *pangas*, *kukris* and hybrids of them all. There is also a vast array of Bowie hunting, survival and bushcraft knives. I have found fixed blades safer and more robust than folding knives. In Arizona I was running through the desert. At the time I had a Cold Steel Tanto folding knife in the cargo pocket of my trousers. While running, the knife unfolded itself and cut a neat hole through my trouser leg and pierced my calf muscle. I didn't feel any pain, and only became aware of it when I felt a wet patch which was blood.

A tracker needs at least two knives. The tracker's day is dictated by the quarry; wherever he goes the tracker follows. Therefore a knife that can cut and slash through soft vegetation and hold its own going through hard vegetation is required. He will also need a general-purpose small knife for cooking, repairing equipment, and, if need be, as a back-up for self-defence. For this knife I generally use a small knife which is horizontally mounted onto my kit belt.

The bigger knife is an Extrema Ratio Kukri. I had a traditional *kukri* given to me. It was an excellent knife, however while I was mounted on a horse and crossing a river the knife was submerged. The result was that the wood and goatskin sheath swelled up and I couldn't get the knife out until it dried out. I decided that was too unreliable and opted for the Extrema Ratio Kukri with the Geocam design. It is truly the best knife I have ever used. It has travelled the world and been used by an unforgiving owner, but it keeps going on and on.

It is always a good plan to see what the locals are using as their cutting tools and to consider using the same, if you can get them. However, never count on buying a knife when you arrive in a country. Often cutting tools are sold in specific markets which can be hard to find, or you arrive and find yourself in transit directly to your destination in the jungle. For this reason I always travel with my belt kit, including my *kukri*.

BACKPACKS, RUCKSACKS AND BAGS

Trackers sometimes have to travel long distances and climb through dense vegetation and enclosed spaces. It is a continuous battle between volume, weight, equipment and performance.

For intercontinental travel, where the destination requires a rucksack to carry equipment, I place the rucksack inside a large-barrel 120 litre barrel bag for airline transit. This way the rucksack straps and fabric are protected from airport handling machinery. At the other end I remove the rucksack from the barrel bag and leave that at base camp.

The Maxpediton backpack holds water, provisions and first aid equipment. Secured to the pack on the left side is a tracking brush that is used for brush-outs.

I use a Karrimor 110 litre rucksack, which was made specifically for me. It has several good compartments and is comfortable for carrying.

For backpacks which should carry enough kit for two to three days I use the Maxpedition Condor. It is a well-compartmentalized pack and has sufficient capacity to pack thermal and waterproof layers. It is ideal for climates where weather is changeable.

My favourite backpack is the Maxpedition Falcon 2. It is small and streamlined. It is extremely well designed and is easy to customize.

BELT

My kit belt contains everything that I need to survive and track. It is permanently configured and there is no variation, apart from removing the kukri. It has evolved through trial and error. It has seen action all over the world and has lasted me well.

The most important factor is to use an extremely thick and rigid belt, sometimes referred to as a duty belt. Its purpose is not to keep trousers up, but more to support the kit that is attached. In fact my method for wearing the belt is at a tilt. For some reason this causes the belt to cinch up to the waist and will stay put even when running at full speed.

It is recommended that the plastic buckle has a two-part release mechanism and a positive action for locking.

The belt consists of Maxpedition roll-up pouches, green LED torch, Bayley Tracker knife, Exstrema Ratio Kukri and powerful white light torch. The boots are Courteneys, with snake-guard tops – ideal for tracking in the bush.

Mounted on both sides there are two Maxpedition pouches which, when not in use, are rolled up and tucked away on the belt. When they are needed they are unrolled and provide convenient storage. I place spent ammunition cartridges into mine, also stones to throw and other bits and pieces. Inside the right-hand side pouch I have a concealed emergency whistle attached to an elastic bungie, There is also a green LED torch and a Leatherman.

Mounted horizontally at the back is a small knife.

HYDRATION AND SUSTENANCE

Among the numerous systems available, I use two. My preferred method of carrying water is in a rigid water bottle. The Nalgene wide-mouth bottles are very good, as you can see the water level. They connect to filtration systems easily and are virtually unbreakable. Where a larger volume of water is required I use a bladder system placed inside my pack. This leads to a pipe through which water can be sipped. I put a turn in the hose and tuck it up high so that it doesn't drag on the ground or touch the ground when not in use. The bladder systems can split and valves fail, plus it is difficult to know how much water has been consumed. I have experienced a burst valve on my hydration system and it emptied very quickly. For this reason the main system for hydration should be a rigid bottle and the bladder system serves only as a back-up.

Water Purification

I exercise a great deal of caution in regard to water supply. Never assume that it is clean! Becoming infected from water-borne diseases will place the tracker in a very bad predicament. He will become weaker, track less efficiently and place himself in danger. To make matters worse, he may well have to continue to drink the infected water and may become seriously ill and dehydrated.

I favour the First Need filtration systems. They are robust and efficient. I have used chlorine and potassium iodide, which require a measuring dosage and do not have any means of filtering the water. I would only recommend these for water purification as a last resort.

Obtaining water can be a dangerous task for anyone, but is especially important for trackers. Try to get water from a position which doesn't leave tracks in the mud or is in a predictable position.

Be careful, as leaning over into water to scoop some up can cause imbalance and may lead to falling into water. Be especially aware of slippery high banks, cold water, vertical banks, fast water and animals in the water like crocodiles, hippos and snakes. For this reason filtration straws can be dangerous.

Cooking Equipment

There is a vast range of cooking equipment available but I keep it simple by choosing to carry a titanium pot, mug and utensils. Titanium is light and very robust. To light a fire I use the easiest method available, which could be either a blowtorch, matches, lighter or ferro rod.

NAVIGATIONAL EQUIPMENT

I keep at least two compasses at hand. The large compass, which is a Silva type flat compass, is usually tucked away where I can get to it easily for map reading. The other is usually very small, referred to as a button compass. This is either on my wristwatch or attached to something I can look at without stopping.

GPS technology is very advanced and I carry a sophisticated GPS which can take photos and marks the photos with coordinates. This is ideal for photographing evidence and spoor. I rarely use GPS because of the difficulty of getting a signal under tree canopies, and the issue of battery life. However, I always have one with me which is easy to access without stopping. If coordinates are required, it is disruptive to stop and refer to a map. By having the GPS mounted on my shoulder straps, I am able to simply read the coordinates and pass them on.

TORCHES

The only torches I carry are mounted on my kit belt, with the exception of my head torch, which is carried in my backpack.

Both torches are compact and the primary torch is a powerful green LED torch, used for night tracking. I have a very powerful white light torch for emergencies and protection. The white light is only used on rare occasions and it has a sequence of flashes, including SOS and stroboscopic, which would disorientate any would-be attacker.

The headtorch is a Petzl. It is not the brightest of torches but it is extremely reliable. It has a red flip-down filter so that it can be used at night without spilling white light and destroying night vision.

OPTICS

Binoculars

In certain conditions tracking may not be an option because the environment and terrain could be hazardous or unfavourable and the ground and environment may offer a tactical advantage to the quarry. To avoid chance contact and before moving into a tactically hazardous area, it should be scanned using optics.

It is very rare for me to track without binoculars close to hand. They are invaluable for scanning the middle and far distance and for oppo-site-bank river tracking. For this reason they need to be easily accessible without having to remove a pack to access them. I wear my binoculars attached to an elasticated chest harness which keeps them close to the chest. The harness makes it easier to run, and they don't drag on the ground when bending over.

Size
Binoculars come in a variety of sizes (defined by the objective lens size). The following is a comparison of pros and cons.

Full-size (common specs: 8 x 42, 10 x 50):
Pros:
- Capture more light and perform better in low light situations
- Usually provide steadier images and a wider field of view

Cons:
- Too big and heavy for backpacking.

Mid-Size (common specs: 7 x 35, 10 x 32):
Pros:
- Balance moderate size and above-average light transmission.
- Good all-around use.

Cons:
- A bit heavy for backpacking

Compact (common specs: 8 x 25, 10 x 25):
Pros:
- The lightest, smallest binocular option for backpacking
- Work well during daytime

Pros:
- Less comfortable during extended periods of use.

Monoculars (single scopes):
Pros:
- The smallest and usually lightest option for viewing distances

Pros:
- Single-eye viewing is usually desired only for short-term usage.

Magnification Power and Effectiveness
Binoculars are identified by two numbers. The first number is magnifi-

cation power, the second is the diameter of the front lenses – take, for example: 7 x 35 binoculars.

The **magnification power** of 7 means that an object will appear seven times closer than it would to your unassisted eye. For example, if you view a target at 200 metres through 7x binoculars, it will appear as though it were 28.6 metres away (200 divided by 7).

The **objective lens diameter** identified in this example by 35, is the diameter (in millimetres) of the objective lenses (those further from your eyes; thus closer to the 'object' being viewed). The diameter of the objective lenses largely determines how much light the binoculars can gather. If you have two pairs of binoculars with exactly the same specifications except for objective lens diameter, those with the larger diameter objective lenses will capture more light. More light means a brighter view, particularly in low-light conditions.

Exit pupil
The exit pupil is a third number used in defining binoculars, that indicates how bright objects will appear when viewed in low-light situations. A higher number means brighter images.

Point your binoculars at a light source, hold them about thirty centimetres in front of your face and peer into either eyepiece. See a small, bright dot? That circle of light is known as the exit pupil – the opening that permits light to exit each binocular barrel and reach the pupils of your eyes.

A large exit pupil also makes it easier to maintain a full image of an object if your hands move or shake.

My favoured binoculars are Nikon. They are rubberized and have withstood some serious abuse. They are small enough to carry around the neck for the duration of a follow-up. They are 7 x 35 and, with an exit pupil of a large 9.3 per cent they are excellent in all conditions.

Night-vision Binoculars

These are extremely useful pieces of equipment, providing observation and intelligence. I have used both the very latest in technology and 1st generation. The latest night vision (NV) equipment is very expensive and restricted for sale, so most people still opt for 1st generation.

My 1st generation binoculars perform well for most conditions. In the same range there is the monocular, however I have found them difficult to focus, so use the more expensive binocular.

I don't take them out on every operation. They are quite bulky and heavy. They are usually stored in a bag that contains my technological equipment.

Night-vision Generations
As mentioned, a night-vision device can be either a 1st, 2nd, 3rd or 4th

generation unit. What this stands for is what type of image intensifier tube is used for that particular device; the image intensifier tube is the heart and soul of a night-vision device.

1st generation

1st generation is currently the most popular type of night vision in the world. Using the basic principles described earlier, a 1st generation unit will amplify the existing light several thousand times, letting you see clearly in the dark. These units provide a bright and sharp image at a low cost, which is perfect, whether you are boating, observing wildlife or providing security for your home. You may notice the following when you are looking through a 1st generation unit.

1. A slight high-pitched whine when the unit is on
2. The image you see may be slightly blurry around the edges (this is known as *geometric distortion*)
3. When you turn a 1st generation unit off, it may glow green for some time

These are inherent characteristics of a 1st generation unit and are normal.

2nd generation

Second (2nd) generation is primarily used by law enforcement agencies or for other professional applications. This is because the cost of a 2nd generation device is higher than a 1st generation one. The main difference between a 1st and a 2nd generation unit is the addition of a micro-channel plate, commonly referred to as an MCP. The MCP works as an electron amplifier and is placed directly behind the photocathode. The MCP consists of millions of short parallel glass tubes. When the electrons pass through these short tubes, thousands more electrons are released. This extra process allows 2nd generation units to amplify the light many more times than 1st generation, giving you a brighter and sharper image.

3rd generation

Third (3rd) generation consists of highly technical components and is significantly better than 2nd generation. The cost is prohibitive and they are controlled items, usually only available to the military.

4th generation

Gated/filmless technology represents the biggest technological break-through in image intensification of the past ten years. By removing the ion barrier film and 'gating' the system, 4th generation demonstrates substantial increases in target detection range and resolution, particularly at extremely low light levels.

With significant improvement in contrast level and in performance under all light conditions, 4th generation represents the top of the line performance in the night-vision market.

Rangefinders
These come in a multitude of forms. They are commonly available and are used by hunters and golfers. They are reasonably compact. Some rangefinders are able to calculate speed of travel, which is extremely useful if the target can be observed travelling.

Heat Detectors
Even using night-vision devices, it can be difficult to detect someone who is concealed. To counteract the situation I have attached a heat detector to the top of my night-vision devices. The detector works on the principle of heat ledges. This is where there is a drop-off in heat of an object's signature as an area is scanned. The heat detector can also be used in the hand. It is extremely useful but takes time and practice to master.

Thermal cameras are being widely used in other industries, thus the prices are coming down. While they are extremely useful in most circumstances, they are not ideal for tracking. They are not robust enough and are quite heavy to be packed away and carried. For vehicular mobile operations it could be useful to have an FLIR (forward-looking infrared) camera.

Tactical Ear
This has the appearance of a hearing aid. It is plugged into the ear and tuned to pick up human voices. To avoid injury from the sound of a

This set of night vision goggles (NVGs) are fitted with a heat detector on top. Using this, even though a target might be camouflaged and not easily visible on the NVGs, their position will show up on the heat detector.

gunshot it cuts out. I have got a tactical ear and wouldn't recommend it for tracking. It does pick up most sounds and, if a swan flies past, it sounds like a jumbo jet. It is very lightweight and easy to forget that you have it in your ear. I have lost mine several times and have had to back-track to find it.

Radios

These are essential to most operations, but also a source of frustration. There are several variations of radios and frequency.

The easiest to obtain is the PMR446 (Personal mobile radio 446 Mhz). They can be purchased in many high street shops and don't usually need a licence. However, in some countries they are legal only with an import licence. They can be useful and broadcast up to 5 kilometres in open terrain. Despite the fact that there are several channels to choose from, you can be guaranteed someone else will hear your broadcasts and they may be broadcasting at the same time.

For operations I use Icom radios. They are robust and powerful. The 'press to talk' (PTT) button and channel selection is easy. It is also possible to plug a remote speaker and microphone into one of the ports.

Most radios can be connected to an earphone and operate either on PTT or VOX (voice operated). I discourage trackers from using an earphone because it reduces the tracker's ability to hear efficiently. If stealth is required, then either bring the radio to the ear temporarily or go off communications and use hand signals.

CHAPTER 19

Real-life Cases

Manhunts occur in a landscape in which the main characters are missing. Throughout the history of mankind, tracking has been used in the ultimate pursuit – the tracking of humans! Many famous manhunts have been well documented as using trackers. In the 1870s the Australian bushranger and bank robber Ned Kelly was found by using trackers. During the Matabele War of 1893 Chief Lobengula in Zimbabwe was found by the Shangani Patrol using trackers. There must be thousands of lesser-known cases in which mantracking has been used to find people.

Mantracking has been used in a multitude of roles, from tracking armed and dangerous people through to the search for clues and tracks of missing children.

This chapter is about two cases in particular, but I also draw a comparison between the well-documented manhunt for Ned Kelly and the manhunt for Raoul Moat. The other real-life case is that of Madeleine McCann, who disappeared while on holiday in Portugal in 2007.

They are two very different scenarios. In the case of Moat and Kelly, both were known to have shot police officers and had gone to ground, and both cases were well observed and documented. Madeleine disappeared mysteriously in the night, and while the aftermath is well documented, little if anything is known about the how and why. It is a difficult puzzle, made more complex by the lack of crucial evidence and the contamination of spoor. In the event of an abduction a tracker would need to find spoor left by the perpetrator or Madeleine before a follow-up could commence.

This chapter is written entirely with hindsight and is only applicable to potential tracking operations and tactics that I would have applied if called to provide tracking expertise at the time. It is not a criticism of the many good men and women who worked tirelessly on both cases, and adopts a no-blame theme. The tactics which I cover in the two cases, with the wisdom of hindsight, may or may not have had an impact on the outcomes.

While the manhunt for Moat ended with his suicide, the optimist in me hopes that Madeleine is still alive, and that maybe one day tracking will play a part in finding her.

NED KELLY

During 1879 the bushranger Ned Kelly and his gang were at large follow-ing the murder of three policemen at Stringybark Creek, Australia. They had evaded a massive police hunt launched immediately after the murders and gone into hiding at various locations in rural Victoria and New South Wales.

The hunt for the Kelly Gang was the biggest and most expensive police manhunt in the history of the colony of Victoria, but it failed to produce quick results. Before long, the police came under increasing pressure to adopt new strategies.

At this point a small group of Aboriginal trackers from Queensland were employed to track the movement of the fugitives.

This use of the trackers was not the preferred choice of the Victo-ria Police. The Chief Commissioner wanted to capture the Kelly Gang without the assistance of outside organizations. But following the Kelly Gang's raid on the town of Jerilderie on 8 February 1879, it was clear that his police force could not cope with the situation and in fact did need such assistance.

The trackers were taken to areas where footprints had been found in the bush, which turned out to be either tracks of innocent people or ones that were too weathered to be of any use. However, they were able to build up a picture of the tracks in the area and, with time, they were able to locate the Kelly Gang to Glenrowan. A shoot-out ensued. Kelly used his suit of armour to no avail and he was arrested.

The use of trackers had a significant effect on finding the Kelly Gang.

RAOUL MOAT

The Raoul Moat manhunt has a striking similarity to that of Ned Kelly. They both went on a shooting rampage and then went to ground. The resemblance is perhaps more about human behaviour than coincidence. If we examine the initial phase of the manhunts, both were able to leave a cold trail, giving no clues as to their whereabouts. This is something that indicates the traits of a very dangerous person, because they have the mindset, skills and motivation to evade capture and commit further crimes. They might even know the very tricks a tracker would use to find them. It is impossible to know whether Moat or Kelly had pre-planned their locations and the method by which they would lie low, or whether it was a sequence of random events. Perhaps it was a mixture of both.

The manhunt for Raoul Moat began after several shootings on 3 July 2010. Nearly twenty-two hours later, the shooting of a police officer was linked to Moat. He was believed to have a grudge against the police. He also made threats in two letters and several phone calls that he would kill any officer who attempted to stop him. After a sighting on the night of 5

July in an armed robbery it was later announced that Moat was believed to be in the Rothbury area.

Police had found objects and signs of occupation in the landscape. There was an abandoned tent, a camp fire, a rambling letter, an abandoned car and discarded mobile phones and other clues as to his movements.

The manhunt lasted almost seven days and was the largest in modern British history, involving 160 armed officers and armed response vehicles. Police deployed sniper teams, helicopters, dogs, armoured anti-terrorist police vehicles from Northern Ireland and a Royal Air Force jet for reconnaissance. During the hunt there were raids and false alarms across the region.

It became evident that Moat was sleeping rough, but how was he able to slip through police lines and get into Rothbury? By this stage the authorities believed that they had contained Moat and they were in control of the situation through saturation policing. However, the police cordon which was referred to as the ring of steel had been no threat to Moat despite the use of dogs. Moat was moving freely despite the best efforts by the police to close the net around him.

It appears that the most likely place where Moat was holed up was in the flood drains in Rothbury, just a few metres under the feet of the police.

The behaviour of dangerous fugitives is that they can be fearless, daring and experience a high sense of invincibility, which could lead them to being reckless. The effect of sleeping rough reduces this feeling of invincibility over time. It is clear that Moat made some appearances in Rothbury, allegedly walking down the street and stealing tomatoes. Was this him feeling invincible, or was he taunting the police? Perhaps he had lowered his guard because he was desperate for food? He was eventually cornered near the entrance to the flood drains.

Author's Comments

From my perspective as a tracker, certain actions might have created a different outcome.

I have conducted training courses for police forces and had ongoing dialogue with both international and national police search authorities. What is very clear is that most police forces do not have sufficient money in the budget for training. Even if they did conduct training, maintaining the skill level required for police trackers is not possible for most officers. However, I have come across many police officers who track in their spare time, and some even self-fund their own tracking courses. They are usually passionate about tracking and fieldcraft. In my estimation, within the UK there are a sufficient number of such officers who could form a highly effective national police tracking team, which could be deployed to manhunts.

A trained tracking team would carry out the following actions.

Briefing Specific to Tracking
I would have agreed what the expectations of the tracking team are and its limitations. I would have agreed a procedure for handling evidence so that the tracking team did not get drawn into evidence processing.

Perimeter Cutting and Containment
While looking for spoor they should be brushing out all junctions and paths. If I am perimeter cutting then I would expect to do this very quickly and would consider ten kilometres a day to be the norm. The brushing out will be done using a stiff brush, or as the US Border Patrol do, dragging tyres behind their vehicles, and it will contain an area in tracking terms. The brush-outs will be monitored. I use this technique regularly. Even the most aware people will not recognize a brush-out unless they are trackers. To combat someone replicating the pattern, my personal brush has a V cut into the bristle which would be very difficult to copy. As described in Chapter 16, brush-outs are only useful if they are checked at a later time.

I have been tracking someone as they inadvertently followed on behind me. Brushing out was the only way that it came to light as they walked through a previous brush-out.

A good brush-out will confirm who walked through and in what direction.

In the Moat manhunt a tracking team would have been busy at work. They would have been doing their best to find spoor at the last-known point while other tracking teams brushed-out and perimeter-cut.

The entrance to the flood drain that Moat was probably using comes into question. The police allege that they checked the underworld of tunnels and there was no sign of human occupation. Given Moat's mobility and the fact that he evidently spent time above ground during the search, it may be that when they checked, he wasn't in there, and perhaps returned later.

I would suggest that a tracking team should have examined the entrance in detail, and perhaps had a good micro-tracker take a look. It is unlikely that a tracker would enter a flood drain system because of the hazards, but at the very least they would have brushed out the entrance. There was good mud and silt for brushing out.

If Moat had used the drain, then his tracks would have shown in the brush-out, and best of all his direction of travel would have been indicated.

The aim of every tracking team is either to catch up with the target or intercept him. In the case of Moat, we will never know for sure how effective tracking would have been, but at least one tracking technique, the brush-out, would have given the power back to police to control the outcome, rather than the other way round.

MADELEINE McCANN

On the evening of Thursday, 3 May between 9.30 p.m. and 10.14 p.m. 2007, Madeleine McCann went missing from Apartment 5A The Ocean Club Resort, Praia da Luz, Portugal.

There have been many theories about what happened to her but there is only one fact which is not disputed: the date and time that she was reported missing.

Once the McCanns had reported her missing the Portuguese Police were slow in their response. Two officers arrived at 11.10 p.m. and the enquiry slowly gathered pace, but crucially the apartment was not considered a crime scene until three hours later, when it was sealed off. In that time around twenty people, including civilians and police, came and went. This is not an unusual practice with missing persons.

Human nature will often deny the harsh reality, hoping that, with the passing of time, the missing person will turn up unharmed. There have been many cases when friends, family and the community have exhausted all possibilities before calling the police. This can be for several reasons, but especially when they are concerned about repercussions for themselves rather than the missing person.

The common sequence of events is a search by friends and family, then the police are called. A police constable will attend and make a first-stage assessment, take a report and may call his superior for a second-stage assessment. There are no alarming remains of a body and it's not as dramatic as catching a crime in progress. There is evidence which indicates that police do not see missing people as a priority. The police constable might upscale the search immediately, or wait for further information and resources.

Author's Comments

Assuming that the police were aware of criminal activity in the area, and given the time of night, the age of the child and vulnerability, the search should have been upscaled immediately and the apartment sealed off. Clearly they were dealing with a very serious situation. Human curiosity is such that we all want to go and take a look for ourselves. We may never know what spoor was damaged or indeed rendered useless by the uncontrolled access.

Crucially, ownership of an enquiry can cause delays. The role of the criminal investigation department is to investigate a crime and compile evidence for a successful prosecution. This requires the area to be sealed off for a forensic investigation.

On the other hand, search officers have a different agenda where the missing person may still be alive. Their priority may not be the evidence, but the search for clues as to the whereabouts of the missing person, and preserving life. They may or may not be given permission to enter the sealed-off zone to find clues. Access is usually by negotiation, and even if trained searchers were not given access immediately, then at least, in an ideal situation, there might have been some useful spoor that only a tracker would spot after forensic evidence has been gathered.

There followed a slow, grinding chain reaction by the authorities setting up porous road blocks, informing border guards and the maritime police. The first twenty-four hours of the search had been squandered.

This case would have been extremely challenging for all but the best trackers and, as referred to earlier in this book, they would have had to count on an opportunistic approach to the follow-up and exploit each and every piece of spoor.

As a result of this a tracking team would undertake a tracking-biased briefing, obtain details of open rough areas in the vicinity from Google Earth, then take the following actions.

Perimeter Cutting for Spoor

A tracker would not need to go into the apartment. Any spoor created in the apartment would have been hard to find, owing to contamination, and at this stage of the enquiry collection of hair or other evidence would be best dealt with by scene-of-crime technicians The further away from the inside of the apartment that the search could be made, the better. This has the advantage that any spoor is less likely to be contaminated and, if found, it would have the effect of closing the time-distance gap.

Exit and ingress may have been different. From the outside I would have checked vegetation and bedding for damage, looking closely for ground spoor. If the exit was by foot, through the front door, down the stairs and immediately into a car, then the skills of a tracker would be limited, but this does not mean that it might not have been possible to locate some spoor.

While one part of the tracking team would be looking for spoor near the apartment, the other tracking teams would be cutting for spoor further afield. They would start close to the apartment, brushing out and then moving to areas further afield.

The ground in this area is very hard, to the extent that rabbits do not live underground in burrows, but above the surface, and wild vegetation is very hardy. There are some tender plants in the early spring. This means that the ability to track on rocks would be a necessary skill. I have trained mantrackers in the Algarve, and they all left the course with the ability to track over rocks and hardy vegetation.

Observing Animal Behaviour, and Especially Bird Dynamics

If a body had been disposed of, it could have been placed into a natural depression or pre-dug hole, but more likely placed under vegetation. This area is well populated by scavengers such as badgers, foxes, corvids and occasionally vultures, so any remains would be dispersed over a wide area. Uncovered remains would have attracted aerial scavengers from several kilometres away. It is an easy task for a tracker to interpret bird behaviour, as described in Chapter 8.

Cutting for Spoor at Route Influencers and Areas of Interest

As time moved on I would have deployed trackers to road bridges that pass over rivers and dried-out river beds. These are common places for remains to be dumped. I have come across several dog remains under such bridges in Portugal.

Within a few hours' drive there is a remote area riddled with old mine-shafts and tunnels, but the dominant vegetation in the region is eucalyptus. Grown in abundance, these are planted in deep furrows on both the level ground and steep inclines. These trees are virtually impossible to track under. Helicopters are of limited use because of the tree canopy, but the landscape is perfect for canine teams and ground searchers.

This mine shaft is an easy drive from Prai de Luz. The wooden slats over the ditch show recent tracks.

Under these challenging conditions a tracking team would cut for spoor at lay-bys and remote parking places and perhaps go out from the parking by 200 metres. They would also check route influencers.

Summary

I have spent several weeks tracking in remote areas of the Algarve. It is a vast, rugged area with large amounts of wilderness, but easily reached by car in a few hours. Without further intelligence as to where Madeleine is, tracking her would not be possible.

If, at a later date, more information comes to light there is chance that trackers would be a useful resource to deploy.

I know that my tracking team would work tirelessly, without reward or recognition, to track someone who has gone missing.

It is my opinion that the police should call trackers into the search for a missing person as soon as possible. It would then be the responsibility of the lead tracker to determine if trackers would be useful and how to deploy them. Where the authorities are concerned about contamination of a crime scene, this should be discussed with the lead tracker and officer in charge of the investigation so that other options could be considered. It may be that the trackers could have a positive outcome by cutting for spoor outside the crime scene.

If trackers had been deployed to the scene within twenty-four hours of Madeleine's disappearance the chances of solving the mystery would have been significantly increased.

Glossary of Terms and Acronyms

TERMS

Action indicators   Features within a track, or related to it, that indicate what the subject was doing, or intending to do.

Aerial spoor   Any spoor above ankle height.

Anti-tracking   Techniques to reduce the amount of spoor or deceive a tracker.

Barrier   A structure or formation which obstructs or hinders the passage of humans or animals.

Bracketing   Used to place time when a track was made between specified limits.

Brush-out   Old tracks in the ground that are removed by using a brush or vegetation.

Cadence   The speed and rhythm of the tracking team.

Confirmed identifiable signature track (CIST)   A track which is confirmed as being that of the target.

Counter-tracking   Hindering trackers by psychological or physical threats, including injury or death.

Follow-up   Trackers commence searching for and following the subject's spoor.

Gait   Movement pattern, including stride, straddle and pitch.

Ground spoor   Any spoor below ankle height.

Indicator track   The last track that will indicate where the next one will be found.

Initial commencement point (ICP)   Where the trackers start the follow-up.

Mantracking   Following human (whether male or female).

Partially identifiable signature track (PIST)   Only partially visible, but identifiable as a track made by the target.

Primary impact point (PIP)   The first contact on the ground made by the feet of the target, usually, but not exclusively the heels.

Red Zone   The period of time in which a tracker's performance is reduced.

Sphere   Including tracks, the entire environment around the tracker and subject.

Spoor   Physical signs of the passage of a human or animal.

Spoor reduction   Reducing the amount of evidence left behind.

Subject/Target   The human or animal that is being tracked.

Terminal impact point (TIP)   The last contact with the ground, made by the feet of the target as they push off. Usually the toes, but this can vary.

Time-distance gap (TDG)   The theoretical distance between the tracker and target.

Track ageing   Using information including track features to establish a time that the track was made.

Tracks   Normally footprints found on the ground but can also refer to line of spoor.

Track-trap   A position in the landscape where the subject is forced to step and leave a track.

Tracking stick   A stick which is purpose-made or improvised to measure and look for tracks.

Trail   A line of spoor or well-worn route used by animals or humans

Zone-in, Zone-out (ZIZO)   The process by which the tracker zones into the environment, including visualization of the follow-up.

ACRONYMS

CCTV	Closed circuit TV
CIED	Counter-improvised explosive device
CIST	Confirmed identifiable signature track
EOD	Explosive Ordnance Disposal
ICP	Initial commencement point
IED	Improvised explosive device
LKP	Last known point
LKS	Last known spoor
NV	Night vision
OP	Observation post
PIP	Primary impact point
PIST	Partially identifiable signature track
PTT	Press to talk (radio button)
SAR	Search and rescue
TDG	Time-distance gap
TOS	Time out for safety
TIP	Terminal impact point
VT	Visual tracker
ZIZO	Zone-in zone-out

Index